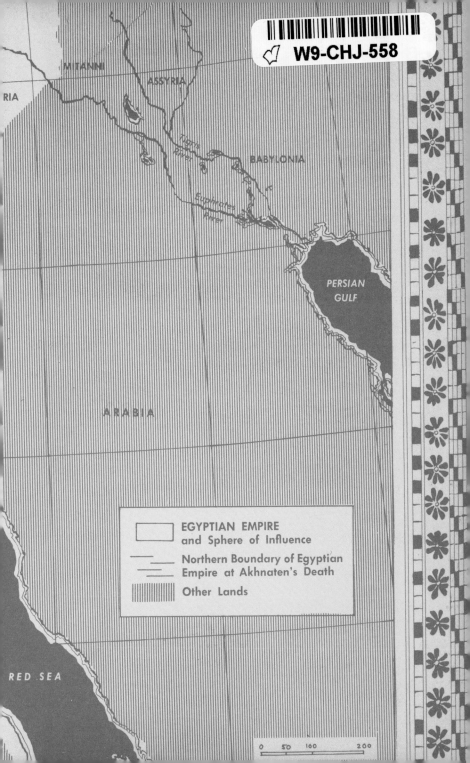

W9-CHJ-558

MITANNI

ASSYRIA

RIA

Tigris River

BABYLONIA

Euphrates River

PERSIAN
GULF

ARABIA

EGYPTIAN EMPIRE
and Sphere of Influence

Northern Boundary of Egyptian
Empire at Akhnaten's Death

Other Lands

RED SEA

0   50   100   200

AKHNATEN
THE REBEL PHARAOH

AKHNATEN
THE REBEL PHARAOH
By ROBERT SILVERBERG

CHILTON BOOKS

A DIVISION OF CHILTON COMPANY
Publishers
Philadelphia　　　New York

Nay I may ask, is not every true reformer, by the nature of him, a priest first of all? He appeals to Heaven's invisible justice against earth's visible force; knows that it, the invisible, is strong and alone strong. He is a believer in the divine truth of things; a seer, seeing through the shows of things; a worshipper, in one way or the other, of the divine truth of things; a priest, that is.

THOMAS CARLYLE
Heroes and Hero-Worship

There is no historical spectacle more tragic and at the same time more repulsive than the fetid disintegration of reformism amid the wreckage of all its conquests and hopes.

LEON TROTSKY
What's Next?

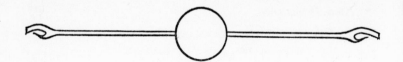

CONTENTS

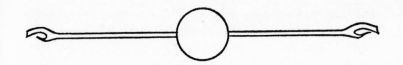

ON NAMES AND DATES

The spelling of ancient Egyptian names has been a matter of scholarly controversy since Champollion and Young first drew meaning from the hieroglyphic inscriptions a century and a half ago. Any phonetic reading from the hieroglyphics is at best an approximation, and the task of transliteration is made more difficult because the Egyptian written language made no provision for vowels.

And so we find Akhnaten's name also spelled Ikhnaton, Ikhnaten, Akhenaton, Akhenaten, Akhunaton, or Ekhnaten—while some of the older Egyptologists read the name even more variously. We find the god of Thebes called Amon, Amen, Amun, and Ammon. The Pharaohs I choose to call Thothmes are sometimes known as Tut-mose or Tuthmosis. I have tried to use the spelling that seems most logical and most attractive, but I am aware that there are some inconsistencies in my usage. The Egyptians were not a logical people, as we understand logic.

A further complication is the use of Greek forms of Egyptian names. Where possible, I use the Egyptian form. Thus I refer to Akhnaten's father as Amenhotep, never as Amenophis. Certain cities, though, are inextricably associated with their Greek names, and so I use such Greek forms as Thebes, Hermopolis, and Hieropolis in preference to the rarely-heard Egyptian names.

The chronology of the Amarna story is similarly uncertain.

Everyone seems to agree, nowadays, that Akhnaten lived during the fourteenth century before Christ, but there is little agreement beyond that. Ancient Egyptian dates depend on a few fixed points, widely spaced—particularly on the date of a certain eclipse whose actual date can be computed accurately. Arriving at dates between the fixed points is a matter of laborious cross-checking and calculation, and one man's findings may be reversed by new evidence a year later.

The scheme of dates I use here is basically that put forth by K. A. Kitchen of the University of Liverpool in 1962. He in turn worked from the "high" chronology suggested by M. B. Rowton in 1960. (Rowton in 1948 had worked out a "low" chronology which would make all events described in this book take place fourteen years later than the dates in his more recent scheme.) It should be understood that when I assign a particular event to the year 1375, say, the margin of error is at least a dozen years in either direction. And, of course, all the dates of the Amarna era should be interpreted as B.C.

ROBERT SILVERBERG

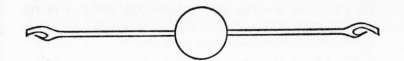

INTRODUCTION

The city of the rebel Pharaoh lies about 160 miles south of Cairo. To reach it from there, you must travel by train at a dignified pace along the western bank of the Nile. The tracks pass close to the edge of the great river at times and at other times veer inland through the cotton-fields of the Nile's fertile valley. Beyond the cotton-fields lies the desert, sweeping away endlessly toward the sunset. Desert dust rolls in over the narrow inhabited strip in white clouds.

The train halts at the town of Mellawi, and the passengers descend. The sun blazes furiously, seeming to occupy at least a quarter of the cloudless sky. No matter where you are in Egypt, you cannot escape the fact of the sun. Between dawn and twilight it glares down, a gleaming disk of light and heat. Clouds rarely hide its radiance. Rain is so rare as to be an improbability. There is no weather in Egypt—only the sun.

From Mellawi, it is a half-mile trip by car to the riverbank. The road is a dirt one, and dusty. Your progress is slow because of the roughness of the road, and slower yet because children and beggars gather round at every moment to greet you and to thrust out eager hands. The journey to Akhnaten's city is a favorite tourist route.

You reach the Nile. It is broad and peaceful, lapping quietly at the fields that slope down to meet it. On the far side, you can see a long row of palms, with the mud-brick village of El Till sprawling behind them. Still further in the distance are brown cliffs forming a backdrop for the scene.

A slow-moving felucca takes you across the slow-moving yellow river. As you cross, you can look southward and see how the river curves round a headland. Thirty-five hundred years ago, an Egyptian Pharaoh came down the Nile from the capital city of Thebes, 250 miles to the south, and, as he rounded that headland, was greeted by his first view of his great new city.

What you will see is far less impressive than the sight Akhnaten enjoyed in the sixth year of his reign. The city of the heretic Pharaoh is all but destroyed now. Nothing but foundations remain. The Pharaoh's enemies did their work well—and time did the rest.

The felucca glides into a landing stage. Guides are waiting here. They will take you to the place called Tell el-Amarna, which was once the city of Akhetaten, "The Horizon of the Disk," built by the Pharaoh Akhnaten, one of the strangest and most fascinating personalities of the ancient world.

At Tell el-Amarna, the cliffs that border the eastern bank of the Nile for much of its length swing inland toward the desert, receding for about three miles, then curving back toward the river some six miles further along. The effect is like a strung bow, with the cliffs as the bow, the Nile as the string. A "bay" of land is formed, sheltered by the cliffs to the east, bordered by the river at the west.

Here, in the middle of the fourteenth century before Christ, the Pharaoh Akhnaten came to dwell in a newly constructed city. Akhnaten had fled the pomp of Thebes, Egypt's capital for centuries. Thebes was dominated by the powerful priests of the god Amon, and Akhnaten would have none of Amon. Akhnaten was a rebel—in a land of conservatives. At a stroke, he swept away the supremacy of Amon, swept away the power of Thebes, and ordered the building of a new capital in an isolated part of Egypt. There he would worship a new god, Aten, after his fashion, and there he would rule the Land of the Nile.

It was a splendid city. On an island in the Nile, just off shore, he caused pleasure-houses and pavilions to be erected. At the edge of the river was the green splendor of the palace gardens, fronting the villas of the nobles. On the broad, flat stretch of the desert, Akhnaten placed the royal palaces and the temples of the new god. And in the cliffs, the "Eastern Mountain," chambers were hollowed out to serve as the final resting-places for the worshippers of Aten.

The magnificence of the city of Akhetaten was short-lived. The rebel Pharaoh died. And his new religion died with him. The new Pharaoh, Tutankhamen, returned to the old capital, Thebes, and to the old religion. The quays at Akhetaten where the royal fleet had moored were abandoned. Desert sand covered the opulent villas, the gardens of colorful flowers, and the carefully tended rare trees. One of Akhnaten's nobles had described the city as "great in loveliness, mistress of pleasant ceremonies, rich in possessions, the offering of the sun being in her midst. At the sight of her beauty there is rejoicing. She is lovely and beautiful: when one sees her it is like a glimpse of heaven." Those words became a mockery. The scorpion and the lizard came to dwell in the deserted halls of the rebel Pharaoh.

The very name of Akhnaten was stricken from the records of Egypt and was forgotten. Later documents called him simply "the criminal of Akhetaten," and then ceased to call him anything at all. Lists of Egypt's kings failed to include his name. The sea of time engulfed him, and he was lost to memory. His city was demolished. No wall was left standing more than a yard above its base. The "lovely and beautiful city," the "glimpse of heaven," endured for less than fifteen years.

When you visit Tell el-Amarna today and stare in confusion and dismay at the dismal remains of Akhnaten's city, you are hard put to detect the grandeur that once was. The ruins are immense, lining the river for miles. But all that can be seen are the stumps of buildings, the traceries of foundations in the sand. The patient toil of archaeologists over nearly three-quarters of a century has revealed the bare skeleton of the city that had been destroyed. Akhnaten himself has returned from the legions of the forgotten. His city, though, is no more than crumbled brick, baking in the eternal sun. A few shards of pottery, some empty tombs, the hint of palaces—nothing more.

Yet it is impressive. The city still conjures up the image of that pathetic, deformed Pharaoh, with his elongated skull and his jutting belly and his swollen thighs, who worked a brief revolution in Egypt.

Why remember Akhnaten? Why write books about this rebel who failed, this defeated dreamer? Of what importance is it that he overthrew one god and replaced him with another? How could it possibly matter to us?

Akhnaten matters, not for what he accomplished, but for what he tried to accomplish. He attempted more than replacing one god with another, one capital with another. He sought to overthrow an entire system of gods and demons, millennia old. He struggled to bring light into the darkness of Egypt's religion. He worshipped one god, and not many.

As we shall see, a current of monotheism was running through Egyptian religion long before Akhnaten reigned. But that current was submerged under a torrent of gods, gods with heads of jackals and heads of beetles, gods who warred with one another and mutilated one another. Akhnaten tried to dam that torrent. He offered Egypt a single god, a god of love, a faith of simplicity and purity.

Egypt rejected the offer. We remember and honor Akhnaten for what he failed to do. We recognize his weaknesses, but we see also his strengths, and we are fascinated by the many-sidedness of his character. One of the archaeologists who has helped to recover Akhnaten's city, J. D. S. Pendlebury, has called the mysterious Pharaoh "the first rebel against the established order of things whom we know, the first man with ideas of his own which ran counter to all tradition, who was in a position to put those ideas into practice."

The aspect of Akhnaten that gives him appeal thousands of years after his death is more than simply his rebelliousness, however. Perhaps the appraisal of the great Egyptologist James H. Breasted can best serve as our key. Breasted wrote:

"He gradually developed ideals and purposes which make him the most remarkable of all the Pharaohs, and the first *individual* in human history."

AKHNATEN
THE REBEL PHARAOH

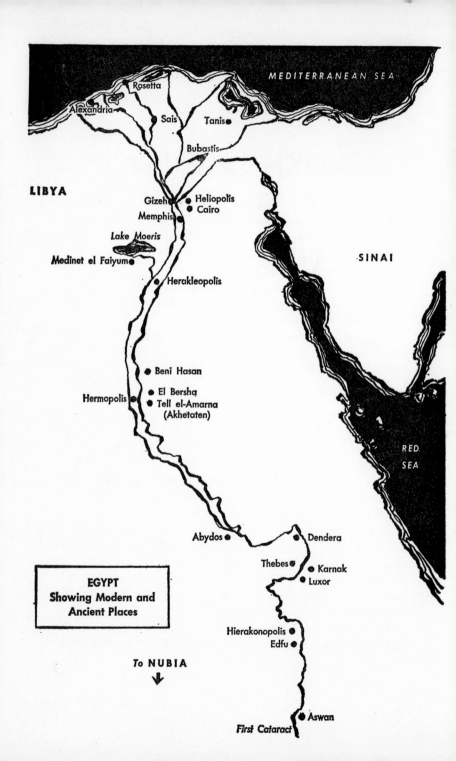

MEDITERRANEAN SEA

Rosetta

Alexandria

Sais

Tanis

Bubastis

LIBYA

Gizeh

Heliopolis

Cairo

Memphis

Lake Moeris

SINAI

Medinet el Faiyum

Herakleopolis

Beni Hasan

El Bersha

Hermopolis

Tell el-Amarna
(Akhetaten)

RED
SEA

Abydos

Dendera

Thebes

Karnak

Luxor

EGYPT
Showing Modern and
Ancient Places

Hierakonopolis

Edfu

To NUBIA
↓

Aswan

First Cataract

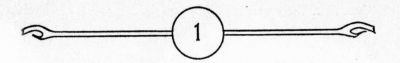

RE, OSIRIS, AND AMON

Fourteen centuries after the failure of Akhnaten's revolution, the Roman satirist Juvenal described the religion of the Egyptians in these stinging words:

"Who knows not, O Volusius of Bithynia, the sort of monsters Egypt, in her infatuation, worships! One part venerates the crocodile; another trembles before an ibis gorged with serpents. The image of a sacred monkey glitters in gold, where the magic chords sound from Memnon broken in half, and ancient Thebes lies buried in ruins, with her hundred gates. In one place they venerate sea-fish, in another river-fish; there, whole towns worship a dog: no one Diana. It is an impious act to violate or break with the teeth a leek or an onion. O holy nations! whose gods grow for them in their gardens! Every table abstains from animals that have wool: it is a crime there to kill a kid. But human flesh is lawful food."

Juvenal wrote as an outsider, and with a pen dipped in venom. He wrote, too, at a time when Egypt's glory had been dead for hundreds of years. The description, though unfair, has a tinge of accuracy to it. Juvenal chose to ignore the spiritual elements of Egyptian religion. But he hit on the most startling aspect of it: the multitude of Egypt's gods.

Egypt had gods of all sorts. More than two thousand different deities were worshipped in Egypt, often hundreds at the

1

same time. There were gods who wore the appearance of human beings, gods who were grotesquely portrayed as humans with animal heads, gods who were natural forces. There was hawk-headed Horus and ibis-headed Thoth; Sekhmet, the lioness-goddess of Memphis; the cow-goddess Hathor; Apet, the hippopotamus-god; Sobek, the crocodile-god; Ubaste, the cat-goddess. There was Ptah, the dwarfed artificer, and the ram-headed god Khnum, and Apis, the sacred bull. There was the sun god, who at dawn was Khepra, the beetle; at noon was Re, the falcon; at sunset was Atum, the creator-god. Egyptians worshipped Geb, the god of the earth, and Nut, the goddess of the sky, and Ihy, the serpent son of Hathor, and Seth, the sinister god of death and decay, and too many others even to list here.

If we put the gods of Egypt in one tumbled paragraph, as I have just done, a sense of impossible confusion results. Juvenal, writing at the tag-end of Egyptian civilization, was thus confused, and so was repelled. But the actual pattern of Egyptian religion was far more orderly.

To understand it—and an understanding is necessary, if we are to know what it was that Akhnaten rebelled against—we must realize two things: that Egypt's civilization spanned thousands of years, and that the Egyptians never discarded anything.

The last vestige of Egypt's independence perished in 30 B.C., with the death of Cleopatra. The real Egypt of the Pharaohs had been dead at least five hundred years by then. But Egyptian history spans more than three thousand years—from Cleopatra back to the first Pharaoh, Menes. Before Menes, there lay perhaps two thousand more years of prehistory during which the civilization of Egypt took shape. We are dealing, then, with a culture which in Akhnaten's time was at least thirty-five centuries old. The roots of Egyptian civilization were as remote to him as he is to us. A land can develop a great many gods in so staggering a span of time, if its inclination runs that way.

The Egyptians were as fertile in their god-making as the Nile Valley was in its bounty of crops. We make the mistake

2

of thinking of Egypt as a united country, and so fail to understand its diversity of thought. Ancient Egypt did not always conform to our idea of a nation.

To begin with, Egypt was two lands. Upper Egypt began in the south, at the First Cataract of the Nile, at the city of Elephantine, and stretched northward, a narrow strip only a few miles wide along the banks of the life-giving river, as far as Memphis. Lower Egypt, the land of the Nile delta, began at Memphis and ran to the sea.

Upper Egypt had a measure of unity, since it centered on the single thread of the Nile. Past Memphis, however, the Nile splits into many mouths. The cities of Lower Egypt, each on its own branch of the Nile, regarded themselves as independent entities, though in extreme antiquity they had been ruled from time to time by a common leader. About 3200, a king of Upper Egypt named Menes conquered all of Lower Egypt, and for the first time the two lands came under one rule. As we shall see, the tendency of Egypt was to collapse into independent cities—but, again and again, there came a unifier out of the south to weld the land together.

By the time of Menes, Egypt had divided itself into forty-two *nomes,* or provinces, and this division persisted through the shifting periods of stability and instability that comprised Egypt's history. Each nome had a sense of pride and independence; each had its own bureaucracy; each had its own local god. In each political subdivision, the god of the most important city was worshipped as the chief god. The inhabitants of each nome were well aware that their neighbors had different gods, every bit as real, though of course less powerful and majestic, than their own. The Egyptologist E. A. Wallis Budge described the situation this way:

"The god of the city in which a man lived was regarded as the ruler of the city, and the people of that city no more thought of neglecting to provide him with what they considered to be due to his rank and position than they thought of neglecting to supply their own wants. In fact the god of the city became the center of the social fabric of that city. . . . The

3

remarkable peculiarity of the Egyptian religion is that the primitive idea of the god of the city is always cropping up in it, and that is the reason why we find semi-savage ideas of God side by side with some of the most sublime conceptions."[1]

A wise conqueror does not try to interfere with the religious beliefs of his subjects. As each nome was brought under the sway of the central government, the local god of that nome was added to the pantheon, no matter what effect that might have on the consistency of the whole scheme. Of course, Pharaoh, ruling from his capital at Memphis, had his own god, and the people of the outlying cities were expected to give lip-service to Pharaoh's god as the high god of all Egypt. But their true religious intensity turned, as it always had, to their own local deity.

Dynasties give way. When Pharaoh ruled from Memphis, one god was considered supreme. When later Pharaohs ruled from Thebes, a different god was promoted to the head of the pantheon. Changing dynasties produced changing fashions in religion. The old gods, though, never were simply thrown away. They were absorbed into the new scheme of things in some lesser capacity.

Over five thousand years, a nation can accumulate quite a host of gods through such practices.

The earliest gods of Egypt were family gods. The great families, dominating a city, made their god the city god. Several gods might be joined to make one new god. A city decimated by famine or plague might turn its back on its god and choose a new one. Family gods and city gods, the national god, the abstract deities of nature, all were divine, all had to be appeased.

The earliest cult to win widespread support in Egypt was probably that of the Mother Goddess. The idea of a primeval mother, who is goddess of the sky and of fertility, has always had a powerful hold on man's imagination. Cave art of 25,000

[1] E. A. Wallis Budge, *Egyptian Religion*.

years ago shows female fertility figures who almost certainly were objects of a Mother Goddess cult. Demeter of the Greeks, Ceres of the Romans, the *Magna Mater* of the Near East, Isis of the later Egyptians, all partook of this ancient concept of worship. It has persisted on into the Christian era too, of course, in the person of the Virgin Mary, who in some parts of the world has come to be revered more deeply than God Himself.

This basic cult of the Mother Goddess probably captivated the Egyptian peasants for thousands of years. She appears now as Isis, now as the cow-goddess Hathor, now in other forms. Whenever the authority of the central government was weakened, the Mother Goddess cult took on renewed life in the Egyptian provinces. At the very end, when the whole weighty edifice of Egyptian culture was toppling, the worship of Isis was supreme in Egypt—and even spread to the conqueror, Rome.

The Mother Goddess did not suit the needs of the Pharaoh. Pharaoh was a man; he needed a male figure of authority to head the family of gods. To meet the political needs of the new unified Egypt that emerged in the time of Menes, certain attributes of the Mother Goddess were borrowed and awarded to masculine gods better able to enhance Pharaoh's prestige.

This process took place during the time of the first five dynasties. Egyptian history is divided into a system of thirty dynasties, beginning with Menes of the First Dynasty, about 3200 B.C., and ending with Nectanebo II in 341 B.C. This framework comes down to us through the work of an Egyptian historian named Manetho, who lived about 300 B.C. Manetho's lists, which reached us in a corrupt and garbled form, have been amplified through more recent historical studies.

The First and Second Dynasties together are known as the Archaic Period, which lasted perhaps from 3200 to 2780. The Third through Sixth Dynasties make up the Old Kingdom, a time of greatness and splendor for Egypt. The famous pyramids of Gizeh are products of the Fourth Dynasty. About 2270, the Sixth Dynasty came to an end, and was followed by a century and a half of political confusion which historians call the First Intermediate Period. The Seventh through Tenth Dynasties ruled then, with one short-lived king succeeding another, and several often claiming the throne at once.

The Eleventh and Twelfth Dynasties are grouped as the Middle Kingdom, a time of renewed vitality for Egypt. About 1776, with the death of the last Twelfth Dynasty ruler, a new period of confusion began; the weak Thirteenth and Fourteenth Dynasties ruled simultaneously, and then, in 1700, invaders from the north conquered Egypt and ruled it for 150 years. The leaders of these invaders, called the Hyksos, were the kings of the Fifteenth, Sixteenth, and Seventeenth Dynasties.

About 1555, the Egyptians expelled the Hyksos, and the Eighteenth Dynasty commenced. This was the dynasty of Akhnaten.

The first four dynasties saw the establishment of the foundation for later Egyptian religious thought. A creation myth—one of many—was codified by priests at the capital, Memphis, and at the nearby city of On (which the Greeks called Heliopolis) in Lower Egypt.

This myth tells how Atum, the creator-god, rose from the primeval abyss of water, creating himself. "I was alone," Atum tells us. "I took courage in my heart. I laid a foundation. I made every form. Many were the forms coming from my mouth."

Atum gave rise to a son, Shu, and a daughter, Tefnut. These two married and also produced a son and daughter, Geb and Nut. Geb was the earth, Nut the sky; Shu and Tefnut served to separate earth from sky and hold the sky-goddess Nut aloft. From the marriage of Geb and Nut there came four children, who also wed one another: Osiris and Isis, Set and Nepthys. These nine gods—Atum, his children Shu and Tefnut, his grandchildren Geb and Nut, and his great-grandchildren Osiris, Isis, Set, and Nepthys, were grouped as the Ennead, the royal family of divinities. A tenth god was Horus, born of the marriage of Osiris and Isis.

In the early days of the Old Kingdom, Atum was the high

god of the official religion. He was worshipped in various forms, for the Egyptians loved to split their gods into separate attributes of the same deity, much as Christian theologians developed the concept of God as a Trinity of Father, Son, and Holy Ghost. At Heliopolis (the name means "City of the Sun"), where a school of theology had been maintained since earliest times, Atum was hailed in three guises: as the beetle Khepra, as the falcon Re, and as the sunset-god Atum.

Khepra, the sacred scarab beetle, was the god of the dawn. The scarab beetle rolls dung into a ball which it hides in a cavity in the earth. It lays its eggs in this dung-ball, and when the young beetles emerge, they push forward through the dung, rolling little dung-balls ahead of them. To the Egyptians, whose taste in symbolism frequently strikes us as strange, the young beetles rolling balls of dung somehow seemed to represent a young sun-god rolling the morning sun ahead of him across the heavens.

Re, the falcon, the hero-god, was the deity of blazing noon. He sailed across the sky in a sumptuous boat, accompanied by a band of lesser gods. Re was the ruler of the heavens, and it was thought that Pharaoh, after his death, ascended to join Re in the solar boat:

Indeed he who is yonder will be a living god, punishing anyone who commits a sin,
Indeed he who is yonder will stand in the boat, causing the choicest offerings in it to be given to the temples,
Indeed he who is yonder will become a sage, who will not be hindered from appealing to God whenever he speaks.

The god of the evening, Atum, was also called Temu. He was represented as an old man, tottering toward sunset.

Of the three forms, Re was by far the most important. In the schools of Heliopolis—which is now a suburb on the northern side of Cairo—the priests taught that Atum-as-Re was the chief of all gods, and, indeed, the *only* god. One hymn to Re declares:

"Thou art the lord of heaven, thou art the lord of earth; thou art the creator of those who dwell in the heights, and of

7

those who dwell in the depths. Thou art the One God who came into being in the beginning of time. Thou didst create the earth, thou didst fashion man, thou didst make the watery abyss of the sky, thou didst form the Nile, thou didst create the great deep, and thou dost give life unto all that therein is. Thou hast knit together the mountains, thou hast made mankind and the beasts of the field to come into being, thou hast made the heavens and the earth. Worshipped be thou whom the goddess Maat embraceth at morn and at eve. . . . Hail, thou mighty being, of myriad forms and aspects, thou king of the world, prince of On, lord of eternity, and ruler of everlastingness! The company of the gods rejoice when thou risest and dost sail across the sky!"

It seems puzzling, to our way of thinking, when the same hymn refers to Re as "the One God," and then refers, a few lines later, to "the goddess Maat," and then to "the company of the gods." But this is the double strand of Egyptian theology. The key is the phrase, "of myriad forms and aspects." Re *was* Maat and the rest of the company of the gods. The monotheistic idea was there, five thousand years ago in the time of the Old Kingdom. Yet, not only was Re worshipped in his many forms, but there was Ptah, the kindly artificer-god, to worship at Memphis, and the various cat-gods and crocodile-gods as well. Consistency was not an Egyptian virtue.

During the Fourth Dynasty, the pyramid-building era, Re was unquestionably the official god of Pharaoh. However, the Pharaohs of the Fourth Dynasty saw *themselves* as gods, living gods, and while Pharaoh worshipped Re, the people of Egypt worshipped Pharaoh—as well as their local gods, of course.

At the beginning of the Fifth Dynasty, the priesthood of Re at Heliopolis managed to assert greater power over Pharaoh. Re, or Atum-Re, came to hold a place higher even than Pharaoh, the king. In his various guises, as Re-Harakhti, the dawn-god of the horizon, or as Re-Atum, the creator-god, or as Re-Sobek, the crocodile-god, he was worshipped everywhere. The king, it was taught, was the son of Re. This was understood literally: that the first king of the Fifth Dynasty had been born to a woman who, though the wife of a priest of Re, had been made pregnant by the sun-god himself. Succeeding Fifth Dynasty kings were also considered of divine blood.

Thus the theology of Heliopolis ruled Egyptian religious thought. Re absorbed, but did not replace, the local gods. The new teaching had political effect, too. Since Pharaoh was divine, he could not dilute the divine blood by marrying a mortal. The wife of Pharaoh had to be herself of the blood of Re. It became customary for the ruler of Egypt to take his own sister as his wife. There was ample precedent for this in mythology, since Shu and Tefnut, Geb and Nut, Osiris and Isis, Nepthys and Set, had all married incestuously. (This should not be thought to mean that brother-sister marriage was practiced commonly in Egypt. Only the Pharaohs did so, to maintain the divinity of the blood-line on both sides.)

During the era of Re's supremacy, there were, of course, other gods worshipped in Egypt. Some monotheistic hymns to Re date from this period, but they do not represent any broad current of feeling. An important goddess was Maat, the goddess of truth, of world-order. *Maat,* as a word and as the goddess who embodied that word, was a vital concept to the Egyptian. Maat meant not simply truth, but stability, permanence, the orderly structure of the world. It was Pharaoh's task always to uphold Maat.

The long reign of Pharaoh Pepi II brought the Old Kingdom to a close. Pepi took the throne in childhood and held it for ninety years, the longest reign in recorded Egyptian history. In his declining years, forces of chaos gained strength in Egypt, and with his death the long centuries of rule from Memphis ended. Egypt collapsed into confusion and misrule.

New gods flourish in such times. Re, the god of the Old Kingdom, was discredited when power fled from Memphis. The rise of the Osiris cult was the result of this time of uncertainty.

Osiris had, perhaps, been a chieftain of Lower Egypt in prehistoric days. Possibly his memory became associated with some crop-god out of Asia, and he was worshipped as a local god at the Delta city of Djedu.

During the Fifth Dynasty, the heyday of Re, Osiris began to take on new importance and a different role. The city of Abydos, in Upper Egypt north of Thebes, came to hail Osiris as a god of the dead. Probably at that time, he was absorbed into the family of Atum and took his place in the official creation myth as one of the four great-grandchildren of Atum-Re, the creator and sun-god.

At Memphis, the capital of the Old Dynasty, and at Heliopolis, the theological center, the Pharaohs worshipped Re. But the sun-god was not popular among the people of Egypt. The peasant in the field toiled under the blazing lash of the sun all day; it was not easy for him to love the god of that sun. The new Osiris-cult gave him a different sort of god, one whom he could understand and identify with emotionally. Osiris had great appeal to the masses of Egypt.

Osiris was a god who had been dead and who rose from the dead. Such resurrected gods are found everywhere in the Near East: Baal of Syria, Adonis of the western Semitic peoples, Dumuzi of Sumer, Telipinus of the Hittites, all die and are returned to life. It is a natural interpretation of the annual miracle of vegetation. The crops are harvested, the plants die, and then, with the return of spring, comes the new yield. The peasant could never be sure that the rebirth would come; only by worshipping the god whose life story symbolized that death and rebirth could he encourage the miracle to happen each year. The resurrection of Christ at Easter is related to this symbolic pattern, certainly.

The most familiar tale of Osiris is the one set down by Plutarch in the first century after Christ. Though a Greek and a latecomer, Plutarch was an accurate reporter by the standards of his day, and his version of the Osiris legend is probably a reliable retelling of a story that was two thousand years old in his time.

According to Plutarch, the god Atum-Re had given to Osiris

10

the task of governing the world. Osiris taught the people of Egypt how to plant seeds and cultivate their crops, and he gave them laws. His brother Set, jealous of Osiris' power, conspired to destroy him. "He secretly took the measure of Osiris' body, and prepared a beautiful, richly-adorned chest, which he brought to a feast of the gods," Plutarch tells us. "When all had rejoiced at the sight of its beauty, Set promised jestingly to give the chest as a present to the one who would exactly fill it when lying in it. All tried it, but it would fit no one, till at last Osiris got into it and lay down. The conspirators then hastened to throw the cover over it, closed the chest on the outside with nails, poured hot lead over it, carried it out to the Nile and sent it drifting toward the sea."

Thus Osiris perished, and the world was plunged into mourning. Chief of the mourners was Isis, the sister and wife of Osiris, the beloved woman who now became the Mother Goddess of Egypt. When Osiris was murdered, Isis fled into the swamps of the Delta and hid there from the wrath of Set. Secretly, she gave birth to the posthumous son of Osiris, the god Horus. While Horus grew up, Isis roamed the marshes of the Delta, searching for the body of Osiris.

After long wandering, Isis came to a far-off city which Plutarch says was Byblos, on the Phoenician coast, where the coffin of Osiris had washed up from the sea. She brought the coffin back to Egypt, but Set discovered it while Isis was tending young Horus, and destroyed the body of Osiris. Set tore the body of Osiris limb from limb, and scattered the fragments to the winds.

Now began a second search. Isis went through the marshes, seeking for the sundered limbs of Osiris. Wherever she found one, she buried it, and men revered each of the many burial places as sacred to Osiris. While Isis was giving burial to the scattered fragments of Osiris, young Horus was challenging Set. Nephew met uncle in a fierce and terrible combat in which each inflicted grave mutilations on the other. Finally, the wise, ibis-headed god Thoth separated them and healed their wounds. Horus was made ruler of the world in place of the dead Osiris,

11

whose spirit soared to the skies. Set, defeated at last, received the consolation of being permitted to ride in the solar boat of Re as it crossed the heavens, using his great strength to ward off enemies of the sun-god.

The story of Osiris thus paralleled the story of agriculture. There was a time of fertility—the lifetime of Osiris—followed by a season of parching drought and the death of vegetation—the time of Osiris' disappearance. Then, thanks to Isis, Osiris was reborn in the form of Horus. Set, the god of storm and destruction, was defeated, and Horus, the returning spring, ruled in his father's place, while Osiris went to dwell in the stars.

This was a story the common people could understand and love. While Pharaoh in his remote palace worshipped the heroic sun-god Re, the people of Egypt gathered in many cities to celebrate the death of Osiris and the triumph of Horus.

There had to be conflict between the two beliefs, the solar worship of Re and the death-cult of Osiris, the religion of light and the religion of darkness. New myths were spawned by the adherents of Osiris which showed Re as a feeble, senile old god whose survival depended on the ministrations of Isis and Horus. One tale told how Re was stung by a serpent that Isis had created:

> The divine god Re opened his mouth
> And the voice of his majesty reached unto heaven.
> His company of gods cried, "What is it? What is it?"
> And the gods cried, "Behold! Behold!"
> He could not answer them.
> His jaw bones chattered,
> All his limbs trembled and the poison invaded his flesh.

Isis, the legend goes on, healed Re, but exacted power from him in return. The old sun-god was forced into retirement, and the new gods came to rule.

Such heresies would have been suppressed, no doubt, in Fifth or Sixth Dynasty times, when Re was the supreme god. But the time of weakness known as the First Intermediate Period saw the general downfall of the old ways. By about 2100, when the strong Eleventh Dynasty had come to power and the

Middle Kingdom had been established, we find the cult of Osiris firmly entrenched in Egypt.

Re still was worshipped at Heliopolis, and the priests of the sun-god managed to effect a compromise with the partisans of the new popular cult. Osiris took over certain powers of Re. He became, for instance, the judge of the dead. All souls had to come before Osiris to be weighed.

The original cult of Osiris had said nothing about a hereafter. In the worship of Re, however, it was understood that the Pharaoh, after his death, would join Re in the solar boat, and so would have a life after death. Ordinary Egyptians, being mortals, would not share the Pharaoh's fate, according to Old Kingdom theologians.

In the Middle Kingdom, the theologies of Re and Osiris were intertwined. Osiris, the dead one, was now considered the lord of the underworld. Pharaoh, who was the son of Re, would *become* Osiris after his death. He would not simply go to dwell with Osiris; he would be identified with the god. The new Pharaoh would be greeted, of course, as Horus. The dead Pharaoh would be reborn as Re. In Pharaoh's death came the rebirth of kingship on Earth and the rebirth of the Sun in the heavens.

Later, the system was extended to embrace everyone. Not merely Pharaoh, but every virtuous Egyptian who died and was buried in the proper way would become Osiris. The promise of an afterlife for everyone was enormously appealing, naturally.

Through a complicated process that took many centuries to mature, Osiris and Re merged into a single deity, and yet continued to be worshipped separately. To the people of Egypt, their god Osiris came to take on certain characteristics of Re; while the nobility and royalty, the followers of the official state religion of Re, saw it as the admission of Osiris into the Heliopolitan theology. As James H. Breasted observes, "The result was thus inevitable confusion, as the two faiths interpenetrated. In both faiths we recall that the king is identified with the god, and hence we find him unhesitatingly called Osiris

13

and Re in the same passage. There are extensive passages in the Pyramid Texts which illustrate the often inextricable confusion resulting from the interweaving of these unharmonised elements. The fact that in such passages both Re and Osiris appear as supreme kings of the hereafter cannot of course be reconciled, and such mutually irreconcilable beliefs caused the Egyptian no more discomfort than was felt by any early civilization in the maintenance of a group of religious teachings side by side with others involving varying and totally inconsistent suppositions."[2]

We need not attempt to untangle the inextricable. Under the hot Egyptian sun, generations of priests spun their intricate theological concepts, and we can at best see them as through a glass, darkly. The religion of Re was the royal and official faith, that of Osiris was the popular one, and a host of local and lesser deities had their cults as well. As time passed the two main cults intertwined, in a way that defeats our more rational way of interpreting such things.

Nor do the complexities of Egyptian religion end here. Out of the turmoil of later political anarchy came yet a third major god: Amon of Thebes.

The city that the Greeks called Thebes (known to the Egyptians themselves first as Wesi and later as Ne or No) was 350 miles south of the Old Kingdom's capital of Memphis. Thebes lay deep in Upper Egypt, and, during the great days of the Old Kingdom, was nothing more than a muddy and unimportant village.

The Eleventh Dynasty, first of the Middle Kingdom, brought sudden importance to Thebes. A southern nobleman named Intef declared himself Pharaoh about 2100, and named Thebes as his capital. A later Pharaoh of Intef's dynasty, Mentuhotep II, marched into Lower Egypt, conquered it, subdued Memphis, and united Egypt under his rule, coming out of the south to do it, as Menes had done more than a thousand years before.

Thebes flourished. Craftsmen from Memphis came up the river to help build Thebes into a capital worthy of the name.

[2] James H. Breasted, *The Dawn of Conscience.*

14

Memphis and Heliopolis, the strongholds of Re, suffered. We have the lament of Khekkeperrisoneb, a Heliopolitan priest of the time of the Twelfth Dynasty: "Maat is cast out, iniquity is in the midst of the council hall. The plans of the gods are violated, their dispositions are disregarded. The land is in distress, mourning in every place, towns and districts are in lamentation. . . ."

Thebes grew great in the time of the Middle Kingdom. And Amon, the god of Thebes, who had been just another minor local god, became the official high god of all Egypt.

Amon's name means "The Hidden One." He may have been originally a god of the harvest, and then a god of the winds. He was depicted always in human form, wearing on his head a circlet from which rose two straight plumes of great length, possibly to represent the tail-feathers of a bird. His wife was Amaunet, later called Mut, meaning "Mother," and their son was the moon-god Khons. Amon of Thebes originally had no part in the Ennead, the family of Atum-Re.

Though Amon became an important god during the Middle Kingdom, his time of supremacy was interrupted by the Hyksos invasion. The Hyksos, sweeping down over Egypt out of Syria, vanquished the ancient land and incredibly maintained their dominion for one hundred and fifty years. When liberation came, it was again from the south. Theban noblemen freed Upper Egypt first, then forged northward, driving the Hyksos ahead of them, at last capturing the Hyksos capital of Avaris in the Delta. Independence returned to Egypt.

It was the time of the New Kingdom and the Eighteenth Dynasty, and now both Thebes and Amon came into their own. The people went on celebrating the mysteries of Osiris, as they had done for a thousand years and more—but the rival priesthoods of Amon and Re carried on a bitter battle for official supremacy.

The result was a theological compromise of a familiar sort. The priests of Amon declared that Amon and Re were one god. The new entity, Amon-Re, was simply the wind-god of Thebes grafted to the old sun-god of Heliopolis. Amon-Re was decreed to be supreme, and the old story of Pharaoh as the son of Re was replaced with a new version in which he was the son of Amon.

It was a heavy blow for the priests of Heliopolis. They found themselves compelled to sing the praises of the usurping deity of the south. Re, demoted, was considered merely one aspect of Amon now. The ancient priesthood of Heliopolis survived the blow, but its political power was gone. Priests at Thebes would dictate the tenets of the official religion of Egypt. More important, priests at Thebes would reap the rich rewards of Pharaoh's generosity. For this was a time of conquest for Egypt. Long held down by the Hyksos, Egypt was unwinding like a coiled spring, bursting out to achieve dominion over the whole Near East. A flood of tribute bounty headed for Thebes—and much of it fell into the hands of Amon's priests.

Amon, "The Hidden One," was no god of love. A hymn to Amon written in the Eighteenth Dynasty declares:

> The gods fawn at his feet,
> According as they recognize his majesty as their lord,
> The lord of fear, great of dread,
> Rich in might, terrible of appearances,
> Flourishing in offerings and making provisions.
> Jubilation to thee who made the gods,
> Raised the heavens and laid down the ground!

Another hymn to Amon, written in the time of Amenhotep III, Akhnaten's father, stresses the tribute-hungry nature of the Theban god:

> When I turn my face to the south, I work a wonder for thee.
> I cause the chiefs of Kush, the wretched, to turn to thee
> Bearing all their tribute upon their backs.
> When I turn my face to the north, I work a wonder for thee.
> I cause all the countries of the ends of Asia to come to thee,
> Bearing all their tribute upon their backs.
> They present themselves to thee with their children
> In order that thou mayest give to them the breath of life.

Amon, gold-greedy, the "lord of fear," was worshipped in dark, mysterious temples of terror. They were vast, somber, awe-inspiring buildings—the temple of Amon at Karnak is the most massive temple ever built, with one single chamber, the Hypostyle Hall, covering an area of 54,000 square feet. Tiny windows admitted only thin shafts of light. Ominous stairways led to subterranean passages, and these to lightless chambers in the walls, out of which rose the hollow, booming chants of Amon's hidden priests. The worshippers crouched in superstitious fright, and only the elect could dare to approach the innermost shrine of Amon himself.

Forbidding though Amon was, he commanded a loyal following. The gold of the Near East flowed into Egypt during the gloriously imperialistic days of the Eighteenth Dynasty, and much of it flowed into Amon's hands. Pharaoh after Pharaoh sought favor in the god's eyes by bestowing the fruits of conquest upon Amon's priests. An inscription at Karnak tells how Thothmes III, the greatest conqueror of that dynasty, gave Amon towns, fields and gardens "of the most excellent of the south and of the north," tons of gold and silver and lapis lazuli. In his thirty-fourth year of reign he gave Amon more than seven hundred Troy pounds of gold from the mines of Nubia and the Sudan; in his thirty-eighth year, about the same amount; in his forty-first year, more than eight hundred pounds. Other Pharaohs were equally generous.

The domain of Amon grew until it vied in splendor with that of Pharaoh himself. The king, forever under the necessity to honor priests or nobles with gifts, was unable to accumulate great wealth. What Amon received, though, Amon kept and never gave back. The god's store of gold grew from year to year. The most fertile fields of Egypt were farmed on Amon's behalf. Palm forests, fish-ponds, meadows, whole towns and villages, an army of scribes and soldiers and farmers, laborers and tradesmen—all this was Amon's, ruled over by a Theban high priest of awesome might.

Just how wealthy the priesthood of Amon was during the Eighteenth Dynasty, we cannot be sure, since the records were destroyed by the reforming zeal of Akhnaten, who obliterated anything that bore Amon's name. But we do have one extraordinary document from the Twentieth Dynasty, a century and a half after Akhnaten, which outlines the extent of Amon's material holdings as restored after Akhnaten's revolution. This is the so-called Papyrus Harris, discovered by natives at Thebes in 1855, purchased by the collector A. C. Harris of Alexandria, and now in the British Museum.

Papyrus Harris, a well-preserved roll 133 feet long, is a detailed list of the benefactions of the Pharaoh Rameses III in the thirty-one years of his rule. He offered gifts to many gods, but the burden of his generosity was directed toward Amon.

In the time of Rameses III, we learn, the Egyptian temples controlled 720,000 acres of Egyptian land, out of about five million cultivable acres—almost 15 per cent of the land! The priesthood of Amon owned 583,000 of these acres; the endowment of Re at Heliopolis was 108,000 acres; that of Ptah at Memphis only 6,850 acres.

Amon, then, owned a tenth of Egypt's land in the Twentieth Dynasty, and probably as much in the Eighteenth as well. His annual income in gold was 26,000 grains, a fortune then or now. The papyrus lists the endless gifts of Pharaoh to Amon: "Gold, silver, real lapis lazuli, real malachite, every real costly stone, copper, garments of royal linen, fine southern linen, colored garments, jars, fowl. . . ." Such entries as "White gold: 310 finger rings" and "Silver: 31 caskets with lids" and "Royal linen: 489 tunics" abound in the list. The priests of Amon rejoiced in gifts of incense and honey, oil and myrrh, butter and goose fat, cinnamon and grapes, pomegranates and cattle.

The wealth of Amon was the doing of the Pharaohs of the Eighteenth Dynasty. There is evidence, though, that the monarchs soon regretted the power of this state within the state that they had helped to create. Although the gifts to Amon never slacken as one Eighteenth Dynasty king succeeds another, we find a certain restlessness coming to trouble the Pharaohs, a fear that Amon is perhaps growing far too mighty.

Thus, in the time of Thothmes IV, the grandfather of Akhnaten, there seems to have been a definite movement on the part of the priests of Re to regain their ancient dominance.

18

Thothmes IV does not appear to have been the direct heir to the throne of his father, Amenhotep II. Yet somehow, through a sort of palace coup, Thothmes IV came to the throne against the wishes of the priests of Amon. A story tells how, before his father's death, the young prince had wandered on a hunting expedition to Gizeh, far to the north of Thebes. There, in the heart of Re's domain, the prince had fallen asleep at noon in the shadow of the Sphinx, and Re had appeared to him in a dream, urging him to clear away the sand that had come to hide the sacred image. If he would do that, Thothmes was told, the kingdom would be his.

The young prince vowed to obey Re's wish. In time, he became Pharaoh, and one of his first official acts was to free the Sphinx from its sandy encumbrance. The title he took as Pharaoh included the phrases, "Chosen of Re" and "Beloved of Re." Certainly his sympathies lay with the sun-god of Heliopolis, and not with the all-too-powerful Amon of Thebes. He let himself be hailed as "Son of Atum and Protector of Harakhti . . . who purifies Heliopolis and satisfies Re."

Thothmes IV was sickly and short-lived. He reigned only a little more than eight years, and was unable to carry his apparent revolution against Amon past the initial stages. He was succeeded by his son, Amenhotep III, called Amenhotep the Magnificent, who ruled with pomp and majesty for nearly forty years, and who is remembered as much for the splendor of his era as for the heresies of his son Amenhotep IV, who called himself Akhnaten.

Amenhotep III was tolerant of all gods. He was willing to continue his father's support of the Heliopolitan priesthood of Re. He allowed the worshippers of the old sun-god to challenge Amon openly. But he was as lavish in his gifts to Amon as his great-grandfather Thothmes III had been.

In the reign of Amenhotep III we hear for the first time of the worship of the sun under another name: not Atum, not Re, not Amon-Re, but *Aten*. Within a generation Aten had inspired a religious reformation and revolution which astonished Egypt and still exerts a fascination today.

19

2

THE GREAT KING PASSES

The New Kingdom of Egypt, which began with the Eighteenth Dynasty in the sixteenth century before Christ, was the time of Egypt's greatest opulence. After generations under the Hyksos heel, Egypt emerged as the world's leading power. It was the time of the glory of Thebes, of the supremacy of Amon. When an Eighteenth Dynasty king moved his capital from Thebes and denied the greatness of Amon, the light of Egypt's brilliant renaissance flickered and died.

There had been earlier times of greatness in Egypt, as in the Fourth Dynasty of the Old Kingdom, when all Egypt hailed Pharaohs as gods and labored to build mighty piles of stone as their mausoleums. But even in those remote and illustrious days Egypt had not had a foreign empire. Nor had there been one when the Middle Kingdom dynasties, the Eleventh and Twelfth, once again made Egypt mighty.

Then had come the Hyksos. The facts about this interlude of foreign rule in Egypt are cloudy. The Egyptians did not write history as such; they left us decrees and autobiographies, self-propagandizing pronouncements, but no chronicles except for lists of kings. What we have is a series of official narratives, carefully edited to provide the best possible view of each period. Naturally, such narratives skip over a time when foreigners held the Egyptian throne.

What we know of Egyptian history has been pieced together from these official inscriptions, from works by such latterday historians as Herodotus, Manetho, and Diodorus Siculus, and from the archaeological evidence itself, which has been a valuable corrective for the errors of the early historians and the self-serving distortions of the Pharaohs. Concerning the Hyksos invasion, a fragment from Manetho tells us:

Tutimaeus. In his reign, for what cause I know not, a blast of God smote us; and unexpectedly, from the regions of the East, invaders of obscure race marched in confidence of victory against our land. By main force they easily seized it without striking a blow; and having overpowered the rulers of the land, they then burned our cities ruthlessly, razed to the ground the temples of the gods, and treated all the natives with a cruel hostility. . . .

Manetho translated the word *Hyksos* as "Shepherd Kings," but we now know that that was a false interpretation; the Egyptians called them *Hiku-khasut,* "Princes of the Desert." Probably they were a mixed band of warrior tribesmen from Syria, Arabia, and Canaan, who descended on a rich Egypt grown lazy, and found it ripe for plucking. They adopted Egyptian customs, writing their foreign-sounding names, Jacob-El and Anath-her and the like, in neat hieroglyphics, and ruling with the aid of a bureaucracy of Egyptian "collaborators." They worshipped their own god Baal and such Egyptian gods as Re and Set as well.

Lower Egypt, which fell first to the Hyksos, accepted the desert princes more or less willingly as their kings. To the people of the Delta, it was a matter of exchanging one foreign master for another, since for centuries Lower Egypt had been under the domination of the Thebans of Upper Egypt.

Upper Egypt never fully surrendered. Probably there were decades of underground resistance and guerrilla warfare around Thebes and the more southerly cities. Gradually the Hyksos relaxed their vigilance. They had grown rich and citified in their conquered land, to which they had introduced such military innovations as the horse-drawn chariot, the war-helmet, scale armor, and new types of swords and bows.

The dispossessed noblemen of Thebes studied the Hyksos weapons, copied them, and mastered their use. A Theban prince named Sekenenre led an open revolt against the Hyksos, but met a terrible death in battle against them, and received a hero's burial from Thebes. The mummy of his hideously mutilated body lies in an Egyptian museum today, all his frightful wounds still evident.

The sons of the fallen leader, Kamose and Amose, carried on the war of liberation. It was Amose, the younger son, who finally drove the routed Hyksos out of Memphis and their own capital of Avaris, forcing them across the Sinai Peninsula and back into their original homelands. Egypt was Egyptian again.

Amose I inaugurated the Eighteenth Dynasty in 1555. Thebes again became Egypt's capital, a vast metropolis sprawling on both sides of the Nile. The Twelfth Dynasty kings had transformed Thebes, an unimportant provincial town, into a major city. The kings of the Eighteenth Dynasty expanded it into a wonder of the ages—"hundred-gated Thebes" of which Homer wrote in awe.

The throne passed from Amose to his son, Amenhotep I. The new king's name symbolized the dominance of Amon in Egypt, for it meant "Amon-is-Content." Where such ancient kings as Khefre and Menkure had taken care to have the name of *Re* form part of their names, the new Eighteenth Dynasty rulers gave honor to Amon.

Amenhotep I commenced his reign by marrying his three sisters, Merit-Amon, Ahotep, and Sat-Kamose. This step—to us so startling—seemed necessary to him in order to cement his hold on Egypt's throne.

The throne of Egypt did not succeed in a direct male line. Rather, the right to rule was transmitted through the eldest daughter of the Pharaoh. Her husband was the heir to the throne. In practice, this was usually the son of the old Pharaoh, since it was customary for the eldest prince to marry the eldest princess. The son of the Pharaoh was also his son-in-law, and took the throne by the latter right.

Amenhotep I, by marrying all three of his sisters, took a

triple hold on his title. No one might challenge his crown by marrying another of the royal princesses.

He ruled about twenty years. He continued his father's work of rebuilding and consolidating Egypt, and when he died the frontiers were at peace, the Hyksos no longer represented any threat, and the damage done by fifteen decades of alien rule had been undone. Egypt had become a commercial center once again. Barges plied the Nile, laden with luxury goods. Busy scribes recorded the new prosperity of the lands, and trade thrived, particularly with the wealthy, important island of Crete.

With internal stability restored, Egypt now turned to foreign conquest. The priests of Amon, growing more powerful from year to year, demanded heavy tributes. The Pharaohs, needing some new source of wealth to feed the appetites of these greedy priests, looked outward, toward the gold-rich lands of Nubia to the south, toward the wealthy merchant-cities of Syria and the Levant.

When Amenhotep I died, the double crown of Egypt came to rest on his son Thothmes I. None of Amenhotep's three wives of royal blood had been able to produce a male heir, and Thothmes was only partly of divine blood, being the son of Amenhotep by a slave-girl. His right to the throne was secured, however, by his marriage to the eldest full-blooded daughter of the king.

Thothmes I initiated Egypt's career of overseas expansion. He had inherited from his father a tightly knit, smoothly run country with an efficient army, and he was hungry for fame. When a ruler of the Sudan, smarting under a defeat at the hands of Amenhotep I, tested the mettle of the new Pharaoh, young Thothmes met the invaders and destroyed them, marched on to Kerma, the capital of the Nubian kingdom of Kush, five hundred miles south of Thebes, conquered it, and forged on two hundred miles beyond it, to the Fourth Cataract of the Nile. There he set a boundary stone to mark the southern limit of his empire.

A few years later, Thothmes I led his battle-hardened veterans northward, into Canaan. His father had made tentative

23

thrusts into that land, by way of driving back the Hyksos, but it was Thothmes I who first brought the territory under Egyptian control. He conquered Canaan (Palestine) and the Phoenician coastal cities, and the whole length of Syria as far as the Euphrates, setting up another boundary-stone at the border of Mesopotamia. He was lord of the greatest empire the world had yet seen, stretching from Asia Minor to the Sudan, and embracing the entire eastern end of the Mediterranean.

The final days of Thothmes I were occupied with domestic enterprises. He spent the last ten years of his life at Thebes, where he built a magnificent temple at Karnak for his god Amon. Gold from every part of the new empire flowed toward Thebes, and much of it went to honor Amon.

The death of Thothmes I created a confused political situation that threatened the stability of the country. There was no male heir of pure blood. Only one of Thothmes' children by his royal wife had survived to adulthood: Princess Hatshepsut. But there was a prince of half-royal blood, the son of Pharaoh Thothmes by a second wife. This boy, named Thothmes also, married his half-sister Hatshepsut. His claim to the throne was thus the same as his father's had been.

Thothmes II succeeded to the throne about 1515 B.C. But the real ruler of the land was Queen Hatshepsut. Hearing of the death of the old conqueror, the provinces of Nubia revolted, and Queen Hatshepsut's energies were involved in suppressing this uprising. There was no time for further foreign expansion; the conquered territories had to be held.

Thothmes II died early in his reign. He, like his father and grandfather, had failed to provide a male heir of the full royal blood, but he, too, had left a son named Thothmes by a secondary wife. Queen Hatshepsut, though, refused to relinquish the throne to this Thothmes, even though he had obtained clear title to it by marrying Queen Hatshepsut's daughter by Thothmes II. Instead, Queen Hatshepsut did something unprecedented in Egypt's long history. She took the throne herself—not as queen, but as king!

Official portraits of Pharaoh Hatshepsut showed her wearing

the artificial beard that was one of the monarch's signs of office. She issued decrees in her own name, built temples and monuments, directed the forces of her army. Thothmes III became a prisoner in his palace, and remained there, unseen and unheard from, for twenty-two years, despite the insistence of the priests of Amon that he be given the throne he rightfully deserved.

At last Hatshepsut died. There followed one of the most amazing reversals of character in history. Thothmes III, the "weakling" prince who had tolerated his usurping stepmother for more than half his lifetime, ascended the throne at last and became one of the most vigorous kings in Egypt's history.

He was nearly forty, and unknown to his people, but he quickly made his presence felt. First, he ordered that Hatshepsut be expunged from history. Her name was to be chipped off every monument where it was carved; the years of her reign were to be removed from all the lists of rulers. Thothmes III decreed that the start of his reign was to be reckoned from the day of his father's death, twenty-two years earlier.

He set out now on a campaign of conquest unparalleled in Egyptian history. Year after year, the armies of Thothmes III drove outward to the north, reconquering cities that had managed to assert their independence during the uncertainties of the last thirty years. The priests of Amon spurred him on. The temple walls of Thebes were covered with battle hymns, like this one in which Amon addresses Thothmes III:

I have come, giving thee to smite the princes of Zahi,
I have hurled them beneath thy feet among their highlands. . . .
Thou hast trampled those who are in the districts of Punt. . . .
I have made them see thy majesty as a circling star. . . .
Crete and Cyprus are in terror. . . .
Those who are in the midst of the great sea hear thy roarings;
I have made them see thy majesty as an avenger,
Rising upon the back of his slain victim. . . .
I have made them see thy majesty as a fierce-eyed lion,
While thou makest them corpses in their valleys. . . .

Twenty years of campaigning left Thothmes III master of an empire greater than that of his grandfather Thothmes I. He marched northward to the Euphrates, setting his own boundary

stone proudly beside that of Thothmes I. He pacified restless
Nubia. He gloried in his own achievements, boasting of his
hunting prowess, telling the world how he hunted 120 elephants
in Syria, how "he killed seven lions by shooting in the completion of a moment and he captured a herd of twelve wild cattle
within an hour." He left us triumphant hymns to his military
achievements, such as this one inscribed on the great stone pylon
he erected in Amon's honor at Thebes:

> Utterance of Amon-Re, lord of Thebes:
> Thou comest to me, thou exultest, seeing my beauty,
> O my son, my avenger, Menkheperre, living forever. . . .
> I have given to thee might and victory against all countries,
> I have set thy fame, even the fear of thee in all lands.

Amon then tells Thothmes III:

> There is no rebel against thee as far as the circuit of heaven;
> They come, bearing tribute upon their backs,
> Bowing down to thy majesty according to my command.
> I have made powerless the invaders who came before thee;
> Their hearts burned, their limbs trembling.

The annals in Karnak listed the booty of Thothmes III:
from the city of Megiddo, 340 living prisoners and 83 hands;
2,041 horses, 191 foals, 6 stallions; a chariot worked with
gold, belonging to the Prince of Megiddo; 892 chariots of "his
wretched army." The list stretches on for yard after yard of
elegant hieroglyphics.

Powerful as Egypt was in the reign of Thothmes III, it was
confronted with another nation which had similarly risen to
eminence within a few generations: Mitanni. This kingdom was
somewhere to the north of Syria, with its capital probably at
Carchemish. It was bordered to the east by Assyria, then a
fairly unimportant state; to the west by the Hittites of Asia
Minor; to the south by Egypt's Syrian empire. The people of
Mitanni were Hurrians, an obscure Near Eastern group, but
their kings were of a different stock, speaking an Indo-European
language related to Sanskrit. It is likely that these Indo-European
conquerors, making war in swift chariots, had ventured into the
Near East about the time the Hyksos were being driven from

Egypt, and had forged a nation for themselves by subjugating the Hurrians.

The northward expansions of Thothmes I and Thothmes III had twice taken Egypt right to Mitanni's southern border. The two mighty nations had not actually come to war, but rather had engaged in diplomatic jockeying that might well be described as a "cold war." During the reign of Thothmes III, diplomats from Mitanni tried subtly to detach the city-states of Syria from their Egyptian allegiance and to win them over to the northern nation.

When Thothmes III was succeeded by his son Amenhotep II, the Mitannian agitations bore fruit. Syria did indeed rebel against Egypt, and the new king hastened northward to restore order.

Amenhotep II was a man of a ferocity we usually associate with the bloodthirsty kings who ruled Assyria seven centuries later. He possessed great physical strength, as an inscription of his reign tells us: "There was no one like him on the field of battle. He was one who knew horses: there was not his like in this numerous army. There was not one therein who could draw his bow. He could not be approached in running." In 1447, the second year of his reign, he marched into Syria to set things right, and in a single campaign of unusual bloodiness put an end to the rebellion there. His record of the campaign is an account of slaughter by the thousands. And, we learn, "The king returned home with his heart full of gratitude toward his father Amon. He had with his own hand struck down seven kings with his battle-axe, who were in the territory of the land of Thakhis. They lay there bound on the forepart of the royal ship, the name of which was 'Ship of Amenhotep II, the upholder of the land.' Six of these enemies were hung up outside on the walls of Thebes, their hands likewise. Then the other enemy was carried up the river to Nubia, and was hung up on the wall of the city of Napata, to make evident for all time the victories of the king."

This demonstration of Egypt's might was enough to cool Mitanni's ambitions for a head-on conflict. When Amenhotep

27

II died, about 1415, the rulers of Mitanni preferred to come to a diplomatic understanding with his successor.

That successor was Thothmes IV, who, as we saw earlier, leaned more toward the worship of Re than toward Amon. Like all three previous kings named Thothmes, Thothmes IV was not the son of the Pharaoh and his divine queen and sister. Rather, he was the child of Amenhotep II by a subordinate wife. For the fourth time in the Eighteenth Dynasty, the royal blood-line was diluted with that of noble but non-royal families.

When Thothmes IV made his way to the throne—a triumph for Re over Amon, under circumstances we do not know—he carried the process a little further. He took as his wife a woman who was not only not his sister, but not even an Egyptian!

She was a princess of Mitanni—Mutenwiya, sister of King Shutarna of Mitanni. By marrying her, Thothmes IV thus contracted an alliance with Mitanni, and put to an end the threat of war between Egypt and its powerful northern neighbor. From then until the eventual destruction of Mitanni by the Hittites, Egypt and Mitanni remained closely allied.

Thothmes IV's reign was brief, and little of historical importance occurred during it. From what we know of the way he reached the throne, we can suspect that Thothmes IV had some idea of curbing the power of the priests of Amon, and of restoring Re's priests at Heliopolis to their old dignity. But none of this was actually done, apparently.

The presence of a Mitanni-born queen lent an exotic touch to the court of Thothmes IV. Mutenwiya arrived accompanied by a full retinue of handmaidens, and into the closed world of the Theban court came foreign ideas, foreign customs. Possibly the influence of Queen Mutenwiya had something to do with her husband's dissatisfaction with the official religion of Amon. Mitanni and the other lands of western Asia were centers of religious speculation. The queen may have brought some subversive new ideas about the nature of God to her husband's thought.

After eight years, Thothmes IV died, and was succeeded by

his young son, Amenhotep III. The new Pharaoh was the full-blooded heir to the throne, the son of Thothmes and Mutenwiya. But he was only half Egyptian. Perhaps Amenhotep III's Asiatic heritage displayed itself in his love of pomp, his easy-going indolence, and his tolerance of strange creeds. Certainly the new king lacked the rock-hewn rigid conservatism of the typical Pharaoh.

He was only a boy when he came to rule, sometime between 1410 and 1406. Probably he was no more than twelve. A Pharaoh needed a queen, whatever his age, and Amenhotep quickly married. He, too, was unconventional in his choice of a bride. Thothmes IV had left no royal sister for young Amenhotep to wed. He took instead a girl of common blood, about ten years old. Her name was Tiy.

Tiy is an unusual figure in Egyptian history, and played an important though enigmatic part in the great upheaval that was to be brought about by her son. Tiy was the daughter of a civil servant and provincial priest, Yuya, and his wife Tuya. During the reign of Thothmes IV Yuya had lived at the royal court, serving as a priest of Min-Re, Re in the form of a fertility god.

Yuya's origins are mysterious. His name itself is not a common Egyptian one, and some have suggested that he was a Syrian prince, brought to Egypt as a trophy during the conquests of Thothmes III or Amenhotep II. We do know that Amenhotep II, in particular, brought many prisoners back with him from Syria and Canaan, including 127 Asiatic princes. (He also brought 3,600 members of a tribe listed in the record as 'Apiru, who may well have been the Hebrews of later renown.)

Tiy may thus have been the daughter of a Syrian who had risen to high rank in Egypt. On the other hand, a small ebony head of Tiy now in the Berlin Museum shows her to have had a definitely Nubian cast of features, and other portraits more recently discovered argue likewise that she was a member of this black-skinned race. It does seem certain that she was not of Egyptian blood, at any rate.

Yuya was granted a number of high titles at the court of the

29

Pharaoh. He was "Prophet of Min" and "Lieutenant-General of the King's Chariots," and also "Divine Father," which may have been a way of saying, "Father-in-law of the Pharaoh." In the past, the father-in-law of the Pharaoh had almost always been the previous Pharaoh; Yuya, a commoner, required some new title to mark his status.

With Tiy as his queen, Amenhotep III ascended the throne of Egypt, taking as his coronation name the appellation, "Neb-maat-re." Every Pharaoh since earliest times had borne five names. Three of them were of religious significance. The fourth was the name which he had received at birth—in this case, Amenhotep. The fifth was the name he took when he was crowned. His birth-name might be a common one—there were many Egyptians named Amenhotep—but there could only be one Neb-maat-re. From the day of his coronation on, Prince Amenhotep was known to his people as Neb-maat-re, King of Upper Egypt and King of Lower Egypt. His coronation name, it will be noticed, paid homage both to Re, the ancient sun-god now somewhat eclipsed by Amon, and to Maat, the goddess who embodied truth and order. (The title Pharaoh, incidentally, did not come into general use as we understand it until the Eighteenth Dynasty. It meant simply, "The Big House," and referred to the palace of the king. By Amenhotep III's time, it had also come to refer to the person of the king himself, through the same process by which we often refer to the President as "The White House.")

Amenhotep III—for so history knows him, though his people called him Neb-maat-re—lost no time in announcing his marriage. On his wedding day, in the first year of his reign, the boy-king caused a series of commemorative scarab-shaped medallions to be issued, bearing the queen's name and ancestry. These scarabs were distributed far and wide through the vast Egyptian empire, letting all know that the new king had taken as his wife a commoner, Tiy, daughter of the priest Yuya.

An undercurrent of change was beginning to stir in Egypt. Old customs were breaking down. King after king had come to the throne under clouded circumstances, and now a woman not at all of the divine blood was queen. Whispers of new religious teachings were heard in the land. Re, so long dominated by Amon, appeared to be returning to influence. The important figures at the new king's court owed no allegiance to mighty Amon. The queen mother, Mutenwiya, was a foreigner from Mitanni, and in the early years of her son's reign she must have wielded great power in Egypt. The "Divine Father," Yuya, was a priest of Min-Re, not of Amon, and he, too, held great power.

Amenhotep III's attitude toward Queen Tiy was new, too. Tiy began to make public appearances at the king's side, something no Egyptian queen had ever done except for the revolutionary Hatshepsut, who had dared to usurp her husband's power and then that of her stepson. Royal proclamations were made in the name of Amenhotep *and* Tiy, ruling jointly—again, something unusual. She received honors that had been offered to no other queen—and she was not even of royal blood.

Though she held unique powers, Queen Tiy was not the only wife of the Pharaoh. Like his father, he found it necessary to make a diplomatic marriage with a princess of Mitanni, and the event is duly recorded on a commemorative scarab bearing this inscription:

"Year 10 under Amenhotep and the Great King's Wife Tiy, whose father's name is Yuya and whose mother's name is Tuya. Marvels brought to his majesty: Gilukhepa, daughter of the Prince of Mitanni, Shutarna, and the chief of her harem-ladies, 317 women."

Amenhotep thus took his cousin of Mitanni as his wife, but this in no way seems to have weakened Queen Tiy's position, as the very phrasing of the announcement indicates. Gilukhepa, though she was a princess of powerful Mitanni, became simply a secondary wife in Amenhotep's harem. There is no record of any children born to Amenhotep and Gilukhepa. But she and her 317 ladies-in-waiting added a further foreign element to Theban palace life. The groundwork for a religious reformation aimed at Amon was being laid.

31

Amenhotep III had inherited a well-ordered empire. Nowhere was the new Pharaoh threatened with revolt. Mitanni was an ally. No other nation was strong enough to challenge Egypt's supremacy. There was no need for Amenhotep III to take to the field year after year on campaigns of conquest, as Thothmes I, Thothmes III, and Amenhotep II had done. The empire they had forged now held together of its own. It was a time when Egypt could relax and celebrate its affluence.

And so the reign of Amenhotep III was one of extraordinary magnificence. Thebes glittered with foreign tribute. The wealthy Pharaoh could afford vast public works. He put thousands of his subjects to work on these huge projects—not pressing them into slavery, as in the Biblical picture of a tyrannical Pharaoh, but hiring them and paying them liberally out of the bottomless well of the royal revenues.

At Malkata, on the western bank of the Nile near Thebes, Amenhotep III caused the construction of a sumptuous palace for himself and Tiy. It was a complex, many-roomed structure of brick and costly woods, rising at the edge of the desert where the Theban hills look down. Its airy rooms, embellished with paintings on stucco, were gay and elegant, in contrast to the stiffly ponderous official style of Egyptian art and architecture that had prevailed till then.

Queen Tiy was given to queenly whims, and Amenhotep III fulfilled them in a regal manner. Piqued because she was not invited by the priests of Amon to play the role of the goddess Mut in a religious festival, Tiy asked her husband for a pleasure-lake on which she could amuse herself. Amenhotep put thousands of laborers—as many as a quarter of a million, according to one estimate—to work building the queen an artificial lake, a mile and a half long by two-thirds of a mile wide, just east of the Malkata palace.

A scarab inscription of Amenhotep's eleventh year of reign records the success of the venture: "His Majesty commanded to make a lake for the Great King's Wife, Tiy. . . . Its length is 3,700 cubits; its width, 700 cubits. His majesty celebrated the feast of the opening of the lake in the third month of the first season, day 16, when his majesty sailed thereon in the royal barge, Aten Gleams."

Only fifteen days elapsed between the time the order to begin work was given, and the time when a no doubt lavish royal party enjoyed a splendid banquet and festival on the water in the royal barge. More significant than the speed with which Queen Tiy's whim was gratified, though, is the name of the barge: "Aten Gleams." It offers a hint of the storm that lay ahead for Egypt.

Aten was a common word in the Egyptian vocabulary. It meant, simply, the visible face of the sun, the solar disk. It had never had any religious connotation. The sun-as-god was known as Atum, or as Re, or as Harakhti, or as Khepra, or as Amon-Re, or as some combination of those names. Aten was merely the word for the sun-as-sun, the object in the sky.

In itself, the name of Amenhotep's barge might have no higher significance. Probably the barge was inlaid with gold, and gleamed with eye-dazzling radiance in the sun; calling it "Aten Gleams" might just have been a way of describing its golden brightness.

But another translation for the name of the barge is "Splendor of Aten," which is something else again—an attempt to glorify the sun. And there were other portents. During Amenhotep III's reign, two royal architects, the twins Suti and Hor, had carved a hymn of praise on a temple wall at Luxor. It began, conventionally enough, with praise for Amon of Thebes, in his role as Amon-Re, the sun-god:

"Thou shootest up at sunrise without fail, Khepra, great one of works. Thy radiance is in thy face, thou Hidden One. Shining metal doth not resemble thy splendors."

Seven more lines of poetry directed toward Amon-Re follow. Then, startlingly, comes this line:

"Hail to thee, O Aten of the day, thou Creator of mortals and Maker of their life! Hail!"

The Aten hailed by Suti and Hor was not the Aten later worshipped by Akhnaten, for Akhnaten's god was abstract and immaterial, while we find Aten described by the twin architects as "thou Great Hawk whose feathers are many-colored"—an ancient depiction of the Heliopolitan god Re.

But it was a beginning. We can see it as a sign of a new cult taking form in Thebes, perhaps nurtured by the women of Mitanni at the royal court, aided in its birth by the sun-worshipping "Divine Father," Yuya, and by his daughter, the unconventional, strong-willed Queen Tiy.

The vast new palace which Amenhotep III built, at a considerable distance from the old palace which adjoined the temple of Amon, was clearly another move in the same pattern. For the new palace's location seems an open indication that the Pharaoh, or those who influenced him, wanted to get away from the presence of the jealous priests of Amon. A building within the new palace complex, reserved for the personal use of the king, was given the name, "The House of Neb-maat-re is Aten's Splendor."

Amenhotep III did not neglect Amon, by any means. An inscription tells us—accurately—that he made "monuments for Amon, the like of which has never occurred." He enlarged the Amon temple at Karnak, which Thothmes I and Thothmes III had already made splendid. Amenhotep added a new pylon, "inlaid with real lazuli wrought with gold and many costly stones; there is no instance of doing the like." The pylons of the temple now "reach heaven like the four pillars of heaven; its flagstaffs shine more than the heavens."

As though not satisfied, Amenhotep turned to nearby Luxor, demolished a small Twelfth Dynasty temple of Amon, and built a new one on colossal scale. Its naos, or shrine, rose high above the Nile, with cornices projecting over the river. A staircase on the south side allowed the priests and devotees to leave the rear of the building and enter boats to take them to their residences across the river. The sanctuary of Amon was at the end of a long, dark hall flanked with immense columns. No sunlight ever broke into the solemn darkness of the holy place. North of the temple, an avenue of sphinxes led to the gates of old Thebes.

On the other side of the river, Amenhotep provided for his

own spiritual welfare, building a mortuary temple for himself where prayers might be said for his departed shade after his death. Here, too, he spared no expense. An inscription tells us, "Behold, the heart of his majesty was satisfied with making a very great monument; never has happened the like since the beginning. He made it as his monument for his father, Amon, lord of Thebes, making for him an august temple on the west of Thebes, an eternal, everlasting fortress of white sandstone, wrought with gold throughout; its floor is adorned with silver, all its portals with electrum [an alloy of silver and gold]; it is made very wide and large, and established forever. . . . It is numerous in royal statues, of Elephantine granite, of costly gritstone, of every splendid costly stone, established as everlasting works. Their stature shines more than the heavens, their rays are in the faces of men like the sun. . . . Its storehouse is filled with male and female slaves, with children of the princes of all the countries of the captivity of his majesty. . . ."

Of all this opulence, "established forever," nothing survives. A later Pharaoh, Merneptah, demolished Amenhotep III's mortuary temple and used the material for a building of his own. All that remains are two immense statues of Amenhotep seated on his throne, the famed Memnon Colossi—so-called because the Greeks, visiting Egypt centuries later, thought they represented Memnon, a dark-skinned warrior from a southern land who had fought on the side of the Trojans in the great war.

The architects were busy in Amenhotep III's reign. Palaces, lakes, temples, colossi—the wealth of Egypt took visible, massive, tangible form. Over all this sprouting magnificence presided Amenhotep and his queen, enjoying the benefits of earlier conquests, and passing their time, perhaps, in thoughts of a new religion whose worship would bypass the troublesome, grasping priests of Amon.

Amenhotep himself does not strike a very impressive figure, for all the greatness of his time. In the early years of his rule, we find him boasting of his prowess as a hunter, much in the manner of such earlier royal braggarts as Thothmes III and

Amenhotep II. A commemorative scarab of his tenth year declares, "Statement of lions which his majesty brought down with his own arrows from year 1 to year 10: fierce lions, 102."

But after the tenth year—the year when the Mitanni princess Gilukhepa joined the Pharaoh's harem—we hear no more of lion-hunting. The portraits of Amenhotep show him growing plump, even bloated. The pleasures of the harem and the pleasures of the royal banquet-hall came to occupy most of his energy. The actual governing of the country, it would seem, was left to Queen Tiy, to her father Yuya, and to the advisers and viziers of the court. Even when trouble developed in the provinces of the empire, in Syria and Palestine, the lethargic, pleasure-loving Amenhotep took no action. The Eighteenth Dynasty had reached its climax of power, and had gone past it. Aging, fat Amenhotep, builder of temples and palaces, was not of the heroic mold.

And what of his son, Prince Amenhotep, the heir to the throne?

We hear little of him through most of the reign of Amenhotep III. We hear of royal daughters born to Pharaoh and Tiy; indeed, late in his life Amenhotep III even takes one of those daughters, Sitamon, as his wife. (Perhaps the priests of Amon were belatedly challenging his right to rule, and the old king sought to legitimize himself by marrying a royal heiress, even though she was his own daughter.) There is no mention, in any of the inscriptions of Amenhotep's early years, of a son.

And so we do not know when Akhnaten was born. We have no idea where he spent his formative years. Probably he lived at the Theban court, closely watched by his mother Tiy—but he could just as well have been travelling abroad, roaming through far countries and picking up strange ideas about the nature of God. Perhaps Egypt's sands still hide some inscription that will tell us about young Akhnaten. Till such a document is found, we can only guess.

Our knowledge of Egypt at the peak of the Eighteenth Dynasty is extensive but intermittent. It is as though we look through opera glasses at a distant stage shrouded in darkness, on which a light gleams fitfully now and then to reveal the actors. Inscriptions, commemorative scarabs, wall paintings, statues, reliefs, tell us something about this era. We see young Amenhotep III crowned, see him taking Tiy to wife, hear of his prowess in the hunt, see him gaining weight while temples and palaces multiply in Thebes, see him corresponding with his fellow monarchs of the Near East—but there are great rifts in the record. And then, suddenly, a strange prince is on the scene, intent on holding the center of the stage.

Amenhotep IV, the eldest and perhaps only male child of the Pharaoh and Queen Tiy, was born about 1400 B.C.—though some Egyptologists think his birth may have come as much as twenty years later. Not anywhere is he mentioned in a royal inscription through the first thirty years of his father's reign. No sons are shown in the family portraits of Amenhotep III and his children. The elaborate tomb of Yuya and Tuya, parents of Queen Tiy, contains funeral gifts from Amenhotep III, his wife, and their daughters, but none from Prince Amenhotep. The man who was to call himself Akhnaten appears abruptly and without introduction.

He was physically deformed. The realistic art style that he helped to sponsor portrayed him with merciless clarity. His head was long, his lips were thick and protruding, his neck so thin it seemed barely able to support the distorted head. His abdomen thrust forward. His thighs were strangely swollen, an odd contrast to the slenderness of his upper body. His knees were in some way wrongly fashioned. His health was poor; indeed, Amenhotep IV may have been an epileptic, sharing the convulsive malady that afflicted Julius Caesar, Alexander the Great, Czar Peter the Great, Byron, Dostoievski, and others who were granted the grim privilege of attaining the lonely heights of eminence.

There is nothing in the background of the Eighteenth Dynasty to explain his odd physical appearance. None of the earlier Pharaohs showed any of Akhnaten's deformities, though it should be noted that the highly conventionalized stylization of court art before his time would have tended to play down any

37

unusual aspect of kingly anatomy. But even the relatively realistic representations of Amenhotep III bear no hint of the prince's misshapen condition. It has been suggested that Queen Tiy was the source of her son's deformity, and certain intimate portraits of the queen do indeed seem to show some of the same physical peculiarities.

The young prince was reared amid Oriental pomp. Court life must have been a long sunny round of Theban festivals and banquets, broken only by ceremonial processions through the Pharaoh's Egyptian dominions. Amenhotep III never deigned to visit the foreign possessions. A Syrian prince would later write to his successor, "Verily, thy father did not march forth, nor inspect the lands of his foreign princes."

All the freight of the world crowded the ports of the Nile, from the Delta to the lower cataracts. Spices, aromatic woods of the Levant, weapons and jewelled ornaments, fine pottery, all found purchasers in the markets of Thebes and Memphis. Caravans and fleets of galleys fanned outward from Egypt along the ancient trade routes, safer now than they had ever been before. It was a time of lazy contentment for Egypt and her king. The gods had never been more kind.

The tomb of Amenhotep III's vizier Khamhat shows the king in paunchy middle age, receiving tribute "from the South and from the North, and from this miserable land of Kush to the region of the river-land Naharain"—from Nubia to Mesopotamia. But the tribute paid to the king was intended chiefly as a spur to his generosity. Foreign monarchs sent gifts to Amenhotep III, hoping that the wealthy monarch would return their friendship many times over.

Thus we find a letter to Amenhotep III from his cousin Dushratta, King of Mitanni, who had succeeded King Shutarna, the brother of Amenhotep III's mother. Dushratta writes:

To Nimmuria [Neb-maat-re], the great king, the king of Egypt, my brother, my son-in-law, who loves me, and whom I love:— Dushratta, the great king, thy father-in-law, who loves thee, the king of Mitanni, thy brother. It is well with me. With thee may it be well, with thy house, my sister and thy other wives, thy sons,

38

thy chariots, thy chief men, thy land, and all thy possessions, may it be very well indeed. In the time of thy fathers, they were on very friendly terms with my fathers, but thou hast increased this friendship still more and with my father thou hast been on very friendly terms indeed. Now, therefore, since thou and I are on mutually friendly terms, thou hast made it ten times closer than with my father. May the gods cause this friendship of ours to prosper. . . .

Dushratta now makes mention of the bond of marriage, covering three generations by now, that linked Egypt and Mitanni. Amenhotep III's father, Thothmes IV, had married Dushratta's aunt, Mutenwiya. Amenhotep III himself had taken Dushratta's sister Gilukhepa as a secondary wife. Now, this letter tells us, Amenhotep III has added yet another Mitanni princess to his harem—Tadukhepa, the daughter of Dushratta. Thus Dushratta was at once the cousin, the brother-in-law, and the father-in-law of Amenhotep III!

Family matters out of the way, the ruler of Mitanni gets down to the real business of his letter:

Now when I wrote to my brother [Amenhotep III] I said, "So far as I am concerned, we will be very friendly indeed, and mutually well disposed," and I said to my brother, "Let my brother make our friendship ten times greater than with my father," and I asked of my brother a great deal of gold, saying, "More than to my father let my brother give and send me." Thou sent my father a great deal of gold: a namkhar of pure gold thou sent him, and a kiru[1] of pure gold thou sent him; but thou sent me only a tablet of gold that is as if it were alloyed with copper. . . . So let my brother send gold in very great quantities, without measure, and let him send more gold to me than to my father. For in my brother's land gold is as common as dust. . . ."

Let my brother send gold in very great quantities. . . . For in my brother's land gold is as common as dust. . . .

From another potentate, Kadashman-Bel of Babylonia, came a letter displaying the same mixture of flattery and peremptory insistence. Kadashman-Bel had sent his sister to join Amenhotep III's harem, and nothing has been heard from the Babylonian

---

[1] *Namkhar* and *kiru* are units of measure that cannot be meaningfully translated because we do not know their modern equivalents.

princess since her arrival in Egypt. Kadashman-Bel thinks his sister may be dead. Why, he asks, has he not been informed?

To this, Amenhotep III replies that Kadashman-Bel had sent no one who could check on whether the princess were alive or dead. "You have sent no one who knows your sister, who could have recognized her, and could have spoken with her. The people whom you sent, there is not among them one who stood near your father. . . . If your sister were dead, why should it be concealed from you?"

Kadashman-Bel, satisfied that his sister still lived, asks now for a daughter of Pharaoh as his wife. He gets a discouraging reply from Amenhotep the Magnificent: "From of old a daughter of the king of Egypt has never been given to anyone." The Babylonian king will not accept that answer. "Why is that?" he asks. "A king are you, and you can do according to your heart's wish. If you give her, who shall say anything against it? . . . There are grown-up daughters and beautiful women. If there is any beautiful woman there, send her. Who shall say: 'She is not a king's daughter'? If, however, you do not send anyone at all, then you will have no regard for brotherhood and friendship."

The argument must have told. The last scrap of correspondence in this series that we have is a letter from Kadashman-Bel to Pharaoh, declaring, "I have ready all that was in the presence of your messenger who brings your daughter."

Ill health troubled the great king as he grew old. His obesity made him sluggish and indecisive. His teeth were bothering him; the mummy of Amenhotep III, discovered at the end of the last century, showed a bad case of dental decay. Late in his life, Amenhotep received the miracle-working statue of Ishtar the Great, an Assyrian goddess, as a loan from his friendly cousin, Dushratta of Mitanni. The statue must have had an invigorating effect on the Pharaoh, for Dushratta had to request the statue back several times before Amenhotep would part with it.

By the year 1377, Amenhotep III had ruled some thirty years. They were not notably taxing years, and he was still only in his forties, but he had aged rapidly. It was the year of his jubilee—a time of religious festival when the king took part in a ritualistic ceremony of rejuvenation. In the mystic ceremony, the king "died" and was "reborn" as a younger and more vigorous man, passing from the Osiris role to that of Horus and Re. Perhaps in prehistoric Egypt the thirty-year festival had been an occasion actually to put the old king to death and place a younger man on the throne, but for thousands of years the ceremony had been purely symbolic.

It appears that Amenhotep III took advantage of the festival to raise his son to the throne by his side. This co-regency of Amenhotep III and Amenhotep IV is anything but a certain historical fact. The record is cloudy. There are Egyptologists who maintain that no co-regency ever existed.

The most important element of evidence to support the co-regency theory comes from a scribbled note in ink found on the pyramid temple of Medum, in Lower Egypt. A scribe had visited the temple about the time of Amenhotep III's jubilee, and had scrawled, "Year XXX, under the majesty of the King Neb-maat-re, Son of Amon, resting in truth, Amenhotep III, prince of Thebes, lord of might, prince of joy, who loves him that hates injustice of heart, placing the male offspring upon the seat of his father, and establishing his inheritance in the land."

Two other proofs of a co-regency are known. A battered limestone block, part of what had been a temple wall, was found a few years ago. It bore the cartouches, or royal insignia, of Amenhotep III and Amenhotep IV, both facing the same way. The cartouches would have faced in opposite directions had Amenhotep IV been the successor of his father, rather than the co-ruler, just as each successive ruler of England faces the opposite way from his predecessor on that country's coinage.

And another limestone slab shows Amenhotep IV pouring a drink for his father. Both of them wear the royal crown of Egypt. It seems fairly certain that, in the closing years of the great king's life, his son ruled by his side as Amenhotep IV.

A year after the jubilee ceremony, Amenhotep III had his tomb made ready for him at Thebes. On the walls of the chapel were inscribed instructions for the maintenance of the king's mortuary temple, with this blistering curse pronounced on any trespasser or on anyone who should fail to keep the temple in good repair:

"Amon shall deliver them into the flaming wrath of the king on the day of his anger; his serpent-diadem shall spit fire upon their heads, shall consume their limbs, shall devour their bodies. . . . They shall be engulfed in the sea, it shall hide their corpses. They shall not receive the mortuary ceremonies of the righteous; the waters by the flood of the river shall not be poured out for them. Their sons shall not be put into their places. . . . The nobles shall not set foot in their houses as long as they are upon earth. . . . They shall belong to the sword on the day of destruction; they shall be called enemies; when their bodies be consumed, they shall hunger, without bread, and their bodies shall die."

Amenhotep III lived on for seven more years. We can be sure that he took little part in the actual governing of Egypt. Rather, he retreated still further into indolent repose, even donning woman's clothing as though to mark his renunciation of royal majesty. No doubt Queen Tiy, royal wife and now royal mother, exercised great power in the land. She was still young and vigorous—young enough to have given birth to a daughter when she had been queen more than thirty years—and she must have served as chief counsellor to the young and inexperienced new king, her son Amenhotep IV. Whether by her inspiration or not, Amenhotep IV spent the seven or eight years of his co-regency performing a series of controversial actions which culminated, finally, in the startling interlude of the Amarna Revolution.

Amenhotep III took little notice of his son's activities. He lived quietly at Thebes, until death came to him about 1369 B.C., after he had ruled the world's most prosperous nation for nearly forty years. The languid, weary, fat old king was no more. Now, as sole ruler, there stood a man of fiery eyes and knifeblade-sharp cheekbones, bizarrely deformed, sublimely unconventional. Egypt was in the hands of Amenhotep IV.

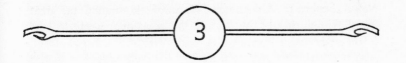

3

A REBEL ON THE THRONE

The new Pharaoh may have been nearly as much of a mystery to his fellow monarchs of the Orient as he is to us. The man who was to bring a sweeping revolution of thought to Egypt came to the throne as an unknown figure.

In the early, hazy years of the co-regency, it seems as though Queen Tiy, and not Amenhotep IV, was the real head of the government. A diplomatic message from Dushratta of Mitanni has survived, dating from the last year of Amenhotep III's life—but it is addressed, not to the old king or to the young co-regent, but to the queen. The letter sends greetings to Tiy, to her son, and to Tadukhepa his bride. (The same daughter of Dushratta who had been sent as a wife for Amenhotep III, and who apparently had become a hand-me-down from the senile king to the harem of his son.) The letter refers to certain negotiations that Tiy is said to "know well," and appeals for continued friendship with Amenhotep III.

By the time this letter had arrived at Thebes, the old king was dead and Amenhotep IV ruled alone. Upon receiving this news, Dushratta wrote, "When my brother Nimmuria [Amenhotep III] died, they proclaimed it, and when they proclaimed it I also learned. He was gone . . . and I wept on that day, and in the middle of the night I sat; food and wine I did not enjoy on that day and I was grieved. . . . But when Naphuria

[Nefer-kheperu-re, Amenhotep IV's coronation-name], the great son of Nimmuria by Tiy his wife the great one, wrote to me: 'I will enter upon my reign,' I said: 'Nimmuria is not dead.' Now Naphuria, his great son by Tiy, his great wife, has placed himself in his stead, and he will not change from its place one thing from what it was before. . . . Tiy, his mother, who was the great wife of Nimmuria, the loved one, is alive, and she will report the words to Naphuria, the son of Nimmuria her husband, that we were on excellent friendly terms."

This letter—with its foredoomed expression of hope that the new king "will not change from its place one thing from what it was before"—is a puzzle. Why should Amenhotep IV need to be told by his mother that Egypt and Mitanni were on excellent friendly terms? Certainly, if he had been co-regent for the past eight years, as the evidence indicates, he would know about the alliance. He should know of it in any case, since his grandmother had been a princess of Mitanni, since another princess of Mitanni had been in his father's harem, and since the daughter of Dushratta was one of his own wives. The letter seems to cast doubt on the whole scheme of a co-regency, and leads one to think that Amenhotep IV had spent his youth in some foreign land, returning to rule only upon his father's death. But that does not seem to have been the case.

There were other letters of congratulation. Ribaddi, a sturdy warrior-prince of the Phoenician city of Byblos and a long-time loyal vassal of Egypt, wrote, saying, "And behold, the gods and the sun and Baalat of Gubla [the god of Byblos] decreed that thou sit upon the throne of thy father's house in thy land." The king of Alasiya, a now-forgotten kingdom that may have been on the north Syrian coast, sent his felicitations, 200 talents (about 12,000 pounds) of copper, and an expression of hope for continued friendly relations with Egypt. A later letter from Alasiya accompanied a flask of good oil to pour on Amenhotep IV's head "now that you have ascended the throne of your kingdom," and asked for such gifts as a gilded chariot, two horses, garments, and aromatic woods. (A little later, the royal correspondent of Alasiya grows a trifle testy. He sends gifts of copper and ivory to Amenhotep IV, but "desires that the customs officers shall not interfere with the men sent in the ship," and a somewhat later letter asks for the quick return of his messengers, as though they were being molested or detained by Egyptian customs officials.)

There were letters, too, from Burnaburiash, the new King of Babylonia, who apparently succeeded Kadashman-Bel about the time of Amenhotep III's death. He began by desiring friendly relations with the new Pharaoh, and suggested an interchange of gifts. A following letter from Burnaburiash to Amenhotep IV strikes a more discordant note: "Naphruria's messengers have thrice come without presents. When 20 minas [equivalence unknown] of gold were sent it was short weight, and when smelted did not amount to five minas." But a betrothal was arranged between the Babylonian king's son and one of the daughters of Amenhotep IV, none of whom could have been more than five or six years old when their father became sole king. Finally, the Babylonian sends a message that must have been a familiar refrain in the Eighteenth Dynasty: "The work on the Temple is great, and vigorously have I undertaken its accomplishment; send me therefore much gold."

Amenhotep IV, to whom all this correspondence was addressed, was probably in his early thirties when he became Egypt's sole king. This—like almost every other fact about the Amarna era—is a matter of considerable controversy. As we shall see, a mummy discovered in 1907 was identified as that of Amenhotep IV, and was found by medical examination to be that of a man who had died some years short of his thirtieth birthday. On the basis of that evidence, it was thought that Amenhotep IV—who is known to have ruled about seventeen years—may have been as young as eight or nine when he was made his father's co-regent.

That would explain such letters to Amenhotep IV as one from Dushratta saying, "And all the words which I have spoken with thy father, thy mother, Tiy, knows them. No one else knows them. But thou mayest ask thy mother Tiy about them. Let her tell thee how thy father was on friendly terms with me."

This letter, written eight years after Amenhotep IV became

co-regent, would make sense if the young king were then in his teens and just emerging from a time when Tiy had ruled in his name. The earlier letter from Dushratta, to Tiy, is written in such a way as to imply that her son would hardly understand a letter, at his age. The evidence of the mummy found in 1907 supported this whole construction, so that for many years it was felt that Amenhotep IV had been a boy-king. This is only partly contradicted by Dushratta's reference, in a letter to Tiy, to his daughter Tadukhepa as Amenhotep IV's wife. Marriage in the teens or even pre-teens was no uncommon event among Oriental royalty.

What is more shattering to the boy-king theory is that it requires us to believe that Amenhotep IV began his great religious reformation when he was only twelve or thirteen. The idea still has its partisans today, but the generally accepted belief—which I share—is that Amenhotep IV was a man of mature years when he became king. He was, in all likelihood, a prince in his early or middle twenties when he was named co-regent, and thus into his thirties when he took sole control of Egypt.

He was married while still only a prince. His wife was Nefertiti, a woman of divine beauty and grace, about whom we know almost nothing but the fact of her loveliness.

Who was Nefertiti?

For a long time she was thought to be identical with Tadukhepa, daughter of Dushratta of Mitanni, who we know was married first to Amenhotep III and then to Amenhotep IV. But this idea was overthrown when research showed that Tadukhepa did not reach Thebes until the thirty-sixth year of Amenhotep III's reign, by which time Amenhotep IV had been co-regent for six years and already had several children by Nefertiti.

Another theory had it that Nefertiti was the daughter of Amenhotep III, either by Queen Tiy or by a subordinate wife. This is an attractive notion, since the new Pharaoh might have been expected to marry his sister or half-sister in order to legitimize his own claim to the throne. However, there is nothing in the record to support this. We know the names of several of Amenhotep IV's sisters, and the name of Nefertiti never appears in that list. We also know of a sister of Nefertiti called Mutnedjmet, who is never referred to as a princess, and so it seems neither of them was of royal blood. This creates a problem. One of Amenhotep III's daughters married a Babylonian prince; another married Amenhotep III himself. The others presumably died while their brother Amenhotep IV was a baby. Why was no royal princess reserved for Amenhotep IV to cement his claim to the throne?

That question must go unanswered. But in recent years the Egyptologist Cyril Aldred has put forth an explanation of Nefertiti's genealogy which, if true, will help to clarify much that is obscure in the history of this era.

We know that a woman named Tiy[1] bore the title of "Great Nurse of the Queen," and was entrusted with the task of rearing young Nefertiti. The husband of this "great nurse" Tiy was a man of common birth named Ay, an important figure in the Amarna story.

Ay was a Pooh-Bah of the Eighteenth Dynasty. He bore a host of titles during the reigns of Amenhotep III and IV: "Master of the Horse," "Foremost of the Companions of the King," "One Trusted by Pharaoh in the Entire Land," and others.

Now, these had all been titles of Yuya, the father of Queen Tiy. Ay and Yuya had also shared a more significant title, that of "Divine Father," which is generally felt to have meant, "Father-in-law of the King." There have been some suggestions that Ay and Yuya were one and the same. But this is obviously impossible, for Ay outlived Amenhotep IV by six years. He could hardly have been old enough to have fathered the wife of Amenhotep III, whose marriage took place fifty-six years before Ay's death. What Cyril Aldred very convincingly

---

[1] Her name is identical with that of Amenhotep IV's mother, but they were separate individuals. To reduce confusion, I refer from this point on to Nefertiti's nurse as "Tiy," and to Amenhotep IV's mother as "*Queen* Tiy."

suggests is that Ay was the son of Yuya, and thus the brother of Queen Tiy. Upon Yuya's death, fairly early in the reign of Amenhotep III, Ay succeeded to his father's many titles.

As for Nefertiti, Aldred and others think she was the daughter of Ay and Tiy, and so the niece of Queen Tiy. This would account for Ay's title of "Divine Father." He, too, was the father-in-law of a Pharaoh. His daughter Nefertiti married Amenhotep IV, just as Queen Tiy, Yuya's daughter and Ay's sister, had married Amenhotep III.

This intricate bit of genealogy is quite significant. It accounts for Nefertiti's birth—and, since she was the niece of Queen Tiy, she was of the royal family, though hardly of royal birth. It also explains Ay's power in the realm, which, as will be seen, grew steadily greater all during the reign of Amenhotep IV and his short-lived successors. The Aldred theory also disposes of the mystery created by an inscription found by the archaeologist Legrain, naming Nefertiti as the daughter of Tiy. That she was—but the daughter of Tiy wife of Ay, not Queen Tiy wife of Amenhotep III.

At any rate, Amenhotep IV and Nefertiti were married, probably when both were in middle or even early adolescence, and Ay, the new "Divine Father," came to hold the same position of importance at the court that his father Yuya once had held. The marriage was fruitful, but apparently Nefertiti bore only daughters. The eldest, Meritaten, was born no later than the fifth year of Amenhotep IV's reign, 1373. About the same time, Queen Tiy produced a child of Amenhotep III's old age, the girl Beketaten.

The names of these daughters are significant. Earlier royal children had been given names which included the divine name Amon in some form. Thus, a daughter of Amenhotep III was named Sit*amon*. *Amen*hotep itself contains Amon's name. But now, only a few years after the young prince has come to share his father's throne, Amon no longer forms part of royal names. We hear of daughters named Merit*aten,* Beket*aten.*

Winds of change were blowing through Thebes.

48

There had been hints of heresy before Amenhotep IV became king. His grandfather, Thothmes IV, had had the political backing of the sun-god priests of Heliopolis, and we have found inscriptions of his declaring that he had fought "with the Aten before him," and that his foreign campaigns were undertaken "to make the foreigners to be like the [Egyptian] people, in order to serve the Aten forever." Amenhotep III had called the royal barge "Aten Gleams" or "Splendor of Aten." Two royal architects had inscribed a prayer to Aten on a Theban wall.

There was no thought in any of this of creating a *new* god. Aten, the disk of the sun, was simply the place where Re, the ancient sun-god, dwelled. At best, Aten might be considered a god who was one of the many forms of the hawk-headed Re.

The priests of Re at Heliopolis had never willingly accepted the merger of their god with Amon of Thebes to produce Amon-Re. To them, Amon was simply a wind-god of Upper Egypt. Their political power, though, was curbed when the Eighteenth Dynasty Pharaohs forced the High Priest of Re at Heliopolis to accept the honorary title of "Second Priest of Amon at Thebes," thereby bringing the whole hierarchy of Re under Amon's control. Thus hampered, the Heliopolitan priests continued quietly to worship their god in their own way. Through some subtle theological evolution, they came to venerate Re most highly in the form of Aten, the solar disk. Probably there was a chapel of Aten at Heliopolis during Amenhotep III's reign.

There may even have been a small chapel of Aten in Thebes itself. During Amenhotep III's reign, there is mention of one Ramose, who is not only a priest of Amon but also "Steward in the Temple of the Aten." A scribe named Pen-buy is cited as "Scribe of the Treasury of the Temple of the Aten." Apparently, in the tolerant days of Amenhotep III, the sun-god in his new form was able to find a foothold in Amon's own stronghold without arousing jealousy.

Amenhotep IV thus found a ready-made cult at hand when he ascended the throne, and he adopted it for his own purposes.

He was not content, however, simply to accept the Aten-cult as he found it. In a series of increasingly bold moves, he transformed and enhanced the obscure solar cult until he evolved from it the noblest religious concept the world had yet seen: the worship of an abstract divinity, the only god of mankind, a god of love and warmth.

Not only had there been an Aten-cult in Egypt before Amenhotep IV, there had also been a strain of monotheism struggling to appear. Even in the Old Kingdom, there had been hymns to Re as "the only god." An ancient Sixth Dynasty text had placed these words in the mouth of Atum-Re:

> I am the Eternal Spirit,
> I am the sun that rose from the Primeval Waters.
> My soul is God, I am the creator of the Word.
> Evil is my abomination, I see it not.
> I am the Creator of the Order wherein I live,
> I am the Word, which will never be annihilated
> in this my name of "Soul."

Such abstract ideas were accompanied by theological interpretations to the effect that all the other gods were simply forms of Re, the Only God. Even Osiris, the death-and-fertility god of the people, was included in the being of Re.

This lofty notion found no followers, and the succeeding centuries were years of a bewildering polytheism. No doubt certain profound thinkers at Heliopolis continued to think of God as a single entity. But even these forerunners of Akhnaten (as Amenhotep IV would be known) were willing to admit other, lesser gods to their seemingly monotheistic schemes.

When Amon engulfed Re and became Egypt's official god, some elements of Heliopolitan universalism seem to have invaded the Theban cult. An Amon hymn of the early Eighteenth Dynasty declares to the god, "Jubilation to thee for every foreign country—to the height of heaven, to the width of earth, to the depth of the Great Green Sea! . . . The solitary sole one, without his peer . . . living on truth every day."

And the hymn of the twin architects Suti and Hor, already mentioned, contained phrases strikingly similar to those Akhnaten would later use in praise of his own god. The hymn of Suti and Hor is polytheistic enough; it is directed not only to Amon but to such gods as Osiris, Anubis, Mut, Khons, Hathor, Isis, Re-Harakhti, the deified queen Nefertiri, and even Aten. But the brothers declared: "When thou crossest the sky, all faces behold thee, but when thou departest, thou art hidden from their faces. . . . When thou settest in the western mountain, then they sleep in the manner of death. . . . The sole lord, who reaches the ends of the lands every day. . . . Shining in the sky, a being as the sun, he makes the season by the months, heat when he desires, cold when he desires. . . . Every land is in rejoicing at his rising every day, in order to praise them."

The elements of the new religion were there: both the long-existing Egyptian tendency toward a monotheism within a polytheism, and the Aten cult itself. Amenhotep IV "invented" neither Aten nor the idea of monotheism, contrary to the usual belief. His real significance is that he seized on these two beliefs—a sun-cult and a single god—welded them together, and lifted his new amalgam high as the religion of the land. Unlike those who had foreshadowed his thinking, Amenhotep IV—as Pharaoh Akhnaten—was able to put his theology into actual operation.

Why did the revolution of Akhnaten come about?

We can only guess at the deformed king's motives. We know that he was impulsive, enthusiastic, emotional. During his early years, Thebes abounded with foreign women and strange ideas. The many Mitanni princesses, his own foreign-born mother Queen Tiy, the Asian princes brought back as booty by earlier conquering Pharaohs, all must have contributed to the ferment of speculation buzzing around the young prince. Perhaps he arrived at his religious beliefs while still a boy—and, coming to the throne in his twenties, set out, with the blazing intensity of a mystic, to make his dreams real.

There is a more cynical explanation, a political one. For generations, the Pharaohs of the Eighteenth Dynasty had had to struggle against the demands of the priests of Amon. Though bloated on gold, Amon never lost his appetite for the yellow

51

metal. Amenhotep IV may have seen the High Priest of Amon as an outright political rival to the king. Amon's wealth was Amon's power, and threatened the age-old stability of Egypt's political system. Perhaps the revolution of Akhnaten occurred primarily to break the power of Amon. A new god was needed, and Akhnaten supplied him, to end the political encroachments of the official religion.

If that were Akhnaten's main motive, rather than religious zeal, he would at least rate commendation for his foresight. Long after the failure of Akhnaten's revolution, the priesthood of Amon grew so powerful that the High Priest of Amon could make and unmake Pharaohs at will—and, ultimately, the two offices became one, Amon's priest taking the throne.

But it does not seem likely that the mainspring of Akhnaten's zeal was the desire to hold political power. His later actions show that he was largely indifferent to worldly ambition. And if he were simply interested in overthrowing Amon, he could have lent his support to Re, rather than devising a new type of worship. It would seem that the Aten heresy arose out of the simmering mysticism within Amenhotep IV, and that the political aspects of the revolution were the work of such calculating advisers as Queen Tiy and her brother, the "Divine Father" Ay.

A raging hurricane may begin with a single cloud on the horizon. The revolution of Amenhotep IV-Akhnaten began quietly, and Amon's priests could hardly have been aware of the storm about to break over them.

As of the year 1377, both the kings of Egypt were outwardly loyal followers of Amon. Pudgy, sleepy-eyed Amenhotep the Magnificent and haggard, long-jawed Amenhotep IV still worshipped at the shrine of the Hidden God, the younger ruler performing all the rituals Amon required of a Pharaoh. Hardly had the festivities of his coronation been concluded, though, than Amenhotep IV gave orders for the building of a new temple in Thebes, midway between Luxor and Karnak.

52

Sandstone for the temple was quarried at Silsileh, where a tablet was raised bearing this inscription:

"First occurrence of His Majesty's giving command to muster all the workmen from Elephantine to Samhudet, and the leaders of the army, in order to make a great breach for cutting out sandstone, in order to make the sanctuary of Harakhti in his name, 'Heat-Which-is-in-Aten,' in Karnak. Behold the officials, the companions, and the chiefs of the fan-bearers were the chiefs of the quarry-service for the transportation of stone."

The decree may have aroused mild surprise in the temple of Amon, but probably nothing more. The new temple, though designed for the unfamiliar worship of Aten, was officially described as being that of Harakhti, a form of Re of Heliopolis. So this was nothing new. Like his grandfather Thothmes IV, Amenhotep IV seemed to show interest in the solar worship of Heliopolis. The priests of Amon had survived Thothmes IV, and, no doubt, they intended to survive any new cult favored by Amenhotep IV.

The Silsileh tablet further indicates the quiet way in which Amenhotep began his revolution. The tablet already depicts the Aten-symbol—the solar disk, radiating streams of light which terminate in human hands—but it also shows the young Pharaoh worshipping Amon. Amenhotep IV doubtless wanted to give the impression that he, like his father, would be tolerant of many gods.

The first temple of Aten rose in Thebes. So, too, did some statues of the new Pharaoh that must have aroused whispers of shocked comment. They were gigantic figures of Amenhotep IV that not only failed to hide his deformities, but actually exaggerated them, showing him as emaciated of face and grotesquely swollen in abdomen and thigh.

The king worshipped at his new temple, and evidently at first what was practiced there was simply the old solar religion of Re. The sanctuary of the temple contained a *benben,* a "Sunstone," polished and pyramid-shaped, an object which had figured in the religion of Heliopolis for thousands of years. The names of such gods as Horus and Set appeared in inscriptions on the walls of the Aten temple. Amenhotep IV had not yet become a monotheist. He was concerned at the start simply with establishing Aten as a form of Re. He chose a name for the new god that stressed this kinship. Aten's full name, which had an esoteric significance we can only guess at, was: "Re lives, Harakhti, rejoicing on the Horizon in his name, 'Heat-Which-is-in-Aten.' "

Step by step, Amenhotep IV declared his independence from Amon. He named his first-born daughter Meritaten, "Beloved of Aten." When a child was unexpectedly born to Amenhotep III and Queen Tiy, she, too, was given a name compounded with Aten, as though to show that the old king was in sympathy with his co-regent's way of thinking. (More likely, it was Queen Tiy who was in sympathy; Amenhotep III apparently could not have cared less which god his son currently worshipped.)

While still avoiding an open break with Amon, the young king sought for converts to Atenism among the Theban nobility. It was a matter of wise politics for the high officials to follow Amenhotep IV's urging. The old king had not much time left to live. One day, probably quite soon, Amenhotep IV would reign as sole king, and would reorganize the "cabinet" of officials who helped operate the government. He would be unlikely to favor those who were not inclined to praise his god.

One of the first important converts was Ramose, the Grand Vizier under Amenhotep III. As was the custom of the day, Ramose had prepared a tomb for himself while he was still in the prime of life. Carved out of the living rock of the hills overlooking Thebes, the tomb of Ramose had been decorated in the conventional style, and lay in wait for its eventual occupant.

The conversion of Ramose to Atenism took place after the tomb had been decorated. It now became necessary to add new decorations and inscriptions. A portrait of Amenhotep IV had already been cut in relief on the tomb wall, showing the king enthroned. It was in the conventional, traditional style of Egyptian tomb art. Following one of the conventions, the artist had suppressed all of Amenhotep IV's physical peculiarities.

Ramose now caused to be added a second portrait of the Pharaoh, done in the realistic style Amenhotep IV had come to favor. This new version, facing the old one, showed the king standing beneath the radiating beams of the sun. It was a merciless portrayal of the king's strange physique. Prayers to Aten were engraved on the walls of the tomb. The solar disk itself was labelled with that intricate title so incomprehensible to us: "Harakhti-rejoicing-in-the-Horizon; in his name: 'Heat-Which-is-in-Aten,' residing in 'Aten-is-Found-in-the-House-of-Aten.' "

Other scenes of the tomb showed Amenhotep IV holding audience, with Ramose appearing before him, now kissing the earth, now kneeling, now standing decorated with gold, now departing with servants who bore the gold collars bestowed by the king, and then leaving the palace and met by congratulating friends carrying flowers. A dialogue between king and vizier also was inscribed on the wall, unfortunately somewhat damaged today. Amenhotep IV is shown saying, "The words of Re are before thee. . . . My august father [meaning Aten] taught me their essence and revealed them to me. . . . They were known in my heart, opened to my face. I understood. . . ."

To which Ramose is shown as replying, "Thy monuments shall endure like the heavens, for thy duration is like Aten therein. . . . Thou art the Only one of Aten, in possession of his designs. Thou hast led the mountains; their secret chambers, the terror of thee is in the midst of them, as the terror of thee is in the hearts of the people; the mountains hearken to thee as the people hearken."

Another Theban noble was Horemheb, a general who bore the honorary post of High Priest of Horus. He, too, saw the light and converted to Atenism in the early years of Amenhotep's reign. Horemheb's tomb, begun early in Amenhotep IV's reign, contained inscriptions praising Re in his ancient form: "Re-Harakhti, great god, lord of heaven, lord of earth, who cometh forth from his horizon and illuminateth the Two Lands of Egypt, the sun of darkness as the great one, as Re," and, in a different place, "Re, lord of truth, great god, sovereign of Heliopolis. . . . Harakhti, only god, king of the gods, who rises in the west and sendeth forth his beauty."

By the fourth year of his reign, Amenhotep IV felt ready to challenge Amon openly. He decreed that the area around the new temple be called "Brightness of Aten the Great," and that Thebes itself be called, "The City of the Brightness of Aten." It is not hard to imagine the effect this must have had on the priests of Amon. It is as though a modern Italian premier were to build a mosque opposite St. Peter's, and then to rename Rome in honor of Mohammed. There would certainly be hurried conferences within the halls of the Vatican.

We have no details of the cross-currents of intrigue that must have swept Thebes in 1373. Obviously a test of strength was drawing near between Amenhotep IV and the High Priest of Amon, and worried courtiers tried desperately to choose the side most likely to win. Meanwhile, disturbing news was coming from beyond Egypt's borders. The Hittites, a powerful but remote people of Asia Minor, were on the warpath. Led by their strong-willed king, Suppiluliumas, the Hittites had marched eastward toward northern Syria, and were menacing Mitanni. In the first foray, Dushratta had defeated the Hittite invaders, and proudly sent samples of the spoils of victory to his friends in Thebes. But Suppiluliumas was known to be a foe worth fearing, and among Amenhotep IV's advisers there were some who looked forward uneasily to further Hittite sallies, not only against Mitanni but against Egypt's own possessions in Syria. At such a critical time, to have Thebes split by a religious dispute could be a calamity for Egypt.

Amenhotep IV took no more notice of the Hittite threat than did his father Amenhotep the Magnificent, dozing in his Malkata palace. Theological problems concerned him more directly. He was formulating the tenets of his new religion, possibly with the help of Re-priests from Heliopolis.

Even in the fifth year of his reign, Amenhotep IV had not

yet turned to monotheism. A letter has survived addressed to him, sent by a royal steward named Apiy who lived in Memphis, and dated in the fifth year of the king's reign, the third month of winter, the nineteenth day. It begins with Amenhotep IV's full title, including the stock phrases, "Great of Dominion in Karnak" and "Ruler in Thebes," and also the slogan "living in Maat [Truth]," which Amenhotep IV had adopted as his own. The letter is concerned with the temple of Ptah, the ancient god of Memphis, whom the Memphites worshipped as the creator of Re. "A communication is this to the Master (Life! Prosperity! Health!) to give information that the temple of the father Ptah is sound and prosperous. . . . The house of Pharaoh is flourishing. . . . The offerings of all the gods and goddesses who are upon the soil of Memphis are complete; complete are they, there is nothing held back from them."

Soon, however, there would be no gods, no goddesses, at Memphis or elsewhere in Egypt. There would be only Aten.

In the sixth year of his reign, Amenhotep IV signalled the scope of his intentions with a series of dramatic announcements. The people of Thebes must surely have gathered in troubled knots on the streets to discuss in hushed tones the decrees of the spindly-bodied young Pharaoh, while messengers hurried outward to bring the bewildering news to all parts of Egypt and to the far-flung provinces of the empire.

First, Amon would be dethroned as the official state god of Egypt. In his lofty place would rise Aten, the god of the solar disk, in all his blazing glory.

Secondly, to symbolize the change in high gods, Pharaoh would change his name, from Amenhotep, "Amon is Content," to Akhnaten, meaning "He Who Serves the Aten" or "Aten is Satisfied."

Lastly, Thebes was to be stripped of its position as capital of Egypt. The Pharaoh Akhnaten and his court would move far to the north, to a place in the desert where no one had ever dwelled, and there would be built the new City of Akhetaten, "The City of the Horizon of the Disk."

4

A CITY IN THE DESERT

The break with Amon was sudden and violent, but it was not carried to completion in a single stroke. It does not seem as though at the outset Akhnaten banned the worship of Amon or any of Egypt's other gods. A year after Akhnaten moved to his new city, it was recorded in Thebes that the Second Prophet of Amon, Aanen, had died and was replaced with one Simut; evidently, the temple at Karnak was still open. The old King Amenhotep and Queen Tiy were still living at Thebes, and Akhnaten apparently did not want to launch full-scale revolution in Egypt while his father lived.

To the peasant tilling the fields in the Delta or at Elephantine or at Memphis, the news, if he heard it at all, must have provoked nothing more than a shrug. Had anything really changed, he might ask? The old Pharaoh still dwelled in the royal palace. The young Pharaoh had quarrelled somehow with the priests of Amon, and, like a sulky child, had withdrawn into the desert and named some new or old god as the official deity. It mattered not at all to the peasant. His god was Osiris, and the bickerings of Theban priests and kings did not impinge on his world.

Akhnaten, though, knew that he had embarked on a struggle to the death. His departure from Thebes may have been as much an act of self-preservation as it was a grand symbolic gesture of independence. Pharaohs had been done to death in their palaces before. The gold of Amon might well buy a skilled assassin's services. The priests of Amon, fighting for their own survival, would hardly have moral objections to the removal of a heretic.

To the site of Akhetaten, then, went the most skilled artisans of Pharaoh, instructed to cobble together a city in the swiftest way. The new capital would rise halfway between the older Egyptian capitals of Thebes and Memphis, 250 miles north of Thebes, 200 miles south of the sun-god's ancient city of Heliopolis. There, the cliffs curved away from the Nile to form a plain on the east bank some three miles deep, stretching in an arc six miles long, and on the yellow sand of this plain Akhnaten's capital would be built.

It was virgin soil, undefiled by temples of the Egyptian gods Akhnaten had come to despise. In Old Kingdom times, the Pharaoh Pepi I had sent an expedition to mine alabaster from the quarries of Hatnub, in the hills overlooking what would, a thousand years later, be the heretic's capital. Later stonemasons had worked at Hatnub, which they called the "Golden Quarry" for its fine stone, and had left their inscriptions. During the Twelfth Dynasty, powerful feudal lords of the family of Thuthotep had used Hatnub stone for their own monuments, which were erected across the river at Hermopolis on a scale worthy of a king. But no one had built on the site Akhnaten chose.

There was little time now for quarrying the superb alabaster of Hatnub. Dressing stone was a slow business, and Akhnaten had the sound of time's winged chariot droning in his ears. Brick, made of mud mixed with straw and left to bake in the sun, was the material out of which the city was constructed, as the impatient Pharaoh confronted the deserts of vast eternity lying before him. There would be time later, when the feverish pace slackened, to face Akhetaten's important buildings with stone.

Foundations were laid out. Walls rose, course after course. The crisp shouts of overseers broke the silence of the desert. Temples, palaces, the villas of nobles, the homes of artisans and merchants—all had to be erected at once and with haste. Perhaps never before in the history of the world had a full-blown city been born at a single command. Akhetaten, in its way, was the ancestor of such modern creations as Washington, Brasilia, and Canberra.

For all the haste, nothing was skimped in the way of magnitude or majesty. The official royal palace, whose frontage was more than two thousand feet, was the largest secular building of the ancient world. The great main road that ran the entire length of the city was broad and imposing, and a mighty viaduct spanned the causeway, leading from the official palace to the smaller royal residence that faced it.

While the city was being built, Akhnaten and Nefertiti remained in seclusion at Thebes. It must have been a time of uncertainty and doubt for everyone. With neither the old king nor the young one exercising royal authority, it may have been that Queen Tiy, a popular figure in the land, held the reins of power during the interlude when Egypt had no capital.

Soon after Akhnaten had ordered construction to begin, he journeyed down the Nile to have his first look at the city of his great dream. The procession must have been a glorious one, as king and court embarked at Thebes and in stately majesty sailed downriver, perhaps in the glittering royal barge *Aten Gleams,* while curious farmers rushed to the riverbanks to catch a glimpse of the perplexing young king.

Amidst the hubbub of construction, Akhnaten formally dedicated the new city by performing a ritual of foundation ceremonies. Boundary tablets were set up marking off the site of the city. The first of these is dated "Year 6, fourth month of the second season, thirteenth day."

The inscription opens with the name of Aten, and then with the full title of Akhnaten, as follows:

"Live the Good God, satisfied with truth, lord of heaven, lord of Aten; live the great one who illuminates the Two Lands; live my father; live 'Harakhti-Rejoicing-in-the-Horizon, in his name, "Heat-Which-is-in-Aten," ' who is given life forever and ever.

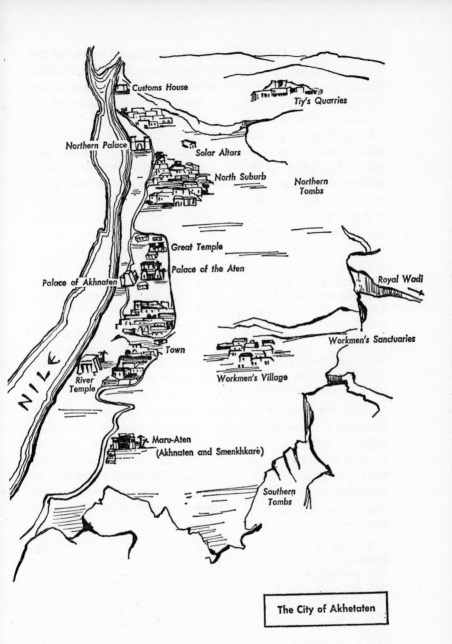

Customs House

Tiy's Quarries

Northern Palace

Solar Altars

North Suburb

Northern Tombs

Great Temple

Palace of the Aten

Royal Wadi

Palace of Akhnaten

NILE

Town

Workmen's Sanctuaries

River Temple

Workmen's Village

Maru-Aten
(Akhnaten and Smenkhkare)

Southern Tombs

The City of Akhetaten

61

"Live Horus: Mighty Bull, Beloved-of-Aten; Favorite of the Two Goddesses: Great-in-Kingship-in-Akhetaten; Golden Horus: Bearer-of-the-Name-of-Aten; King of Upper and Lower Egypt, Living in Truth, Lord of the Two Lands: Nefer-khepru-re-Wanre; Son of Re, Living in Truth, Lord of Diadems: Akhnaten, great in duration, given life forever and ever . . . whose beauty Aten created . . . offering the earth to him that placed him upon his throne, supplying his eternal house with millions and hundred-thousands of things, exalter of Aten, magnifier of his name: Akhnaten."

After a similar, but more concise, titling of Nefertiti, the boundary stone declares:

On this day the king was in the City of the Horizon of Aten. His Majesty (Life! Prosperity! Health!) ascended a great chariot of electrum [an alloy of precious metals], appearing like Aten when he rises from his horizon; he filled the Two Lands with his loveliness. On beginning the goodly way to Akhetaten, at the first exploration of it which his majesty made, in order to found it as a monument to Aten . . . he caused that a great oblation should be offered, consisting of bread, beer, oxen, calves, cattle, fowl, wine, gold, incense, all beautiful flowers. On this day was founded Akhetaten for the living Aten, that favor and love might be received, on behalf of King Akhnaten.

After the sacrifices, the king toured the city, inspecting the buildings that had been begun. Then, returning to his starting point, he declared, "Bring me the companions of the king, the great ones and the mighty ones, the captains of soldiers, and the nobles of the land in its entirety." This was done; and—the boundary stone tells us—"They lay on their bellies before his majesty, kissing the ground before his mighty will." Then, says the boundary stone:

And his majesty said unto them, "Ye behold the City of the Horizon of Aten, which the Aten has desired me to make for him as a monument in the great name of my majesty forever. For it was the Aten, my Father, that brought me to this City of the Horizon. There was not a noble who directed me to it; there was not any man in the whole land who led me to it, saying, 'It is fitting for his majesty that he make a City of the Horizon of Aten in this place.' Nay, but it was the Aten, my Father, that directed me to make it for him. . . . Behold the Pharaoh found that this site belonged not to a god, nor to a goddess, it belonged not to a prince, nor to a princess. There was no right for any man to act as owner of it."

Akhnaten then uttered a prayer to Aten:

Whether he is in heaven or in earth, every eye seeth him without failing, while he fills the land with his beams and makes every face to live. With seeing whom may my eyes be satisfied daily, when he rises in this temple of Aten in the City of the Horizon, and fills it with his own self by his beams, beauteous in love, and lays them upon me in life and length of days for ever and ever.

Next, the boundaries of the city were solemnly delimited:

I will make the City of the Horizon of Aten for the Aten, my Father, in this place. I will not make the City south of it, north of it, west of it, or east of it. I will not pass beyond the southern boundary stone southward, neither will I pass beyond the northern boundary stone northward to make for him a City of the Horizon there; neither will I make for him a city on the western side. Nay, but I will make the City of the Horizon for the Aten, my Father, upon the east side, the place which he did enclose for his own self with cliffs, and made a plain in the midst of it that I might sacrifice to him thereon: this is it.

This is it. Nor would the headstrong king be swayed by those around him. The decree continues:

Neither shall the Queen say unto me, "Behold, there is a goodly place for the City of the Horizon in another place," and I hearken unto her. Neither shall any noble nor any man in the whole land say unto me, "Behold, there is a goodly place for the City of the Horizon in another place," and I hearken unto them. Whether it be downstream, or southwards, or westwards, or eastwards, I will not say, "I will abandon this City of the Horizon."

The Pharaoh then vowed to build a great temple for his god, to "make all works which are necessary for the Aten, my Father," and to build palaces for himself and for his queen. He took care, too, to make funeral provisions for the royal family. Since the time of Thothmes I, the rulers of the Eighteenth Dynasty had been buried in tombs in the Theban hills, at a place we call today the Valley of the Tombs of the Kings. That burial-ground was holy to Amon, and the rebellious Pharaoh could hardly accept eternal rest in the consecrated place of a god he loathed. No, he would lie in Aten's domain:

There shall be made for me a sepulchre in the eastern hills; my burial shall be made therein . . . and the burial of the Great Wife of the King, Nefertiti, shall be made therein, and the burial of the King's Daughter Meritaten shall be made therein. If I die in any town of the north, south, west, or east, I will be brought here and buried in the City of the Horizon. . . . The tombs of the High Priests and the Divine Fathers and the priests of the Aten shall be made in the eastern hills, and they shall be buried therein. The tombs of the officers, and others, shall be made in the eastern hills, and they shall be buried therein.

The final lines of the foundation stone are battered and broken, and it is impossible to make much of them. They refer, it appears, to other projects of the king—the building of granaries, the planting of fruit and shade trees, the celebration of festivals.

There is also one mysterious, incomplete sentence that seems to tell of conflict between Akhnaten and the priests of Amon since the fourth year of his reign:

For as my father Re-Harakhti Aten liveth . . . the words [?] of the priests, more evil are they than those things which I heard until the year four, more evil are they than those things which I have heard in . . . more evil are they than those things which King Neb-maat-re heard, more evil are they than those things which Menkheperre [the coronation-name of Thothmes IV] heard. . . .

No sooner had the engravers of this extensive boundary stone finished their work than they had to begin over. A second daughter had been born to Akhnaten and Nefertiti, and had to be added to the text.

The birth of Princess Meketaten must have been a bitter disappointment to Akhnaten. He already had one daughter, Meritaten, through whom the throne of Egypt would descend. He had ordered the new city in the awareness that Nefertiti was with child. If she gave him a boy, the continuation of his dynasty would be assured; he could marry the new prince to

Meritaten, and proclaim him the heir to the throne. The people of Egypt, with their love of established institutions, would be more likely to follow a Pharaoh whose line was certain to endure. The innovations Akhnaten planned would be less difficult to achieve if he had a son.

The child was a girl. The new boundary stone, which bears the name of this second daughter, reflects Akhnaten's disappointment in a toughening of his phraseology. Now he adds a solemn oath to his earlier vows: "This is my oath of truth which it is my desire to pronounce, and of which I will not say 'It is false' eternally for ever."

The revised inscription also includes a series of puzzling phrases which may simply have been traditional forms not meant to be interpreted literally, but which appear to be vows that, once he has taken up residence in Akhetaten, he would never leave the city:

The southern boundary stone which is on the eastern hills. . . . I will not pass beyond it southwards for ever and ever.
The middle boundary stone which is on the eastern hills. . . . I will not pass beyond it eastwards for ever and ever.
The northeastern boundary stone by which I have halted. . . . I will not pass beyond it downstream for ever and ever.

The final statement of the new inscription is Akhnaten's declaration that his oath, and the tablet recording it, will both endure forever. In words that seem all the more ironic in the light of later events, Akhnaten promised, "It shall not be erased. It shall not be washed out. It shall not be kicked. It shall not be struck with stones. Its spoiling shall not be brought about. If it be missing, if it be spoilt, if the tablet on which it is shall fall, I will renew it again afresh in the place in which it was."

When the ceremonies of dedication had ended, Akhnaten and his family apparently returned to Thebes. Tadukhepa, the daughter of King Dushratta of Mitanni, had arrived at court by this time as a bride for Amenhotep III, but she passed quickly into the harem of Akhnaten.

The events of the seventh year of Akhnaten's reign are unknown to us. No doubt he visited Akhetaten frequently, residing in a luxuriously appointed tent while watching the city of his vision become real. At Thebes, he seemingly issued no decrees, and passed much of his time out of sight of his people. The priests of Amon intrigued against him, but to no avail. Akhnaten remained secluded, perhaps in poor health much of the time, his fragile body racked by the strain of the steadily more bitter conflict with Amon. The new baby must have been a solace to him, for Akhnaten loved children; later in his reign, when his new city's walls were decorated with murals of the royal family, he enjoyed having himself portrayed fondling his tiny daughters.

Akhetaten neared completion. Along more than five miles of the plain rose the palaces and temples and dwelling-places, to which, as Akhnaten's eighth year of co-regency began, the artisans were giving the finishing touches. The time had come to leave Thebes permanently.

On a day in 1371 or 1370, the first of the royal barges left Thebes. The king and queen were aboard, with their children. A third daughter had been born to Nefertiti, and had been named Ankhesenpaaten. Aboard the foremost barge, too, there no doubt rode Ay, the "Divine Father," and his wife Tiy.

Other barges carried the nobles of the court. General Horemheb and the Grand Vizier Ramose doubtless made the journey with their king, as did other, younger men, opportunists who had thrown in their lot with Aten and his prophet. It was a glittering procession, that string of barges drifting with solemn dignity down the Nile to Akhetaten.

A glorious city awaited them. Majestic thoroughfares ran the length of Aten's capital. At the south, the King's Way went past the pleasure palace of Akhnaten, where all the beauties of nature had been gathered to divert the king. When he entered his garden of delight, Akhnaten would pass first through a hall of thirty-six columns, and then to a small artificial lake beyond, around which were planted trees and shrubs gathered from every part of the known world. In the pond, colorful Nile fish slipped past the bright gaiety of lotus-flowers and water-lilies. Past this lake was a larger one, with a quay from which Pharaoh might embark for a banquet on the waters. At the north end of the larger lake there rose a colonnade where the royal ones might sit in the shade, studying the splendor of Aten as reflected on the smooth surface of the waters. Nearby were the wine cellars, where, thirty-two centuries later, men would find wine jars marked with the date of the vintage, and such comments as, "Very good wine."

North of the pleasure garden was the great bulk of the official state palace itself, facing onto the King's Way. Five hundred pillars testified to the power of Pharaoh. The courtyards of the palace were painted in the lively, vigorous style that Akhnaten favored; ducks and fish and jumping bulls sported on the colorful pavements, against a background of plants and flowers and trees. Adjoining the monumental state palace was the smaller residence of Akhnaten, and a private temple for the king's devotions. To the north lay the great main temple of Aten, and nearby were the official buildings, the Hall of Foreign Tribute, the Taxation Office, the Foreign Office, and the Archives, or "Place of the Correspondence of the King." At the very northern end of the city was another royal palace and a customs house, and then the cliffs curved back to the Nile to close the arc.

It was a city born of a dream, and there had never been one like it: a city rising in shining newness, every building sparkling in Aten's light, a city that had been planned in advance and not merely permitted to grow helter-skelter. Later, true, the plan would give way. The nobles and wealthy men of Akhetaten built their villas at the intersections of the main roads, leaving the middle of each block empty, and, gradually, the houses of the poor would come to fill those spaces, mean hovels crowded together, gaining access to the main roads through narrow lanes and winding alleys. Akhetaten would look more like a real city, then. Now, as the emigrants from Thebes reached it, it was somehow unreal, an insubstantial phantom that might well melt away before one's eyes. "She is lovely and beautiful," one noble said of the new city. "When one sees her, it is like a glimpse of heaven."

Akhnaten's first act, on reaching his city to stay, was to repeat his oath of the sixth year, and to have his words engraved on a new boundary stone:

The oath was repeated in year eight, first month of the second season, eighth day. The King was in the City of the Horizon of Aten, and Pharaoh stood mounted on a great chariot of electrum, inspecting the boundary stones of the Aten. . . .

He rededicated the city to his god with these words:

And the breadth of the City of the Horizon of Aten is from cliff to cliff, from the eastern horizon of heaven to the western horizon of heaven. It shall be for my Father Re-Harakhti Aten, its hills, its deserts, all its fowl, all its people, all its cattle, all things which the Aten produces, on which his rays shine, all things which are in . . . the City of the Horizon, they shall be for the Father, the living Aten, unto the temple of Aten in the City of the Horizon for ever and ever; they are all offered to his spirit. And may his rays be beauteous when they receive them.

Amenhotep III had remained at Thebes when his son moved to his new city. We hear no more of the old king. We are not even certain of the year of his death, though it may well have been 1369, within a year after Akhnaten's final departure from Thebes. In the eighth or ninth year of Akhnaten's co-regency, Amenhotep III died, and Akhnaten became sole ruler.

All that had gone before had merely been a prelude. Akhnaten now declared war on the gods of Egypt.

Freed of the last restraint on his authority, the heretic acted with stunning vigor and decision. He ordered that the temples of Amon be closed. Amon was proscribed. He was to be worshipped no longer. Nor were the festivities of Osiris to be celebrated again, nor those of Ptah, the benevolent artificer of Memphis. Isis, the divine wife and mother, was to be no more. There was to be no talk of the conflict of Horus and Set. Mut and Khons, Sobek and Sekhmet, Geb and Nut, Shu, Tefnut, the whole elaborate pantheon, the hundreds of gods accumulated by the Egyptians in their thousands of years of civilization, all were banned, all were declared mere specters.

There was only one god, and that god was Aten.

Not even Re of Heliopolis was spared. Aten had absorbed him. The image of Re as a falcon was universal in Egypt, but Akhnaten's god was no falcon. There would be no attempt to represent Aten as an animal nor even as a man, as Amon had been depicted. Aten was an abstract principle, and the symbol of the Aten was the solar disk, radiating diverging beams of light terminating in human hands, a striking image that told every mortal how the hand of Aten reached everywhere, into the hidden places of the world, into the hearts of men.

Akhnaten's chief enemy was Amon. His campaign of persecution against the other gods was sporadic and intermittent. But his war against Amon was relentless.

The king was not content simply to cut off the lavish revenues that had been Amon's for two hundred years, nor to close the temples and make beggars of Amon's once-haughty priests. The very name of Amon, Pharaoh decreed, was to be obliterated!

Squads of hatchet-men set out through Egypt, instructed by Pharaoh to hack the name of Amon from every inscription in the land. It was a formidable task. We can imagine Akhnaten's hirelings scaling the vast monuments of Karnak and Luxor, mallet and chisel in hand, and chipping away with zeal and fervor at the hieroglyphics so lovingly carved by generations of craftsmen.

The attack was not directed solely against the hymns in praise of Amon. The hated syllables were to be stricken wherever they appeared, even if only in the innocent form of *amon,* the word for "hidden." Thus, even the names of kings had to be marred, if they contained the forbidden word.

The first kings of Egypt who included Amon's name in their own were the several Twelfth Dynasty Pharaohs called Amenemhet. In Akhnaten's own dynasty, though, there had been four kings named Amenhotep, counting Akhnaten himself. Wherever the name of Amenhotep was found, it had to be re-

69

moved, even in inscriptions referring to Akhnaten himself by his earlier name of Amenhotep IV.

This made it necessary for Akhnaten to turn the chisels against the inscriptions of his own father, paunchy, kindly Amenhotep III. It was an act that forfeited much popular sympathy for the heretic. The people of Egypt might have watched the overthrow of Amon without much concern—but they could have nothing but hatred toward a man who destroyed his own father's immortal spirit.

For in the magic power of a man's name lay his hope of eternal life. The Egyptians had believed since earliest times in an afterlife. In their methodical way they had divided men into eight component parts. There was the *khat,* or physical body. This was subject to decay after death, and from prehistoric times the Egyptians had sought ways of preventing that decay through mummification. There was the *ka,* or "double," a kind of guardian spirit or ghost, that remained by a man's side through his life and became separated from him upon death, only to rejoin his *khat* at the will of the gods. There was the *ba,* the "soul," which the Egyptians somehow distinguished from the *ka.* There was the *ab,* or "heart." There was the *khu,* or celestial spirit of a man, and the *sekhem,* the embodiment of his vital power, and the *khaibit,* or shadow. Distinguishing among these ghostly manifestations is beyond our modern perceptions.

The eighth component of a man was the *ren,* his name. It was one of the most important. A man whose name was blotted from memory was a man destroyed. A nameless being cannot be introduced to the gods, and so could have no resurrection at the time when the gods beyond the grave met the dead man, pronounced his name, and welcomed him to the company of the immortals. This power of the name was all-important. In an old myth, Isis gained dominance over Re by keeping from him the knowledge of his true name. (That this belief was not confined to Egypt is shown by the third chapter of Exodus, in which Moses says to God, "Behold, when I come unto the children of Israel, and shall say unto them, The God of your fathers hath sent me unto you; and they shall say to me, What is his name? what shall I say unto them?" God's reply is, "I AM THAT I AM. . . . Thus shalt thou say unto the children of Israel, I AM hath sent me unto you.")

It was the duty of a son to keep his father's tomb in good repair, to perpetuate his name, to maintain his memory. Akhnaten, in the frenzy of his hatred for Amon, hammered his father's name to oblivion wherever he found it, though he left untouched the old king's coronation name, Neb-maat-re, because it contained the names of Maat, the goddess of truth and justice, and of Re, still thought to be an aspect of Aten. Akhnaten had no quarrel with Re, and to the end he respected Maat, not as a goddess but as an abstract force of good. Where he could, he had his agents paint in "Neb-maat-re" in place of "Amenhotep III," to spare his father's spirit.

He gained no love by this act of sacrilege. The campaign of iconoclasm went on, no matter what. Egypt may have murmured in displeasure, but no hint of those murmurs reached Pharaoh in his secluded city. The hatchet-men moved from temple to temple, searching for the name of Amon. Sometimes they chipped out the names of other gods, sometimes not. They did attempt to obliterate each of the gods at his main temple, at least. For instance, the goddess Nekhbet ruled at el-Kab, and her name was hacked out at her temple there, though not at other places. It was too much work to try to destroy every reference to every god. The three hieroglyphs that formed Amon's name were the main target. Amon's wife, Mut, also had to be obliterated. It happened that Mut's name was also the word for "mother," represented by the hieroglyph of a vulture. It was necessary, of course, to use the word "mother" in Akhnaten's own inscriptions mentioning Queen Tiy, but to avoid any reminder of Mut he decreed a new spelling for the word, one which did not use Mut's vulture-symbol. Where the old spelling appeared in inscriptions it was often chiselled out, even when it simply meant "mother," and not the forbidden goddess Mut.

There was one other significant removal. Any general reference to "the gods" in the plural was hacked away when found. There was to be no further talk of gods; only of "God."

No quarter was given. From the Delta to the Sudan, the workmen plied their chisels. Temples, palaces, private homes, even tombs were invaded. Harmless paintings of the sacred goose of Amon were defaced. In far-off Nubia, the shrines of Min-Re, the special god of the old "Divine Father" Yuya, were desecrated.

The old gods were banished. Amon was overthrown; Osiris, the god of the masses, now had to be worshipped in hiding. All Egypt shook with the impact of the deeds of this mad young king. And Akhnaten, remote and serene in the City of the Horizon, fondled his baby daughters, lovingly embraced his beautiful wife Nefertiti, and joyfully offered praise unto Aten.

A painting in the tomb of Meryre, High Priest of Aten, shows us the Pharaoh setting out for the great temple of his god. No Egyptian king before Akhnaten had ever permitted himself to be pictured driving through the streets of his capital in his chariot, but Akhnaten was a pioneer in artistic styles as well as religious thinking.

The procession shown in the painting is magnificent. Two runners holding staves aloft rush forward, clearing a path for Akhnaten. Then comes Pharaoh himself, standing in an ornately decorated chariot. Akhnaten wields whip and reins with his own hands, while two fiery, richly caparisoned horses snort and stamp as they prance along. Colored ostrich plumes rise from the tossing heads of the steeds of Pharaoh as he rides toward the temple, a breathless bodyguard panting along on foot beside his chariot.

The queen, guiding her own chariot, is close behind her royal husband. Two of the young princesses follow in a chariot of their own, the older one grasping the reins, the younger leaning affectionately against her sister. Behind them are six carriages of court ladies, and six more of court officials. Slaves brandish staves and badges of office; ribbons flutter in the breeze; the brilliant sun makes every plume and banner glow radiantly.

The townspeople run from their houses to catch a fleeting view of the great ones as their chariots flash by.

Now the royal party approaches the temple. Meryre waits by the gate to greet Pharaoh. Four slaves kneel by him, waving aloft colored fans of ostrich plumes. Fat bulls are led forth, their massive necks garlanded gaily with flowers. Girls in flowing robes beat tambourines; trumpeters play a ringing salute to Akhnaten as he arrives.

The king enters the building, passing through the outer gate, and coming to two huge pylons rising behind a pillared portico. Each pylon supports five towering masts from which crimson pennants fly. Between the pylons are the swinging doors of the inner gate, which are always left open to symbolize the loving way Aten welcomes worshippers.

An open court lies beyond. In it stands the high altar, under the open sky. Nothing is hidden in the worship of Aten. A flight of steps leads to the top of the altar, but Akhnaten goes by it, through a second courtyard, a third, a fourth. Here are the pillars of a colonnade, and the royal party halts a while in the cool shade. Then onward, through a fifth court and into a sixth, past another altar, and finally into the seventh courtyard, where the highest altar of all stands in Aten's light. All is bright, open, airy here. Today, since Pharaoh is here, the temple is heaped high with flowers and bright cloth ornaments.

Akhnaten and Nefertiti stand at the high altar. Offerings of vegetables, fruit, flowers, geese, and joints of meat surround the royal pair. Bronze bowls filled with burning oil top the altar. Akhnaten and Nefertiti lift their right hands and scatter fragrant spices on the flames.

Pharaoh is bare down to the waist. All the fragility of his body is exposed: the elongated head, the flimsy neck, the hollow chest. But his skin is tanned by the sun. A skirt of fine linen covers the lower part of his body.

Nefertiti is clad in a soft, flowing robe, so fine that the slender loveliness of her body is clearly visible within it. A red sash is tied round her waist, its ends drooping to the ground. Neither she nor Pharaoh wears jewels or ornaments.

73

Behind the king and queen, two little princesses stand, honoring Aten in their own way by rattling the systrum, a small tinkling musical instrument. Meryre, the High Priest of Aten, is bowing to the king. Another priest burns incense. Eight blind musicians, fat and old, sing a hymn to Aten while clapping their hands. A harpist plays.

Thus did Akhnaten honor his god. There were no elaborate rituals, no prostrations before idols, no occult incantations. Akhnaten had no room in his beliefs for demons, for images of gods, for all the extensive furniture of religiosity that his ancestors had accumulated in their thousands of years of life along the Nile. He took what he wanted from the Heliopolitan worship of Re, but he discarded much. The cult of Aten, though it had firm roots in the soil of Egyptian theology, was something quite new, a bold departure from what had gone before.

There were precedents for many elements of Akhnaten's new religion. We have already seen several times how hymns to Re and later to Amon had displayed monotheistic tendencies. The most advanced thinkers of Egypt had long thought of a god who embraced all gods, a supreme deity who had created the world and ruled it through his many guises.

Even the idea of a totally abstract, non-tangible god had occurred to the Egyptians before. Though Ptah, Atum, Re, Amon, and the other creator-gods and sun-gods had always been depicted in corporeal form, either as a human with the head of a beast or as a man, one god had always been abstract. This was Hep (or Hapi, or Hap), the Nile-god. The Nile was the source of Egypt's life; its annual flood brought fertile topsoil out of Ethiopia, and on the river's mercies the whole land depended. Yet the Nile never figured as a prominent deity, as did the sun. Perhaps the Nile was too sacred even to worship. A Nile-god existed, but men feared him rather than worshipped him. A scribe of the Eighteenth Dynasty set down this hymn to the Nile-god:

He cannot be sculptured in stone in figures whereon is placed the White Crown. He cannot be seen. Service cannot be rendered to him. Gifts cannot be presented to him. He is not to be ap-

74

proached in the sanctuaries. Where he is is not known. He is not to be found in inscribed shrines. No habitation can contain him. There is none who acteth as guide to his heart.

Nowhere in Egyptian literature do we find prayers or petitions addressed to this unseen, unknown god. But in Old Kingdom texts there sometimes are found references to a divine power without a personal name, an abstract being referred to as *neter,* "The god," in a context that could almost be taken as "God."

Probably these concepts were known to the priests at Heliopolis whose teachings influenced Akhnaten so greatly. Another influence may have come from the Mitanni women at the royal court.

Mitanni was ruled by an aristocratic class of Indo-Europeans, or Aryans, who had brought with them out of central Asia the gods of early India, the gods celebrated in that collection of Sanskrit hymns known as the Vedas. An important Aryan god, worshipped no doubt in Mitanni as well as in Vedic India, was Surya, the rising and setting sun, the source of light and heat, and thus the lord of life. Surya was the Dyaus-Pitar, the "Heaven-Father," from whose title the Greeks derived *Zeus* and the Romans *Jupiter.* Of him, we are told in the Indian hymns, is born all life and warmth: "He raises his long arms of gold in the morning, rouses all beings from their slumber, infuses energy in them, and buries them in sleep in the evening." Savitri, the Vedic god of the sun shining in full strength, is an exact equivalent of Re: "the golden-eyed, the golden-handed, and golden-tongued." And the Vedas speak of Varuna, another solar deity:

Light-giving Varuna! Thy piercing glance doth scan
In quick succession all this stirring active world.
And penetrateth, too, the broad ethereal space,
Measuring our days and nights and spying out all creatures.

All this Aryan imagery would find a place in Akhnaten's own hymns to the Aten.

Our actual knowledge of Akhnaten's religion is limited largely to those hymns, found in varying degrees of intactness on the

75

walls of tombs at Akhnaten's capital. The actual ethical and moral precepts of Atenism have not come down to us. Some critics of Akhnaten have said that the religion had no formulated scheme of ethics, that it was simply an emotional cult, depending for its appeal on that "oceanic" feeling of one-ness with the universe which forms part of so many Oriental religions.

It is hard to accept this idea. We can be fairly sure that Akhnaten's religion had aspects more profound than the mere singing of lovely hymns and the burning of incense. Inscriptions at Akhetaten speak of the religion as "the teaching"—but the teaching, whatever it was, has not survived. Undoubtedly the scriptures and commandments set down by the king and his priests, written on papyrus or carved on stone, were rooted out and destroyed utterly in the wave of vindictive anti-Atenism that swept Egypt after the death of the heretic.

Our knowledge of Akhnaten's religion has to be based primarily on the hymns. But we can, by approaching it negatively to see what the religion was *not,* manage to see how it differed from previous religious practice in Egypt.

The Aten was an abstract, intangible god. That much is clear. There were no images of Aten, only the solar symbol. Akhnaten was careful to point out that the solar disk itself was not God, but only a symbol of God. Aten was a life-giving, intangible essence; not the sun or even the face of the sun, but the *heat which is in the sun.* Other gods were worshipped in their image, but the sun-symbol of Aten was no more Aten than the cross, to a Christian, is God.

Aten was the power of creation. The great hymn declares, "O sole God, whose powers no other possesseth, thou didst create the earth according to thy desire, while thou wast alone." Out of the heat, out of the energy, that was God came all the universe. The rays of Aten remain as visible signs of his love for his creation: "Thou art in the sky, but thy rays are on earth." . . . "Thy rays embrace the lands, even all that thou hast made. . . ."

A formless essence, a loving force, invading all of time and

76

space—this, the hymns say clearly, is Aten. It is very different from any earlier Egyptian concept. Nor does it bear much relation to the original Hebrew concept of God. Like Akhnaten, the Hebrew patriarchs prohibited all graven images of the deity: "Thou shalt not make unto thee any graven image, or any likeness of any thing that is in heaven above, or that is in the earth beneath, or that is in the water under the earth." Yet Genesis declares, "God created man in his own image," and the God of Abraham and Moses walks in a garden in the cool of the evening, and possesses face and form.

Aten was a kindly god. "When the chicken crieth in the egg-shell," says the hymn, "thou givest him breath therein, to pre-serve him alive." Nothing escapes Aten's glance, not the smallest detail of existence on earth: "All flowers live and what grows in the soil is made to grow because thou dawnest. They are joyful before thee. All cattle skip upon their feet; the birds in the marsh fly with joy, their wings that were folded are spread, uplifted in adoration to the living Aten, the maker."

Aten is light. His beams play over all things, bringing joy to man and bird and flower. Akhnaten's joy in Aten's light is perhaps best described in the words of a man who probably never knew of the heretic Pharaoh, the nineteenth-century art critic Ruskin, who wrote in 1873 of "the breathing, animated, exulting light, which feels and receives and rejoices and acts—which chooses one thing and rejects another—which seeks and finds and loses again—leaping from rock to rock, from leaf to leaf, from wave to wave, glowing or flashing or scintillating according to what it strikes, or in its holier moods absorbing and enfolding all things in the deep fulness of its repose, and then again losing itself in bewilderment and doubt and dim-ness, or perishing and passing away, entangled in drifting mist, or melted into melancholy air, but still—kindling or declining, sparkling or still—it is the living light, which breathes in its deepest, most entranced rest, which sleeps but never dies." [1]

There is no longer any recognition of the somber mysteries of hidden Amon—nor of that other hidden god, Osiris the dis-

[1] Ruskin, *Modern Painters,* Volume I.

membered, god of the darkness of night. Akhnaten never mentions Osiris. In the tombs of Egypt for a thousand years, since the rise of the cult of Osiris, men had had inscribed texts of an almost liturgical quality, retelling the tale of Osiris and asking for that god's intercession in the next world. There were many of these liturgies; the most famous to us is *The Book of the Dead,* but there were such standard texts as *The Book of Opening the Mouth, The Book of the Two Ways, The Book of the Dweller in the Underworld,* and *The Book of Gates.* All these texts, with their incantations and spells, their depictions of Osiris as the weigher of souls, their cloud of gods and demons, are banished from the tombs at Akhetaten. The monsters and demigods, all the courtiers of Osiris, are consumed in the blaze of Aten's pure light.

Akhnaten's belief in an afterlife is hard to interpret. We know of no funeral services or rituals that he offered in place of the discarded Osiris cult. The apparatus of the old tradition, the Last Judgment and the Field of Reeds, the Field of the Grasshoppers, the Field of Offerings, the Block of Slaughter, the Five Pits of the Underworld where the wicked were burned —all play no part here. There is no talk of hell in Akhnaten's hymns.

The Atenists did not live wholly in the present, though. The king and nobles, at least, had tombs. Perplexingly, there does not seem to have been a cemetery at Akheteten for commoners; though the city was occupied at least fifteen years, no burial-places have ever been found by archaeologists. Were the bodies of the dead cast into the Nile? Were they burned and scattered in the desert? Only mystery faces us here.

It may very well have been that Akhnaten did not teach an afterlife. Early Judaism, which, as we will see, may be indebted to Akhnaten for many of its tenets, says absolutely nothing about life after death. Hamlet's "undiscovered country" may have had no place in the thinking of Akhnaten. The religion of Heliopolis supplied him with the solar boat of Re, in which the souls of the virtuous departed might ride. But Akhnaten declined to adopt that feature of the Heliopolitan theology. The hymns tell us that when Aten is not in the sky "the earth is in darkness like the dead," and all things "sleep in their chambers, their heads are wrapped up, their nostrils are stopped, and none seeth the other." But nowhere do we find an expression of belief that those dead will rise again when Aten shines.

Nowhere, either, is there mention of Aten's jealousy, his hatred, his vengeance. Aten is no stern Jehovah, thundering against wickedness from on high. We hear over and again of Aten's compassion, his tenderness, his love, and, in the sweetness and purity of Aten we find a concept of God that amazingly foreshadows the kind of deity found in the preachings of Christ.

There is much, then, in Akhnaten's religion that links it to Judaism and Christianity. The forbidding of idols of God gives it a point in common with Judaism (and with Islam). The emphasis on the loving goodness of God is a bond with Christianity, as is the frequently repeated insistence that Aten watches over all beings, the great and small. (Compare the text of Akhnaten's hymn with Christ's words: "Ye ask who are those that draw us to the kingdom if the kingdom is in heaven? The fowls of the air, and all the beasts that are under the earth or upon the earth, and the fishes in the sea, these are they which draw you, and the kingdom is within you.")

Atenism is a religion of delight, of joy, of happiness. "O Lord, how manifold are thy works!" Akhnaten cries. "The whole land is in joy and holiday because of thee! They shout to the height of heaven, they receive joy and gladness when they see thee." Aten is the lord of peace, the lord of truth: "I have set truth in my inward parts," says one of his followers, "and falsehood is my loathing; for I know that the King rejoiceth in truth."

The king did, indeed, rejoice in truth. The goddess Maat was never forbidden by Akhnaten, though there were no temples or religious ceremonies dedicated to her. But how—if he conceded the divinity of Maat at all—can we call Akhnaten a true monotheist?

When we consider whether Akhnaten was or was not a monotheist, we enter onto treacherous terrain, onto the quicksand of semantics. It is difficult, perhaps impossible, for us to understand the monotheism of Akhnaten. More than thirty centuries have passed. We must try to penetrate not only an alien language but alien ways of thought that refuse to conform to our notions of logic.

Jehovah was described as "great above all other gods"—a phrase that admits the existence of other, less worthy deities. Aten, though, stands alone, without rivals. "O sole God, whose powers no other possesseth," one hymn declares, while other verses exclaim, "O sole God, beside whom there is no other." Of Aten is it written, "Thou art alone, but infinite vitalities are in thee by means of which to give life to thy creatures."

Yet the name of Aten contains references to three earlier gods: Re, Horus (Harakhti), and Shu (the god of heat and light). The intricate phrase, "Re-Harakhti, rejoicing on the Horizon in his name, 'Shu [Heat]-Which-is-in-the-Aten,' " hardly sounds monotheistic to us. It is more the double Egyptian monotheism-within-polytheism that has little meaning for us, except when compared with the Christian Trinity. Perhaps the original name of Aten sounded too polytheistic to Akhnaten himself, for, in the ninth year of his reign, he altered the title as the result of some unknown theological decision, revising it to drop Horus and Shu: "Re lives, Ruler of the Horizon, who rejoices on the Horizon in his name, 'Re the Father, who has returned to Aten.' " Even so, that retains the name of Re of Heliopolis, and Re's name was openly used throughout Akhnaten's heresy, even forming part of the king's own coronation name, Nefer-kheperu-re, "Beautiful is the form of Re," and his secondary name, "Wan-re," "Sole one of Re." Then, too, there was his continued tolerance of Maat. He referred to himself by the epithet, "Living in Truth," to the end of his reign.

The modern scholars who refuse to see Akhnaten as a monotheist point to his tolerance of such names as Re, Harakhti, and Maat to claim that he was doing no more than others had done before him in Egypt: combining the attributes

Amon of Thebes.

Courtesy of The University Museum, Philadelphia, Pa.

Ptah of Memphis.
*Courtesy of The University Museum,
Philadelphia, Pa.*

Osiris.
*Courtesy of The University Museum,
Philadelphia, Pa.*

Isis nursing Horus.

Horus.

Metropolitan Museum of Art.
Rogers Fund, 1934.

Bes.

Courtesy of The University Museum,
Philadelphia, Pa.

Amenhotep III as a young man.
Courtesy of The Brooklyn Museum.

Amenhotep III in old age.
Courtesy of The Brooklyn Museum.

Tell el-Amarna tablet, 18th Dynasty.

Courtesy of The Oriental Institute, The University of Chicago.

Akhnaten and Nefertiti.

Akhnaten.

Nefertiti.

Courtesy of the Staatliche Museen, Berlin.

Limestone statuette of Nefertiti.

Courtesy of the Staatliche Museen Zu Berlin, Berlin.

Akhnaten and his family worshiping Aten. Note how rays from the disc terminate in hands. The hands near the eyes of Akhnaten and Nefertiti bear the symbol of life.

Courtesy of The University Museum, Philadelphia, Pa.

The Royal Couple with three daughters.

Verlag Gebr. Mann, Berlin, 1961.

A daughter of Akhnaten.

*Courtesy of The University Museum,
Philadelphia, Pa.*

Statue of Akhna
from Karnak.

Courtesy of the
Egyptian State Tou
Administration.

Sculptor's model of the
head of Queen Nefertiti.

*Courtesy of the
Egyptian State Tourist Administration.*

Smenkhkare.
Courtesy of The Brooklyn Museum.

Tutankhamen and Ankhesenamen: portrait from the throne of Tutankhamen, found in his tomb.
Photograph by Harry Burton, The Metropolitan Museum of Art.

Reconstruction of the Commercial Quarter in Akhetaten.

Garden Court, North Palace, Akhetaten.

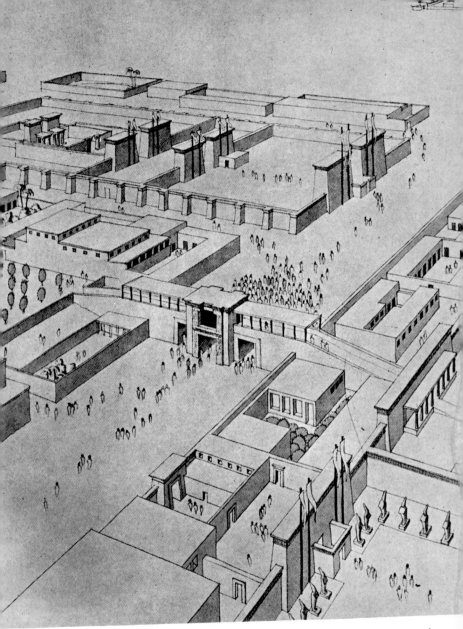

Reconstruction of the Central Quarter in Akhetaten. A bridge connects the King's House and the Royal Chapel (left) with the Great Palace (right). The Window of Appearances is in the center of the bridge.

Egypt Exploration Society.

of many gods into one. Long before, Egyptians in one district had seen the sun-god as the beetle Khepra; others had seen him as the falcon Re; others as the doddering old man Atum, and the theologians of Heliopolis had combined these varying local forms into the single god Atum-Re. Later, Osiris and Re had been merged for reasons of public policy, and still later, Amon and Re. Could it not be said that Akhnaten, merging the various forms of Re into his Aten, was simply following an age-old practice by which a new cult achieved domination over an old one? Amon, Re, Atum, and others had all been called "sole god" in their turn.

Another objection to Akhnaten's monotheism lies in the fact that he found it necessary to obliterate the names of other gods, which to us seems childishly vindictive. It is as though he felt those other gods would continue to exist as rivals to Aten until their names were hacked away. If Aten were the only true god, and Amon had never existed, why go to such trouble to destroy the record of earlier spiritual ignorance?

A defense of Akhnaten is that he acted for reasons of propaganda. In his mind, perhaps, Amon and the other gods had never existed; but to make the break more dramatic, he ordered the obliteration, the symbolic destruction of Amon. It would not be the only time that a prophet found it necessary to make concessions to the superstitions of his people.

Perhaps this same policy of concession led Akhnaten into his most baffling departure from pure monotheism: he evidently encouraged the worship of *himself* as a god!

Pharaohs in Egypt had long asserted their divine origin, as sons of Re or of Amon. In the pyramid era, the great kings had had themselves worshipped as deities, and down through the centuries some Egyptian kings had claimed the same homage in their own lifetimes. It was quite common for a king to be worshipped after his death, since he was then one with Osiris and Re; temples devoted to various Pharaohs existed all over Egypt.

There is some reason to think that Amenhotep III, at some point in his long reign, was willing to allow himself to be worshipped as a living god. There is no doubt that Akhnaten took that same glory upon himself.

The hymns to Aten are not at all ambiguous on the matter. The most famous hymn is entitled "the worship of the Aten by the King Akhnaten and the Queen Nefertiti," as though Aten were the personal god of the king alone. The hymn states explicitly that only Pharaoh knows the god: "Thou are in my heart, there is no other that knoweth thee, save thy son Akhnaten." It is clearly indicated that Akhnaten is the son of Aten: "O living Aten, born in the sky every day, he begets his august son Wan-re [Akhnaten]." The king is thus making the same claim of divine descent that earlier Pharaohs had made in relation to Re and then Amon.

The paintings in the tombs of courtiers at Akhetaten demonstrate that Akhnaten alone worshipped the Aten, while the rest of his people worshipped *him*. Inscriptions on the murals refer to the king as "the unique one of Re," "the beloved son of Aten," and the prayers of the courtiers are addressed not to Aten but to the king.

Thus the "Divine Father" Ay asks Akhnaten for long life: "May thou grant to me a good old age as thy favorite; may thou grant to me a goodly burial by the command of thy *ka* in my house. . . . May I hear thy sweet voice in the sanctuary when thou performest that which pleases thy father, the living Aten."

Even when a courtier addresses Aten directly, it is purely on behalf of the king: "May thou make thy beloved son Akhnaten to live with thee forever, to do what thy heart wishes, and to behold what thou dost every day, for he rejoices in the sight of thy beauty. . . . Let him remain here, until the swan turns black, until the raven turns white, until the mountains stand up to walk, and until the sea runs up the river. And may I continue in service of the good god [Akhnaten] until he assigns to me the burial that he gives."

We can be sure that no word was inscribed in anyone's tomb at Akhetaten without the direct approval of Pharaoh. Akhnaten knew, and did not object to it, that his courtiers were referring to him as "the good god."

It is a familiar pattern in the history of religion for a prophet to be made divine by his followers. Jesus, regarding himself as a simple teacher, never declared himself to be the physical son of God; only after his death did Christian theologians interpret Jesus' teachings in such a way that he could be said to be not only God's son but God Himself. Mohammed, who insisted, "There is no god but God," has been given a quasi-divine position in Islam, though he is worshipped only as God's prophet. Most ironically, Buddha, who denied the existence of any actual deity, has been made the object of an intricate religious cult. Only Moses, of all the great law-givers, has never given rise to any blurring of the monotheistic idea.

The case is different with Akhnaten, since apparently he welcomed the divine accolade, while Jesus, Buddha, and Mohammed would certainly have rejected any such concepts in their own lifetimes. Akhnaten's self-deification is a disturbing dilution of his great ideal. Did he think that only in that way could he maintain royal authority? Perhaps Egypt was prepared to accept a Pharaoh only if he claimed to be divine. Yet Akhnaten permitted himself to be depicted informally, in a style that borders close to caricature. There was nothing austere about him. He appeared in public dressed simply, smiling, his wife and daughters at his side. In the tomb paintings, we see him nibbling at meat, playing with his children, kissing Nefertiti, putting his arm around her in public. Would one who felt he needed to claim divinity to bolster his authority let himself be portrayed so casually?

The other explanation is less attractive. There are those who feel that Akhnaten, isolated in his remote city, surrounded by flattering courtiers, cut off from the hostile murmurings of his people, genuinely saw himself as divine. These critics show a steady evolution of Akhnaten's fanaticism. The Aten religion begins first as one of many, then is exalted to become the highest religion, and then the *only* religion. Having achieved that much, Akhnaten, a physically weak, possibly mentally unstable man, passed on into that realm of delusion where he regarded himself as not simply the prophet of Aten, but the divine representative of Aten on Earth, to whom prayer should be addressed.

The mystery of Akhnaten's motives can never be unraveled. Certainly he weakens the concept of Aten as the sole god, by offering himself as a subsidiary deity. His religion was, perhaps, the closest possible approach to monotheism in an Egypt where the king was held to be divine and where God could be worshipped as having at once one and many forms. It was not the pure monotheism of the Jewish prophets, of Jesus, of Mohammed. Unless we are misinterpreting the few Atenist texts we now have, Akhnaten's religion fell somewhat short of that pure monotheism.

The texts on which we base our entire knowledge of Akhnaten's religion come from the Amarna tombs. (Amarna, as noted before, is the modern name for Akhetaten.) Excerpts from the hymns are inscribed on the walls of the tombs of the nobles and courtiers, and it appears that two main hymns were in use: a long hymn recited by the king himself, and a shorter one recited by his officials.

No single complete text of either hymn exists. The great royal hymn in a nearly complete version was copied by an archaeologist in 1883, but the copy contained inaccuracies, and a third of the inscription was later destroyed by the vandalism of modern natives of Amarna. In 1894, James Henry Breasted put together a composite version of the shorter hymn in his doctoral dissertation, *De Hymnis in Solem sub Rege Amenophide IV Conceptis,* while the archaeologist Norman de Garis Davies assembled the text of the longer hymn from five separate fragments in his *Rock Tombs of El Amarna.* In 1905, Breasted translated both hymns into English, and his lyrical, graceful version is the one used below.

The Aten hymns are in the great tradition of Egyptian sacred literature. They contain little that is really new; some of Akhnaten's actual phrases are anticipated by earlier hymns to

84

less exalted god-conceptions. But in their simplicity, their purity of concept, they transcend their literary ancestors and shine brightly in the ranks of the world's most noble devotional poetry.

The "long hymn" comes mostly from the tomb of Ay, the "Divine Father." The introductory text calls it "A hymn of praise of Harakhti, the living one exalted in the Eastern Horizon in his name of 'Heat-Which-is-in-the-Aten,' " and is offered by Ay in the names of Akhnaten and Nefertiti:

Thy dawning is beautiful in the horizon of heaven,
O living Aten, Beginning of life!
When thou risest in the eastern horizon of heaven,
Thou fillest every land with thy beauty;
For thou are beautiful, great, glittering, high over the earth;
Thy rays, they encompass the lands, even all thou hast made.
Thou art Re, and thou hast carried them all away captive;
Thou bindest them by thy love.
Though thou art afar, thy rays are on earth;
Though thou art on high, thy footprints are unseen.

When thou settest in the western horizon of heaven,
The world is in darkness like the dead.
Men sleep in their chambers,
Their heads are wrapped up,
Their nostrils stopped, and none seeth the other.
Stolen are all their things, that are under their heads,
While they know it not.
Every lion cometh forth from his den,
All serpents, they sting.
Darkness reigns,
The world is in silence:
He that made them has gone to rest in his horizon.

Bright is the earth, when thou risest in the horizon,
When thou shinest as Aten by day.

The darkness is banished
When thou sendest forth thy rays;
The Two Lands [Egypt] are in daily festivity,
Awake and standing upon their feet,
For thou hast raised them up.
Their limbs bathed, they take their clothing,
Their arms uplifted in adoration to thy dawning.
Then in all the world, they do their work.

All cattle rest upon their herbage,
All trees and plants flourish;
The birds flutter in their marshes,
Their wings uplifted in adoration to thee.
All the sheep dance upon their feet,
All winged things fly,
They live when thou hast shone upon them.

The barques sail upstream and downstream alike.
Every highway is open because thou hast dawned.
The fish in the river leap up before thee,
And thy rays are in the midst of the great green sea.

Thou art he who createst the man-child in woman,
Who makest seed in man,
Who giveth life to the son in the body of his mother,
Who soothest him that he may not weep,
A nurse even in the womb,
Who giveth breath to animate every one that he maketh.
When he cometh forth from the body on the day of his birth,
Thou openest his mouth in speech,
Thou suppliest his necessities.

When the chicken crieth in the egg-shell,
Thou givest him breath therein, to preserve him alive;
When thou hast perfected him
That he may pierce the egg,
He cometh forth from the egg,
To chirp with all his might;

He runneth about upon his two feet,
When he hath come forth therefrom.

How manifold are all thy works!
They are hidden from before us,
O thou sole God, whose powers no other possesseth.
Thou didst create the earth according to thy desire,
While thou wast alone:
Men, all cattle large and small,
All that are upon the earth,
That go about upon their feet;
All that are on high,
That fly with their wings.
The countries of Syria and Nubia,
The land of Egypt;
Thou settest every man in his place,
Thou suppliest their necessities.
Every one has his possessions,
And his days are reckoned.
Their tongues are divers in speech,
Their forms likewise and their skins,
For thou, divider, hast divided the peoples.

Thou makest the Nile in the nether world,
Thou bringest it at thy desire, to preserve the people alive.
O lord of them all, when feebleness is in them,
O lord of every house, who risest for them,
O sun of day, the fear of every distant land,
Thou makest also their life.
Thou hast set a Nile in heaven,
That it may fall for them,
Making floods upon the mountains, like the great sea,
And watering their fields among their towns.

How excellent are thy designs, O lord of eternity!
The Nile in heaven is for the strangers,
And for the cattle of every land, that go upon their feet;

But the Nile, it cometh from the nether world for Egypt.
Thus thy rays nourish every garden,
When thou risest they live, and grow by thee.

Thou makest the seasons, in order to create all thy works:
Winter bringing them coolness,
And heat that they may taste thee.
Thou hast made the distant heaven to rise therein,
In order to behold all that thou didst make,
While thou wast alone,
Rising in thy form as living Aten,
Dawning, shining afar off, and returning.

Thou makest the beauty of form, through thyself alone.
Cities, towns, and settlements,
On highway or on river,
All eyes see thee before them,
For thou art Aten of the day over the earth.

Thou art in my heart;
There is no other that knoweth thee,
Save thy son Akhnaten.
Thou hast made him wise in thy designs
And in thy might.
The world is in thy hand,
Even as thou hast made them.
When thou hast risen, they live;
When thou settest, they die.
For thou art duration, beyond thy mere limbs.
By thee men liveth,
And their eyes look upon thy beauty
Until thou settest.
All labor is laid aside
When thou settest in the west.

When thou risest again
(Thou) makest (every hand) to flourish for the king.

Since thou didst establish the earth,
Thou hast raised them up for thy son,
Who came forth from thy flesh,
The king, living in truth,
The lord of the Two Lands, Nefer-khepru-re, Wan-re,
The son of Re, living in truth, lord of diadems,
Akhnaten, whose life is long;
(And for) the great royal wife, his beloved,
Mistress of the Two Lands, Nefer-nefru-aten, Nefertiti,
Living and flourishing for ever and ever.

Perhaps the most interesting theme of this majestic hymn is not the lovingness of Aten, nor even the one-ness of him, but his universality as a deity. Here we have an idea quite new to Egypt.

Even the most lofty thinkers at Heliopolis had never conceived of Re as more than god of Egypt. Even when hailing Re as "sole god," they understood him to be only sole god along the Nile; other lands, it was assumed, had gods of their own, but those gods were no concern of any Egyptian. Other Egyptian priests were even more parochial in their thinking, hailing their god as "sole god" but placing the limits of his dominion at the boundaries of their own city or province, as though he were some sort of feudal prince.

Akhnaten's god is a universal one, and not by accident. The Eighteenth Dynasty was the first in Egypt to rule over a foreign empire. Akhnaten was Pharaoh not only of Egypt but of much of the known world. Universal tribute flowed toward Egypt. Akhnaten's response was to offer the world its first universal god. He offered not Amon, so inextricably associated with Thebes, not Re of Heliopolis, not Ptah of Memphis, not any local deity, but Aten, the lord of the solar disk, whose benevolence extended toward every man.

Here is Akhnaten's real innovation. The worshipper of Marduk in Babylon had no interest in what god reigned at Nineveh. Those who bowed before Baal at Byblos did not yearn to impose him on the people of Mitanni. The stiffnecked Hebrews, making burnt-offerings to fierce Yahweh in the wastelands of Palestine, desired not at all to share with others the god who had chosen them. Akhnaten offered his god to all humanity, not at the point of a sword but in meekness and humility. Not till Jesus would a prophet make a similar gesture to the world.

The universality of the new god is strikingly demonstrated in the hymn. Syria and Nubia are specifically mentioned—indeed, they are mentioned before Egypt herself! We know that Akhnaten caused temples to Aten to be constructed in those lands. Far up the Nile in Nubia, five hundred miles south of Thebes, rose the temple of Gem-Aten where the modern town of Dulgo now stands. The site of the Aten temple of Syria is unknown today. Within Egypt, there were temples of the new god at Heliopolis, Hermopolis, Memphis, and other cities.

The tongues of men, Akhnaten declares, "are divers in speech, their forms likewise and their skins"—but all are creatures of Aten, and all are welcome in Aten's temple. Most touchingly, Akhnaten describes how God, who has provided Egypt with the bounty of the Nile, has "set a Nile in heaven that it may fall" for the people of foreign lands—rain, all but unknown in Egypt. "The Nile in heaven," Akhnaten declares, "is for the strangers. How excellent are thy designs, O lord of eternity!"

The shorter hymn lacks the majesty, but not the eloquence, of its great companion. It recapitulates some of the ideas of the long hymn, and adds new lines of joy and wonder:

> Thou risest beautifully, O living Aten, Lord of Eternity;
> Thou art glittering, beautiful, strong;
> Thy love is great and mighty,
> Thy rays are cast into every face.
> Thy glowing hue brings life to hearts,
> When thou hast filled the Two Lands with thy love.
> O God who himself fashioned himself,
> Maker of every land,
> Creator of that which is upon it:
> Men, all cattle large and small,
> All trees that grow in the soil.

They live when thou dawnest for them.
Thou art the mother and the father of all that thou hast made.
As for their eyes, when thou dawnest,
They see by means of thee.
Thy rays illuminate the whole earth,
And every heart rejoices because of seeing thee,
When thou dawnest as their lord.

When thou settest in the western horizon of the sky,
They sleep after the manner of the dead,
Their heads are wrapped up,
Their nostrils are stopped,
Until thy rising comes in the morning,
In the eastern horizon of the sky.
Their arms are uplifted in adoration of thee.
Thou makest hearts to live by thy beauty,
And men live when thou sendest forth thy rays.
Every land is in festivity:
Singing, music, and shoutings of joy
Are in the hall of the Benben-house,[2]
Thy temple in Akhetaten, the seat of Truth [Maat],
Wherewith thou art satisfied.
Food and provision are offered therein;
Thy pure son performs thy pleasing ceremonies,
O living Aten, at his festal processions.
All that thou hast made dances before thee,
Thy august son rejoices, his heart is joyous,
O living Aten, born in the sky every day.
He begets his august son Wan-re [Akhnaten]
Like himself without ceasing,
Son of Re, wearing his beauty, Nefer-khepru-re, Wan-re,
Even me, thy son, in whom thou art satisfied,
Who bears thy name.
Thy strength and thy might abide in my heart.
Thou art Aten, living forever. . . .

[2] The *benben* was a pyramidal polished stone which occupied the place of honor in the temples of Re at Heliopolis. Akhnaten made use of it for his religion.

Thou hast made the distant sky to rise therein,
In order to behold all that thou hast made,
While thou wast alone.
Millions of life are in thee to make them live,
It is the breath of life in the nostrils to behold thy rays.
All flowers live and what grows in the soil
Is made to grow because thou dawnest.
They are drunken before thee.
All cattle skip upon their feet;
The birds in the marsh fly with joy,
Their wings that were folded are spread,
Uplifted in adoration to the living Aten,
The maker. . . .[3]

[3] Here the text breaks off.

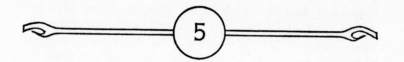

5

ΛTEN IS SΛTISFIED

The middle years of his reign were tranquil ones for Akhnaten. He dwelled in the City of the Horizon, in a round of ceremonies and festivities, and, so far as we know, never left the city. Nefertiti was always at his side. The royal family grew; a fourth daughter was born, a fifth, a sixth. The queen was unable to give Pharaoh a son.

Only one moment of darkness marred the sunny joy of those years. Death took Meketaten, Akhnaten's second daughter. The little girl died in the twelfth year of Akhnaten's reign, and the fourth or fifth year since he had moved permanently to the new city. Two moving reliefs carved in Akhnaten's own tomb show the scenes of mourning in the palace at the death of the royal daughter. Nefertiti, grasping her husband's wrist for support, peers forward to look at the small figure on the bier, while servants of the king tear their hair and rend their clothes in lamentation, and the surviving princesses weep. A woman, perhaps a nurse, is shown leaving the room carrying a child at her breast, as though Nefertiti had recently been delivered of a seventh daughter, but no mention is made elsewhere of that baby.

The Amarna tombs give us a matchless picture of life in Akhnaten's city. No one was ever buried in those tombs, not even Akhnaten himself; all were left empty when the city was abandoned after the death of the Pharaoh. There were two groups of tombs, hollowed out of the rocky cliffs east of the city. Each tomb consisted of a forecourt, a hall supported by columns of rock, an inner chamber, and several adjoining rooms. On the walls of the tombs gleam the famed Amarna paintings, bringing Akhnaten and his city to vivid life.

The tombs somehow escaped the vengeance of Amon, and went untouched when wrecking crews demolished Akhetaten in the reign of Pharaoh Horemheb. They have not been so fortunate in more recent times. Two hundred years before Christ, the soldiers of Ptolemy came through the area, visited the tombs as sightseers, and scribbled comments in Greek that still survive: "Having ascended here, Catullinus has engraved this in the doorway, marvelling at the art of the holy quarriers." And: "Autrales. . . . I have been here." Some centuries later, a band of persecuted Coptic Christians adopted one tomb as a catacomb, and, with a fanaticism that recognized no beauty, defaced several of the "impious" reliefs. In our own day, despite the vigilance of guards, villagers at Tell el-Amarna have vented their displeasure at those set in authority above them by slipping in to destroy some of the remaining reliefs.

Luckily, the paintings have been copied and published, and so are beyond the reach of ignorance and vindictiveness now, no matter what fate befalls the originals.

The great charm of the Amarna paintings is their unique style. It has been called realism, but it is more than that, for the Amarna murals are not "realistic" in our sense of the word. Rather, the artists have been given free play. Imagination runs unfettered. In his search for Maat, the king, "living in truth," insisted on truth in art, and asked his artists to be true, not to a conventional technique showing things as they should be, but to things as they really were. The truth Akhnaten sought in art was the inner truth, not necessarily the truth of the eye. Thus, one remarkable scene shows Akhnaten and Nefertiti together. At a glance, it appears to be a single figure. You look more closely and see a double outline, and too many arms and fingers. The king's outline and the queen's have been *superimposed*—

and the artist captures the harmony of Akhnaten and Nefertiti unforgettably in this inspired linking.

The fluid, free style of Amarna art marks a sharp break with past traditions, but is not without ancestry. A new liveliness had entered official Egyptian art to some extent as early as the reign of Thothmes IV, and great freedom of conception was evident in many works executed under Amenhotep III. No doubt Akhnaten, seeing the beginning of an artistic revolution, seized on it and carried it to its remarkable fulfillment.

In the great days of the Old Kingdom, when Re had been Egypt's supreme god, artistic effort had reached a peak in the land of the Nile. Those early artists had captured something of the "truth" Akhnaten sought; he may even have known of certain works of art (found by nineteenth-century archaeologists at Heliopolis and Abydos) which actually anticipated the realistic long-jawed, long-headed style in which Akhnaten himself was depicted.

Early in the Old Kingdom, what had been a supple and free style of artistic representation hardened into an inflexible tradition. A strangely contorted posture became a universal style. Human beings were shown with their heads in profile, but the profiled eye was shown as if in front view, as were the shoulders. The chest and the lower part of the body were weirdly pivoted to be at once a profile and a front view, but the wrist was done in profile, as were the feet. In addition, ironbound laws governed the position of the feet: when one arm or foot was shown in advance of the other, it always had to be the one furthest from the spectator. A figure facing right could only have its left arm or foot advanced, and vice versa. A second law, even more arbitrary, required the Egyptian artist to depict all figures as though they were facing to the right, turning their right sides toward the spectator. When the needs of composition made it necessary to show a figure facing left, the design was simply reversed, so that a short staff held against the right thigh in a right-facing figure would still be held against that thigh (and thus would pass *behind* the figure) in a leftward-facing representation.

In the Old Kingdom, the best and boldest of artists departed from this rigid canon whenever they pleased. Figures turn their back on us, advance the wrong leg, and commit many other artistic "crimes." But after the period of chaos that followed the Old Kingdom, it became almost a subversive act for Middle Kingdom and New Kingdom artists to vary from the old dogmas. The artistic rules were followed slavishly, and what had been a vigorous and vital art degenerated into a stiff, lifeless one. All Pharaohs were shown not only in the same postures but with more or less the same features and physiques. Composition of large scenes never varied. Generations of weary artists submerged their personalities in meeting the demands of conventional art.

As we have noted, the artists were beginning to rebel by the middle of the Eighteenth Dynasty. They started to draw figures with the nearer arm outstretched, to use a looser line, to make background details more lifelike. Though representations of gods and kings remained as stiff as ever, it became possible to depict slaves, servants, dancing-girls, and animals in realistic poses. The conflict is made clear by the paintings of the time, which show, side by side, noble figures in conventional poses and slaves in realistic ones.

Akhnaten carried the artistic revolution to its ultimate. The artist was set free. Maat was to be his guide. Pharaoh might now be shown casually leaning on a stick, while Nefertiti dangles a bouquet of flowers before his nose. Informal family scenes replaced the formal pharaonic poses. Gaiety, relaxation, beauty —these were the new rules of the day.

The pursuit of Maat sometimes led the artists to the old dead end of conventionality. Akhnaten had given orders that he was to be shown "warts and all"—in complete fidelity to his unusual anatomy. The artists accordingly portrayed him in an unforgettable way, setting him apart from every ancient ruler by showing his haggard face, his sharp elbows, his protruding belly, his swollen thighs. But, as if all too willing to exchange one artificiality for another, they began to paint first Nefertiti and the royal children, then every courtier of the city, in the same style! The

Amarna murals throng with men and women of spindly necks and heavy legs. It was strange homage to Pharaoh to have one's self shown in his guise. Perhaps, if Akhnaten's revolution had survived, all noble Egyptians thenceforth would have been drawn in the heretic's shape, no matter how they might actually have looked.

Though Amarna art has its mannered and artificial side, it represents a bold step away from the past. For the first time in the history of Egyptian art, hands and feet are drawn correctly, members of the royal family are shown in natural, lifelike positions, and artists depart from frigid monumentality to provide human touches of warmth and charm. Many of the Amarna innovations served to influence later Egyptian art.

There seems no doubt that Akhnaten himself was directly responsible for the new style. Chief among the architects and sculptors responsible for Akhetaten was Bek, son of Men and grandson of Horamu, third in a line of master-builders. At Aswan in Upper Egypt, Bek obtained red granite to decorate the new city, and he left a large commemorative tablet on the rock there. The tablet shows Bek in gala costume, holding a bouquet of flowers before an altar above which is the Aten-symbol. Bek is paying homage to Akhnaten, who stands to the left of the altar, but the king's figure has been obliterated by later enemies. Bek is shown as saying:

I give praise to the Lord of the Two Lands, obeisance to Wan-re [Akhnaten], I, the chief of works in the Red Mountain, the assistant whom his majesty himself taught, chief of sculptors on the great and mighty monuments of the king, in the house of Aten in Akhetaten, Bek, son of the chief of sculptors, Men.

Bek may simply have been offering ritual homage when he called himself "the assistant whom his majesty himself taught." Certainly Akhnaten was not himself a skilled artist, for a king would have no opportunity to acquire such craft. But, from what we know of him, it seems likely that Akhnaten "taught" Bek artistic freedom and unconventionality of execution, if not actual technique.

Another inscription of Bek's has survived—his tombstone,

which appeared on sale in the open market at Cairo late in the nineteenth century. It provides us with a shred of evidence that the Aten-worshippers did indeed look forward to an afterlife. The inscription begins with praise of Aten, who is asked to "vouchsafe a complete good life, united with the reward of honor, joy of heart, and a beautiful old age, in favor of the artist of the king, the sculptor of the lord of the land, the follower of the divine benefactor, Bek."

Bek asks, using phrases from ancient prayers for the dead, "That his soul may appear, that his body may live, that his foot may march out to all places." He hopes, too, that "the king may grant me to drink wine and milk," and that "the king may receive the sacrifice of the dead" on behalf of the sculptor's wife, the lady Ta-hir.

Bek and his corps of assistants did a masterly job. Thanks to them, the city of Akhnaten comes to life for us. The artists showed every detail of city life, even showed themselves at work, as in one lovely little scene in which "the overseer of the sculptors of the Queen Tiy," by name Yuti, is depicted at work on a statue of Akhnaten's young sister Beketaten. The sculptor sits on a low stool, putting the last touch of paint on the child's statue. At the same time he is supervising the work of two nearby apprentice sculptors who are carving an arm and a limb for another statue, using a third sculptor or slave as their model.

The sculptors and artists were kept busy. Not only did the palaces and villas of the city have to be decorated, but the tombs as well, nineteen tombs in the limestone cliffs to the south of the city, six to the north. The southern tombs belonged to such notables as Nefer-kheperu, the governor of Akhetaten; Apiy, the royal scribe and steward; Mahu, the chief of police; Paatenemheb, commander of the royal troops (this seems to be General Horemheb wearing an Atenist name); and May, the royal chancellor and "bearer of the fan of the king's right hand." The southernmost tomb, the most imposing in the city, was that of Ay, the "Divine Father."

Ay's tomb, like most of the Amarna tombs, was left unfinished when the city was abandoned. It was to have had

98

twenty-four pillars supporting the main chamber, but only fifteen were ever cut. Though the walls had been sized for a series of murals, only one wall actually was decorated.

Ay was Akhnaten's closest confidant, and perhaps the most important man in Akhetaten next to Pharaoh himself. In the reign of Amenhotep III, Ay was not a powerful political figure, but as "Divine Father" in Akhnaten's reign he held a clutch of high titles, and undoubtedly had the ear of the king. If he was, as we think, the father of Akhnaten's dearly loved Nefertiti, it would explain a good deal of Ay's preeminence.

As the token of that preeminence, Ay tells us himself, "I was one favored of his lord every day, great in favor from year to year, because of the exceeding greatness of my excellence in his opinion. He doubled for me my favors like the number of the sand; I was the first of the officials at the head of the peo- ple. . . . I am a true witness, devoid of evil; my name has penetrated into the palace, because of my usefulness to the king, because of my hearing his teaching."

That "teaching" is set forth nearby, for here is the text of Akhnaten's great "long hymn." Its noble phrases share the wall with more of Ay's smug self-praise. "I am the truthful one of the king," Ay declares. "I am at the head of the princes, the companions of the king, the first of all the followers of his majesty."

Strikingly vivid scenes show Akhnaten marking his apprecia- tion for Ay's services in a tangible way. The murals tell us that on two occasions Pharaoh honored Ay with munificent gifts. We see the "Divine Father" going to the palace in a chariot escorted by servants and fan-bearers. The people of the city gather round as Ay stands in the palace courtyard, and Akhnaten and Ne- fertiti appear at the "Great State Window" of the palace. They are dressed lightly, in soft robes, and the king, smiling, extends a hand in greeting to the cheering multitude.

Then, in succeeding panels, the story unfolds. Pharaoh turns to his treasurer and orders him to decorate Ay. "Put gold on his neck, and on his back, and gold on his feet, because he has heard the doctrine." The treasurer signals to slaves; jewels are brought forward, golden chains, vases of ointment. The king and queen stand beaming under the Aten-symbol; the treasurer officiously writes down the value of each gift on his tablet; the servants entwine the throat and neck of Ay with chains of gold. Happily, Ay lifts his arms toward Pharaoh, and Akhnaten favors him with a pleasant smile from the balcony.

On a second occasion was the "Divine Father" honored this way. No doubt he had risen in Pharaoh's estimation, for now he travels to the palace with almost regal splendor, squadrons of runners and fan-bearers escorting him, Syrian and Nubian soldiers forming his bodyguard. Ten scribes follow Ay to write down the words of Pharaoh.

Again Ay comes before the royal balcony, accompanied this time by his wife Tiy. A stunning honor is granted him: the entire royal family appears in the window. King and queen are there, and the young princess Ankhesenpaaten is in Nefertiti's arms, while Meritaten and Meketaten stand by their parents. Akhnaten leans comfortably on a colored cushion, basking in Aten's warmth, and tosses a necklace of gold down to Ay. Then the queen drops chains of gold to her father, and the two older princesses, joining in the fun of it, excitedly scatter bracelets. Ay and Tiy are pelted with a rain of wealth. It is impossible to carry everything, let alone wear it. Ay adorns himself with seven thick necklaces and nine massive bracelets; the servants carry the rest. Nefertiti beams; above her is the inscription: "The heiress, great in favor, lady of grace, sweet of love, Mistress of the South and North, fair of face, gay with the two plumes, beloved of the living Aten, the Chief Wife of the King, whom he loves, lady of the Two Lands, great of love, Nefertiti, living for ever and ever. . . ."

The dazzled Ay moves out of the courtyard. His friends gather round to view his gifts, and dance and jump for joy. The servants of Ay kiss his feet, and throw themselves in the dust before the gifts. Shouts of happiness ring out, carrying all the way to the doors of Ay's own dwelling.

The porters there exchange puzzled glances. "For whom is

this rejoicing being made?" they ask. One of them sends a boy to find out, ordering him: "Run! Hasten! See what this great rejoicing means!"

"I go! I go!" the boy answers, and soon he is back. "They are rejoicing over Ay, the 'Divine Father,' and over Tiy. They have been made people of gold!" And a sentry calls out, "Pharaoh (Life! Prosperity! Health!) has given them millions of loads of gold and all manner of riches!"

From the walls of Ay's tomb, the silent voice of the "Divine Father" endlessly recites self-congratulatory words: "I was eminent, possessing character, successful in opportunities, contented of disposition, kindly. . . ." And history, knowing that Ay ultimately placed himself upon the royal throne under mysterious and perhaps dishonorable circumstances, frowns.

Another who enjoyed the favor of Akhnaten during those golden years was one Meryre, High Priest of Aten. In the early days of Atenism, Akhnaten himself had held the title of High Priest or "Chief Seer," an honor derived from the old Heliopolitan Re cult. Once the new religion had been established, Akhnaten freed himself of that responsibility, and conferred it on Meryre.

The tomb of Meryre contains a mural more than a hundred feet long, depicting incidents in the High Priest's career. A key scene, of course, is Meryre's investiture with the title, "Chief Seer of the Aten in the City of the Horizon of Aten." Akhnaten again stands at a window of the palace, leaning forward over brightly colored cushions piled on the sill. Nefertiti and one of the princesses stand by him. Ribbons flutter from the delicate pillars supporting the roof of the gallery outside, in which Meryre kneels. Officials pompously hold standards and red and blue ostrich-plume fans.

A lady of Meryre's household named Tenr, probably his wife, advances and sings a version of the hymn to Aten: "Thy rising is beautiful, O Living Sun. . . . O living Aten, beside whom there is no other, who heals the eyes with his rays, the maker of all things that are. . . . Grant thou thy beloved son, living in truth, Akhnaten, that he may live with thee forever. . . ."

Akhnaten now commands Meryre to rise. He declares, "Behold, I make thee High Priest of the Aten for me in the Temple of the Aten in the City of the Horizon of Aten. I do this for love of thee, and I say unto thee: O my servant who hearkenest to the teaching, my heart is satisfied with everything which thou hast done. I give thee this office, and I say unto thee: thou shalt eat the food of Pharaoh, thy lord, in the house of Aten."

The onlookers crowd around Meryre and hoist him to their shoulders. The new High Priest cries jubilantly, "Abundant are the rewards which the Aten knows how to give when his heart is pleased." He is presented with the insignia of his office by Akhnaten, and with gold and silver. A chariot waits to take the High Priest back to his villa; women with tambourines, who will head the procession, impatiently drum and dance with excitement as Meryre is honored.

In another scene, Meryre is rewarded for having successfully collected the dues of the temple from the farms on the far bank of the river. The High Priest stands proudly before Akhnaten in front of the bulging granaries of the temple; the king leans on his staff, and turns to address his treasurer:

"Thou treasurer of the chamber of silver and gold! Reward Meryre! Hang gold necklaces around his throat, and place gold at his feet, for he was obedient to the teaching of Pharaoh." Attendants rush forward to heap riches on Meryre; scribes write down an account of the event; Meryre returns to his villa accompanied by dancers and singers.

The wall paintings of Meryre's tomb tell us, too, what the house of an important man of his day looked like. Two houses are shown, one drawn from the front, the other from the side. Possibly they both belonged to the High Priest. Both had roughly the same plan.

Each house was rectangular, and surrounded by a wall which could be entered only on the short side in front of the house. Within this doorway was a courtyard, which servants scrupulously swept and wet down every day. The rear wall of the court formed the front of three small inner rooms. The center room led inward to a great hall beyond it, a dining hall supported by pillars. Meryre's dining table stood in the center of the hall, covered with dishes, bowls of fruit, loaves of bread; smaller adjoining tables held roast meat and flowers. Ponderous wine jars were built into the rear wall of the hall. Arm-chairs stood at either side of the table, and next to one of them we can see a basin with a jug of water.

A narrow courtyard separated the dining hall from the bedrooms and storerooms. A special antechamber led to the bedroom, in which stood a large bed, heaped high with pillows. There were two kitchens and a bakery nearby. Oddly, the only way for servants to get from the storerooms and kitchens to the street was through the main dining hall, and they had a door of their own to use, so they could pass through without disturbing Meryre and his guests. Meryre's houses, and the other great houses of Akhetaten, all were of only one story. Here, again, was a departure; in Thebes, houses of the nobles had two levels.

The tombs of Akhnaten's other courtiers indicate a love for the king, a reciprocated warmth that is probably more than mere flattery. The tomb of May, the royal chancellor, "hereditary prince, count, wearer of the royal seal, king's-attendant in his august barge, chief of all works of the king," shows us May declaring, "I was a man of low origin both on my father's and on my mother's side, but the king established me. . . . He caused me to grow . . . by his bounty when I was a man of no property. . . . He gave me food and provisions every day, I who had been one that begged bread." May must have been one of the "new men," those who vaulted to sudden prominence when Akhnaten shattered the power of Amon and that god's followers.

Another who rose swiftly was Panehesy, a priest of Aten. "When I knew not the companionship of princes I was made an intimate of the king," says Panehesy, giving thanks to Akhnaten, "who maketh princes and formeth the humble." Mahu, the chief of police, also a favorite of Akhnaten, rose the same way from lowly birth. His tomb gives us a hint of tense wariness behind the sunny tranquility of the city. Evidently nomad tribes, wandering through the desert, were a menace to Akhetaten, for one scene in Mahu's tomb shows the police chief being awakened early one morning—a winter morning, it seems, for a servant kindles a small fire as Mahu listens to a report of trouble outside the city. He calls for his chariot, goes to the scene of the disturbance, and gets his men; we next see Mahu, plump and proud, handing over two crouching, bound criminals to the governor of the city. "Examine these men whom the foreigners have instigated," Mahu requests. Spies, perhaps? Or assassins plotting against Pharaoh? The tomb does not tell us.

Mahu was one of the most devout worshippers of Aten, one of the most loyal followers of Pharaoh. We see him kneeling before his king, while policemen shout Akhnaten's praises, acclaiming the "Good Ruler," and adding a chorus with a Gilbert & Sullivan touch: "He promotes, in masses, in masses. He shall live eternally like the Aten."

It was necessary for Pharaoh to ride out with Mahu occasionally to inspect the city's defenses. We see Akhnaten setting out from the palace in his chariot, taking the reins himself as was his custom; Nefertiti and Meritaten ride with him. Mahu is shown waving goodbye to the royal family as they leave, but then, in a later panel, he is amusingly portrayed running alongside the chariot, panting in obvious discomfort as he tries to keep pace with Pharaoh's spirited horses. Akhnaten speaks to the queen, and now and then addresses a few words to the breathless Mahu. Princess Meritaten, meanwhile, mischievously adds to the police chief's problems by poking the rumps of the horses with a stick, spurring them on even faster. (This scene has been tragically destroyed by modern vandals.) Fifteen policemen trot in front as Pharaoh's bodyguard, and the rays of the Aten extend their benevolent hands toward the royal chariot.

Another chariot scene is found in the tomb of Ahmose, "Veritable Scribe of the King," "Master of the Estate of Akhnaten." This tomb of the northern group shows Akhnaten and Nefertiti on their way to the temple in the golden chariot. Akhnaten negligently holds the reins, but he is facing Nefertiti, chatting with her as the chariot rolls along. Between the royal couple is Princess Meritaten, peeping over the edge of the chariot to stare at the handsome steeds.

Pharaoh may have been something less than an accomplished driver, despite the nonchalant pose he strikes here. Archaeologists uncovering the houses of the workmen in Akhetaten came upon a child's toy, a chariot driven by a monkey, with another monkey as passenger. The horses are rearing and prancing, nearly out of control, while the monkey-driver hauls on the reins and tries desperately to get matters into hand. The monkey's head and neck, interestingly enough, are elongated in just the style of Akhnaten's. The toy—it is in the Cairo Museum today—seems an unmistakable caricature of the king in difficulties with his chariot. We can easily imagine Akhnaten grinning as he sees the clever little model—though certainly no one knowingly would have brought it to his attention. Yet this king, who was so slyly lampooned by his subjects, proclaimed himself the living incarnation of God! It is hard to see how Akhnaten's subjects could make sense out of the king's mixture of easy informality and mystic austerity.

One whose role in the history of the times may have been dark and sinister built a tomb for himself in the southern group. He was Tutu, "The Chief Mouthpiece for the Foreign Countries," Akhnaten's Foreign Minister or Secretary of State. Tutu's offices were at the northern end of the city; there, he received and read the correspondence that reached Pharaoh from foreign monarchs, and took such action on it as he thought necessary. It seems, as we will see later on, that Tutu for reasons of his own kept much of the incoming diplomatic mail from Akhnaten's eyes, serving his own ends but hardly those of his king or of his country.

Yet Tutu was outwardly loyal and devout. The walls of his tomb contain excerpts from the Aten hymns: "I come with praise to Aten, the living, the only god, lord of radiance, who makes light when he rises in heaven." More fulsome than Tutu's praise of the Aten is Tutu's praise of Tutu; he asserts, with that bland self-satisfaction so common to Egyptian courtiers, "I am the favorite servant, who hears his teaching, and his marvelous things are in my body without ceasing. I will speak truth to his majesty, for I know that he lives therein. . . . My voice was not lifted up in the king's house, nor was my step too broad in the palace. I took not the reward of lying, nor expelled the truth for the violent."

We see the Foreign Minister being honored by Akhnaten. Beside the king is Nefertiti, dandling two babies on her knee, while representatives of Syria, Nubia, Mitanni, and other foreign lands stand by bearing tribute. Akhnaten says, "O great ones who stand before the king, my purpose is to confer an exceptional reward equal to a thousand of which are done to men. I give it to the Chamberlain, Tutu, because of his love for the king his lord."

And Tutu—perhaps already conspiring with foreign princes against Akhnaten—replies, "O my good lord, a ruler of character, abounding in wealth, great in duration, rich in monuments! Thy every command is done; they come to pass as in the care of Aten, the Lord, the living Aten. . . . Thou controllest the entire land; Syria, Ethiopia, and all the nations. Their hands are outstretched in praise of thee. . . ."

Of all the tombs, the most important for the light it sheds on the events of these years of Akhnaten's reign is that of Huya, the northernmost sepulchre of Amarna. Huya was the son of an important official of Amenhotep III, and under Akhnaten had accumulated such titles as "Superintendent of the House," "Overseer of the Royal Harem," "Steward in the House of Queen Tiy," "Superintendent of the Treasury," "His Majesty's Brave in Cavalry," and many more.

As superintendent of the treasury, Huya was in charge of receiving tribute sent to Akhnaten from abroad. A scene in Huya's tomb shows Akhnaten on a splendid throne-chair, a palanquin of wood covered with gold foil, borne on the shoulders of eighteen soldiers, accompanied by fan-bearers and shade-bearers, as he goes to inspect the tribute. It is the twelfth year of Akhnaten's reign. Beside him in the palanquin is Nefertiti, her arm resting tenderly around the king's waist. The armrests beside them are in the shape of sphinxes, rising above glistening golden cobras. A priest walks before the palanquin, sending up clouds of incense, while dancers skip nimbly in the roadway ahead of the procession. An inscription beside the scene declares:

Year twelve, the second month of winter, the eighth day. . . . The King and Queen of Upper and Lower Egypt, living forever, made a public appearance on the great palanquin of gold, to receive the tribute of Syria and Ethiopia, and of the west and the east. All the countries were collected at one time, and also the islands in the midst of the sea; bringing offerings to the king when he was on the great throne of the City of the Horizon of Aten, in order to receive the imposts of every land and granting them in return the breath of life.

The six princesses follow the royal couple, the younger ones attended by nurses. The party reaches the pavilion where the tribute-ceremony is to be held, and Akhnaten and Nefertiti take their places upon a double throne, resting their feet on hassocks. Again, the queen's arm slips around Akhnaten's waist, and she takes his left hand in hers. The princesses gather around the throne. One holds a young gazelle; another strokes the graceful beast's head.

Now the tribute-bearers of the vassal kingdoms pass before the king, who is diverted from their solemn homage by a corps of wrestlers, tumblers, and dancers in the background. Long-robed Syrians drop before the throne and lift their hands high in greeting. Magnificent Syrian horses are presented; chariots, bows, spears, shields, ivory tusks, daggers, and other gifts are displayed to Akhnaten and placed on the ground near the royal pavilion. Wild animals, among them a tame lion, are led past by their keepers. Slaves are marched forward, handcuffed, but neither heavily bound nor whipped as they go by, for the gentle Akhnaten will abide no cruelty. Several lovely girls, gifts from Syria to the king's harem, walk by, and then handsome vases of metal and costly stone are exhibited to the king.

The Libyans offer ostrich eggs and ostrich feathers. The tribute of Nubia and the Sudan, carried by Negroes decked in feathers, comprises bars and rings of gold, bags of gold dust, shields, weapons, tusks, cattle and antelopes. A slave comes past with a panther to match Syria's lion. Akhnaten sits quietly, perhaps bored by this display of worldly wealth. None of it results from his conquests. He has never led an army into battle. He is no more of a warrior than his father was. All this tribute comes to him by the grace of his great-great-grandfather Thothmes III, the world-conqueror, the empire-builder. Egypt has not had a true warrior on the throne since the death of Thothmes III's son Amenhotep II, more than half a century before. The empire has run on its own momentum ever since. But that momentum is soon to run down.

A second great event took place not long after, also in Akhnaten's twelfth regnal year, and for our knowledge of it we are again indebted to Huya's tomb. Queen Tiy, who had remained in Thebes after Amenhotep III's death, came to pay a ceremonial visit to Akhetaten, and perhaps to take up permanent residence there.

Queen Tiy had been sympathetic to her son's heresy from the first, and had publicly revealed her adherence to the new creed by naming the last of her children Beket*aten*. Yet she had chosen to remain in Thebes for the past four years. Perhaps she had served as her son's line of contact with the key figures of that still important city, keeping a watchful eye over the resentful Thebans lest they rise up in rebellion against the king who had shamed them. However, now she chose to see her son, the Pharaoh.

It fell to Huya to make all ready for the visit. Akhnaten had provided a palace for her in his city, but it had rarely if ever been occupied, and now it had to be decked out in all the pomp worthy of the queen mother. Tiy was then a woman in her early fifties, but, unless Akhnaten's truth-loving artists have deceived us, she was still strikingly beautiful, with the slim, youthful look of a woman half her age. She came accompanied by her daughter Beketaten, who was perhaps seven or eight years old, and thus younger than at least one of her six nieces.

Huya arranged the royal feast of greeting, but with unusual modesty allowed himself to be portrayed as an insignificant, almost invisible figure in the banquet scene. The royal family occupies the center of attention. Streaming Aten-rays illuminate the scene; Akhnaten sits facing his mother, Nefertiti is seated behind the king, and two of the royal princesses occupy low chairs at their mother's side. Young Beketaten sits beside Queen Tiy.

It is a charmingly relaxed scene. Queen Tiy wears her royal headdress, consisting of a disk, two horns, two tall plumes, and two small serpents, all probably fashioned of gold. Her graceful gown is transparent enough to reveal the beauty of her figure. Akhnaten, bare to the waist, slouches backward in an unflattering pose; a gleaming golden serpent is mounted on his forehead, and he wears sandals. Nefertiti, like her mother-in-law, is garbed in a diaphanous linen robe. The three children seem to be naked.

Tables piled high with food surround the royal group. Joints of meat, dishes of sweets, vegetables, pomegranates and other fruit, bread and cakes, tempt the diners. Jars of wine are decked with ribbons. Akhnaten holds in his right hand a large broiled bone from which he nibbles meat; perhaps it is a skewer of shish kebab. Nefertiti takes a dainty bite of a whole roast duck. Queen Tiy, while pondering the heavily laden table before her, offers some tidbit to Beketaten, who reaches for it gladly. Huya moves to and fro in the background, seeing to the details of the banquet, diligently tasting each dish before it is placed before the royal family. Two groups of musicians perform in turn; four Egyptian girls regale the feasters with harps and lutes, and then what seems to be a band of foreign musicians play, one musician strumming a standing lyre taller than a man.

Elsewhere in the tomb we see a scene of the evening, after the banquet. It is cooler, now, and Akhnaten has donned a linen mantle. He and Nefertiti and Queen Tiy drink wine from golden bowls, while the little princesses help themselves to fruit from overflowing bowls. Little Ankhesenpaaten climbs on the footstool of her mother's chair, tugging at Nefertiti's skirts, while stuffing some juicy morsel into her mouth. Huya again hustles about, gesticulating to the waiters, who fill the drinking-bowls. Once again, musicians play in the background.

A third scene from Huya's tomb shows a more solemn moment in Queen Tiy's visit. Akhnaten is escorting his mother to the temple. Perhaps it is a special temple set aside for the use of the queen mother, for it is twice labelled in the mural, "Temple of the Shadow of Re of the Great King's Wife Tiy." It must have been an unusually handsome building of great size. We see Akhnaten leading his slender, youthful-looking mother by the hand, ushering her through two great swinging doors into the main court. An altar rises in the midst of the courtyard; a more private altar lies beyond, flanked by statues of Akhnaten, Queen Tiy, and Amenhotep III. Behind the king and queen mother come Princess Beketaten and her two ladies-in-waiting. Huya and an official in foreign costume—two tiny, stooping figures—precede Akhnaten. Courtiers carrying ostrich-plume fans follow Beketaten. Outside the temple wait policemen, charioteers, fan-bearers, porters, and temple attendants, crying, "The ruler of the Aten! He shall exist for ever and ever!" As the queen mother goes by they shout, "She who rises in beauty! She who is patron of this temple of Aten!"

Perhaps it was one of the happiest moments of Akhnaten's life, as he led his mother hand in hand into her temple of Aten in the city he had spun into reality in the desert. Soon after, though, death took Akhnaten's second daughter, Meketaten, and shadows of gloom descended on the City of Aten's Horizon. The death of Meketaten is depicted in the tomb Akhnaten had intended for himself—a solitary tomb, in a lonely, jackal-infested spot in the hills. Here, a passage descended into the hill, to a rock-cut hall, its roof supported by four columns. A sarcophagus of pink granite, intended for Akhnaten, rested here. A small chamber adjoined it—planned as Nefertiti's tomb, or possibly that of Meketaten. On the walls of that chamber are the scenes of lamentation.

Having buried one daughter, Akhnaten soon would lose an-

110

other in marriage to a foreign prince. Since his coronation, Akhnaten had carried on correspondence with Burnaburiash, King of Babylon. Midway in Akhnaten's reign, Burnaburiash had asked for one of Akhnaten's daughters as a wife for his son. Kadashman-Bel, the father of Burnaburiash, had similarly procured a royal Egyptian princess, one of Akhnaten's sisters, as a bride.

Akhnaten was eager to remain on friendly terms with the Babylonian monarch, and without much prodding he offered his fourth daughter, Neferneferuaten, to Burnaburiash's son. Neferneferuaten was probably no more than five at the time of her betrothal, but she was the oldest available princess. As we will see, Meritaten and Ankhesenpaaten, the first and third daughters, were probably already betrothed to Egyptian princes, while Meketaten, the second daughter, was dead, or at least sickly, at the time of the correspondence.

The marriage was performed by proxy, and Neferneferuaten remained with her parents for the time being. We know this from a letter sent to Akhnaten by Burnaburiash, which mentions that he is sending "a necklace of 1,048 stones" as a gift to "Pharaoh's daughter, the wife of his son"—which can only mean that the princess still resided in Egypt.

The correspondence between Egypt and Babylonia takes on a darker hue a short time later. A quarrel develops between Babylonia and Mitanni, and Akhnaten, perplexed by this split between two of his allies, tries to offend neither of them and succeeds in offending both. While this prickly situation was developing, Burnaburiash fell ill. Somehow, Nefertiti failed to send a letter of good wishes to the Babylonian king, and Burnaburiash, irritated by the omission, writes coldly to Akhnaten, telling him that he is sending the usual gifts required by etiquette, but that only a small part of his gift is to be bestowed upon the "mistress of the house," Nefertiti, since she had not cared to ask after his health.

Soon Burnaburiash had a much more serious complaint to register. The caravan of Tsalmu, Burnaburiash's messenger, had twice been plundered en route from Babylon to Akhetaten.

111

Both times, the incident had occurred on Egyptian territory, and therefore, Burnaburiash insisted, Akhnaten must make good the losses.

For the caravan of a royal messenger to be plundered on Pharaoh's soil was something new in Eighteenth Dynasty times. It would never have happened in the reign of Amenhotep III, and certainly not while any of the earlier, stronger kings of the dynasty held power. Times were changing. The world beyond Akhetaten was becoming a place of uncertainty. Whispers of intrigue and revolt in the foreign empire of Egypt were heard. It was said, in the capitals of Mitanni and Babylonia and the Hittite land, that Egypt's king was a dreaming mystic who could not and would not command the armies of the world's greatest power, and that anything might happen as the unrest grew.

Akhnaten gave no sign that he knew what was happening. In a letter to a Syrian prince, he calmly assured the vassal, "I am very well, I the sun in the heavens, and my chariots and soldiers are exceedingly numerous; and from Upper Egypt even unto Lower Egypt, and from the place where the sun riseth even unto the place where he setteth, the whole country is in good cause and content."

But the country was not content, nor was all well. While Akhnaten chanted hymns in his spotless capital, men of more sturdy fiber plotted the end of Egypt's empire.

6

AN EMPIRE SLIPS AWAY

Thothmes III, the first world-conqueror, had built a vast domain. From deep in Nubia to the northern reaches of Syria, Pharaoh's word was law. Beyond the Egyptian possessions in Syria lay the friendly buffer state of Mitanni, and north of Mitanni lay the end of the world.

Mitanni was flanked with hostile states. To the east, there was Assyria, not then the fierce state that would descend on the world "like a wolf on the fold" centuries later. Still eastward, south of Assyria, was Babylonia, which maintained friendly relations with Egypt, possibly out of fear of the Assyrians. To the west of Mitanni were the Hittites, their empire sprawling over the whole length of Asia Minor.

The Near East had tasted Hittite fury many times. In 1590, while Egypt still wrestled with the Hyksos yoke, King Mursilis I of the Hittites had thundered eastward on a march of conquest such as the world had never beheld. Leaving his capital of Hattusas behind, the Hittite monarch had marched first to Tunip (Aleppo) in Syria, three hundred miles away. Conquering Tunip, Mursilis smashed on, five hundred miles further to the east, blazing a trail through the land of the Hurrians that later would become Mitanni, and attacked Babylon itself.

The great city had fallen to Hittite might almost without a battle. Returning to his own capital, though, Mursilis was assassinated by his brother-in-law, and the world had respite from the Hittites as they quarrelled among themselves. Not for seventy years did the Hittites unite behind a single king again, and more than a century passed before they could think of foreign conquest. It was a century of great political change. Egypt threw off the Hyksos and entered into the glittering pomp of the Eighteenth Dynasty. Indo-European invaders, related, it seems, to the Hittite kings, conquered the Hurrian lands and virtually overnight built the powerful kingdom of Mitanni. In the three-cornered political situation, Egypt first allied herself with the Hittites against Mitanni, at a time when Mitanni chariots rumbled through the sacked Hittite capital; then, several generations later, Egypt and Mitanni allied themselves through royal marriages as the Hittites grew in strength. Egypt was thereby making use of a policy diplomats have never forgotten: a strong nation must ally herself with the second strongest of her rivals. When Mitanni was powerful, Egypt made overtures to the Hittites; when the Hittites grew too strong, Egypt consorted with Mitanni.

About 1380 B.C., late in the reign of Amenhotep III, there came to the Hittite throne a man sometimes called "The Charlemagne of the East," who rejoiced in the sinuous name of Suppiluliumas. He longed to repeat the exploits of Mursilis, the Hittite conqueror of Babylon. Suppiluliumas prodded first at Mitanni, in the third or fourth year of Akhnaten's co-regency with his father. Dushratta of Mitanni threw the invaders back. For six years, Suppiluliumas strengthened his hand in patience. He sent ambassadors to Akhnaten at the new capital. Akhnaten, though, had little to say to the belligerent Hittite, and the correspondence faltered quickly and broke off. Once again, Suppiluliumas challenged Mitanni, but Dushratta's soldiers stood firm in the mountain passes, and the Hittites were thwarted.

By the tenth year of Akhnaten's reign, word had certainly reached Suppiluliumas that Pharaoh was a strange, unworldly man, bored by warfare, interested only in the company of women and children, more eager to chant hymns than to see Egypt's pride defended. Unable to make headway against

Mitanni, the Hittite king did what no one would have dared to do in the previous century: he set out to conquer Egypt's Syrian possessions.

Canaan and Syria, lying along the eastern end of the Mediterranean, had never been unified lands, and had fallen easily to the armies of Thothmes I and Thothmes III. The dominant political unit in the Levant was the city-state, ruled by a local prince or even by an oligarchy. In time of trouble, the city-state closed its gates and concentrated on its own defense, without thought of aiding its neighbor. Egyptian conquerors had simply gobbled up city after city. The Pharaohs had not attempted to interfere with the local dynasties. They had left each city-state in the hands of a puppet prince, who was permitted to rule so long as he continued to show loyalty to Egypt by making the proper tribute remittances. Now and then, some crafty princeling would be able to form a coalition of several cities and rise in revolt against Egypt, but such uprisings were always short-lived, ending in disunity and confusion when Pharaoh's troops arrived.

Late in the reign of Amenhotep III, the Hittites had already begun to foment intrigue in northern Syria, with the intent of detaching some of the local princes from their Egyptian loyalty. It was a time of plush affluence in Egypt; Amenhotep III had little interest in what took place at the remote northern end of his empire; young Prince Amenhotep IV was, perhaps, already preoccupied with theological matters.

The Hittite strategy was to encourage a Syrian prince named Abd-Ashirta to carve out a state of his own in northern Syria, while continuing to give lip-service to Egypt. After Abd-Ashirta had consolidated his position, the Hittites would ally themselves openly with him, move southward skirting Mitanni's southern borders, and devour the rich cities of the Mediterranean coast.

Abd-Ashirta and his son Aziru were quite willing to play the Hittite game for their own ends. If Egypt asked them why they were suddenly extending their sway to other cities, the two desert princes could reply, "To protect Egyptian territory against the Hittites." To the Hittites, Abd-Ashirta and Aziru could explain their maneuvers as the necessary preliminaries to inviting the invaders to cross into Egyptian land. In their own minds, they were conscientiously serving the welfare of themselves, but neither Pharaoh nor Suppiluliumas needed to know that.

Gradually northern Syria came under the "protection" of the sly father and son, while the Hittite armies moved closer all the time to what had once been the Egyptian empire's border. The first serious Hittite thrusts into Egyptian territory were made near Beirut, in the valley of Amki along the Litani River. Abd-Ashirta and Aziru, meanwhile, had taken control of a strip of coastal cities, including Irqata, Ardata, and Shigata. They were in a position to have resisted the Hittite advance, if they cared to—indeed, as Egypt's vassals, they were bound by oath to do so—but they quietly feathered their own nests while the Hittites advanced.

Even in the reign of Amenhotep III, Aziru's ambitions had caused concern in Syria, and such local governors as Akizzi of Qatna, west of Damascus, had asked the old king for help against Aziru. "If troops do not march this year, he will get the whole country," Akizzi warned Amenhotep III, pointing out also that the Hittites had burned a nearby city. Amenhotep III, old and sick, took no action. Perhaps he was unable to make head or tail out of the conflicting complaints of the Syrian princelings, for the correspondence shows them contradicting each other at every point.

We find a prince named Itakama suddenly setting up a kingdom of his own at Kadesh and allying himself with the Hittites. Akizzi of Qatna warns Amenhotep III against this prince's treachery, and another local prince named Namyawaza also writes to Thebes to denounce Itakama. But then Itakama himself writes to Pharaoh, accusing the loyal Namyawaza of wronging him, and declaring his own loyalty! Itakama offers to drive out of Syria both Namyawaza and a marauding tribe of desert dwellers called the Khabiri, also known as the 'Apiru, and evidently a branch of the people we know as Hebrews.

Into this already intricate situation, the sly Aziru injects himself. Caught between the Hittites on the north and Itakama's new kingdom on the south, Aziru busies himself by moving west-ward to complete the job of conquering the coastal strip. He can then offer a different story to everyone. If the Hittites ask him what he is doing, he can tell them he is consolidating a path for them from the north to Itakama's friendly city of Ka-desh. If Itakama raises objections, Aziru can give him the same answer—that he is just another Hittite ally, and they are all working together. While if Pharaoh bestirs himself to question the proceedings, Aziru can say, as before, that he is uniting Syria on behalf of the Egyptians against the Hittite invasion.

Soon after, Aziru and Abd-Ashirta allowed the Hittites through to join their allies at Kadesh. About this time, Akhnaten must have summoned Aziru to Egypt to give an accounting of himself. Probably Pharaoh had been prodded by a letter from Burnaburiash of Babylon, complaining of unrest in Syria and the interruption of trade. Aziru went to Egypt, no doubt to present a glib and convincing picture of his loyalty to the Egyptian king. Meanwhile, Abd-Ashirta, Aziru's father, wrote to Akhnaten's foreign minister, Tutu, asking him to defend Aziru at court and obtain his speedy release. It seems as though the Egyptians were holding Aziru as a hostage against his fa-ther's continued loyalty—but not for long, since soon Aziru was back in Syria.

Northern Syria had now been carved up among Itakama, Aziru, and his father, and the Hittites themselves. Aziru next turned his attention to a more southerly prize: the coastal strip of Phoenicia, lying between Syria on the north and Palestine on the south. Here were the rich mercantile cities of Byblos, Sidon, Tyre, and Simyra. They were in strong hands, however, Byblos in particular being ruled by Ribaddi, a doughty warrior loyal to Egypt. Aziru's first forays against Byblos and Simyra were un-successful, and he turned eastward instead, to the city of Niy, which he captured, putting its king to death. He explained both to the Hittites and to the Egyptians that he had done this in their own best interests.

The city of Tunip (Aleppo) in Syria had maintained its in-dependence of Aziru and the Hittites during all this, and now found itself wholly isolated. The governor of Tunip wrote an unhappy letter to Akhnaten, begging dismally for help:

To the King of Egypt, my lord. The inhabitants of Tunip, thy servant. May it be well with thee, and at the feet of our lord we fall. My lord, Tunip, thy servant, speaks, saying: Who formerly could have plundered Tunip without being plundered by Thothmes III? The gods of the King of Egypt, my lord, dwell in Tunip. May our lord ask his old men if it not be so. Now, however, we belong no more to our lord, the King of Egypt. . . . If his soldiers and chariots come too late, Aziru will make us like the city of Niy. If, however, we have to mourn, then the King of Egypt will mourn over these things which Aziru has done, for he will turn his hand against our lord. And when Aziru enters Simyra, Aziru will do to us as he pleases, in the territory of our lord the king, and on account of these things our lord will have to lament. And now Tunip, thy city, weeps, and her tears are flowing and there is no help for us. For twenty years we have been sending to our lord the king, the King of Egypt, but there has not come to us a word—no, not one.

The letter from Tunip is a tragic document. It would have been easy enough for Akhnaten to have saved the city from Aziru. The ports of Byblos and Simyra were still loyal; Egyptian troops shipped there could have marched inland to Tunip. Itakama could have been crushed, Aziru pushed into line, and the Hittites thrust back into Asia Minor.

Akhnaten did none of these things. He sent no aid to Tunip. Was it out of pacifist convictions? Was he willing to let Egypt's enemies devour all of Syria and Phoenicia? Or is the explanation a simpler one: that Tutu, Akhnaten's foreign minister, a known friend of Aziru's, simply kept the Tunip letter and others like it from Pharaoh's eyes?

Akhnaten sent no troops. He received letters from Abd-Ashirta and Aziru, staunchly proclaiming their loyalty to Egypt, and he went to Aten's temple, day after day, while the empire slipped away.

Akhnaten had no stronger ally than Ribaddi of Byblos, a robust warrior-king of the Phoenicians who fiercely resisted Aziru until strength left him. In a long series of anguished letters,

Ribaddi tells Akhnaten of the rebel encroachments, and denounces Aziru and Abd-Ashirta, all to no avail. We see him warning Akhnaten that Aziru is a friend of the Hittites, and a false vassal of Egypt. He begs for aid, telling Pharaoh that in the chaos the marauding Khabiri will destroy everything. When Aziru attacks Simyra, Ribaddi again asks for help, knowing that if Simyra falls, his own city of Byblos will not be able to hold out for long. Then Zimrida of neighboring Sidon goes over to Aziru's side, and Aziru and Zimrida march against Tyre at the head of a mixed army of Phoenicians, Syrians, and Khabiri.

To Ribaddi's warnings are now joined those of Abimilki, King of Tyre. Abimilki, faced with the attack of Aziru and Zimrida, addresses Akhnaten at great length, effusively avowing his loyalty to Akhnaten and to Aten:

Seven and seven times I fall at the feet of the king, my lord. I am the dirt under the feet of the king, my lord. My lord is the Sun-god who rises over the lands day by day, as ordained by the Sun-god, his gracious father. . . .
On my belly, on my back, I bear the word of the king, my lord. As for him who hearkens to the king, his lord, and serves him in his place, the Sun-god shall rise over him, and the sweet breath from the mouth of his lord shall give him life; but as for him who hearkens not to the word of the king, his lord, his city shall perish, his dynasty shall perish, his name shall not exist in the whole land forever. . . .
Behold, I have said to the Sun-god, the father of the king, my lord, "When shall I see the face of the king, my lord?" But behold, I am guarding Tyre, the great city, for the king, my lord, until the mighty power of the king come out unto me, to give water for me to drink, and wood to warm me.
Further: Zimrida, the king of Sidon, has written day by day to the criminal Aziru, the son of Abd-Ashirta, concerning everything that he heard from Egypt. Behold, I have written to my lord, for it is good that you should know.

A later letter from Abimilki to Akhnaten is less effusive and considerably more grim. Abimilki is penned up in Tyre by Zimrida's army, and lacks water and wood. He asks "for twenty men" to guard the city—a figure of speech meaning a whole army. The Hittites, he says, are quiet at the moment, but

119

Itakama and Aziru are taking town after town. The next letter from Abimilki repeats the plea for wood and water. "Why has it not been sent?" he asks, as though Akhnaten has not even deigned to reply to his earlier letters. Zimrida and Aziru in their ships are besieging the island city. Is there no help to come from Egypt?

While Abimilki is besieged, Aziru makes himself master of Simyra. Ribaddi's letters to Akhnaten report first, "Simyra is like a bird in a snare," and soon after, "Simyra, your fortress, is now in the power of the Khabiri."

With the fall of Simyra, Abimilki loses heart. He defects to the enemy, joining Aziru and Zimrida in rebellion. Tyre, Sidon, and Simyra have all freed themselves from Egyptian ties now, and only Byblos, held by the loyal Ribaddi, is still faithful. Aziru's armies hammer at the gates of Byblos, but Ribaddi stands fast, despatching letter after letter to Akhnaten asking for help.

Akhnaten sends no troops. Instead, he writes a mild letter to Aziru, asking him once again to come to Egypt and explain himself. But Aziru has made that journey once; he does not care to expose himself to imprisonment again. Realizing that he can openly defy the pacifist Pharaoh from a distance, Aziru replies to Akhnaten, saying, "I am being slandered." Everything he has done, Aziru declares piously, has been done on Akhnaten's behalf. He cannot come to Egypt at this moment, for he must remain in Syria to defend Tunip against the Hittites. Akhnaten has also ordered Aziru to rebuild the city of Simyra, which he destroyed while capturing it, and Aziru agrees to do this—in a year or so, since he is currently much too busy fending off the Hittites. As for the tribute due to Egypt, Aziru assures the king that it will be paid as usual. Apparently at least a token tribute did continue to flow from Syria to Egypt during these troubled years.

No doubt Tutu, Aziru's friend at court, managed to convince Akhnaten that all was well in the Levant, for Ribaddi's continued letters, though they grew more desperate, produced nothing in the way of Egyptian military assistance. It was as though

Akhnaten had decided that Egypt's foreign empire was a needless encumbrance, hindering the true worship of Aten, and could safely be dispensed with. Aziru never failed to stress his loyalty to the new religion in his letters; that may have impressed Akhnaten.

Unable to get aid from Egypt, Ribaddi turns now to other Syrian and Phoenician cities still safe from Aziru's clutches. He asks for soldiers to help him defend Byblos against "that dog, Abd-Ashirta" and his son. Leaving Byblos, Ribaddi journeys to nearby Beirut to obtain reinforcements, but while he is gone the people of Byblos revolt, overthrowing Ribaddi and offering the city to Aziru. Ribaddi is marooned in Beirut, and soon after that city also surrenders to Aziru, and the old soldier flees into the open country. After adventures unknown to us, he somehow regains control of Byblos, and continues the hopeless struggle against Aziru.

The letters to Akhnaten record the steady deterioration of the situation. Only three cities in Phoenicia remain loyal to Egypt, Ribaddi writes . . . and then there are two . . . and then just Byblos. His favorite figure of speech recurs again and again: "I am shut up and cannot get out of my city; I am like a bird caught in a net." Famine threatens. There is no grain left in the beleagured city, and the farms lie beyond the walls. Will Akhnaten send him grain, soldiers, horses, water, money, anything? Ribaddi will fight on to the death against Abd-Ashirta and Aziru, but he needs help. "What dogs the sons of Abd-Ashirta are! And they act according to their heart's wish and cause the king's cities to go up in smoke!" Ribaddi writes.

Still Akhnaten holds his hand. He seems unwilling to make war on Aziru, an avowed convert to Atenism. The empire is crumbling, but Pharaoh takes no action.

A long letter from Ribaddi shows him in the depths of despair:

I have written repeatedly for troops, but they were not given, and the king did not listen to the word of his servant. And I sent my messenger to the palace, but he returned empty-handed—he brought no troops. And when the people of my house saw this, they ridiculed me like the governors, my brethren, and despised me.

Ribaddi's own brother, we learn, rebelled against him when he saw the old prince unable to get aid from his Egyptian ally. "He committed a crime and drove me from the city," Ribaddi writes from exile. "Let the king not restrain himself at the deed of this dog!"

Ribaddi himself would come to Egypt, but he cannot. He is exhausted from the long struggle, first against Aziru, then against his own brother. His possessions have been taken from him; he has endured exile, starvation, siege, and now the gods of Byblos, angry with him despite his valor, have visited sickness upon him: "I am an old man, there is grievous illness in my body, and the king, my lord, knows that the gods of Byblos are holy, and the illness is severe; and my sin I have redeemed by a vow to the gods." Was his sin, perhaps, the embracing of the heretical faith of Aten? Is he now backsliding into the Baal-worship of his ancestors?

Still, he is undaunted. "Let the king hear the words of his servant, and let the king, my lord, give archers, and let them take Byblos, lest rebellious troops and the sons of Abd-Ashirta enter it. . . . Let my lord know that I would die for him. When I am in the city, I will protect it for my lord, and my heart is fixed on the king, my lord. . . . Let the king not ignore this grievous deed which was done to the lands of the king, my lord. . . ."

Later letters show Ribaddi returning to Byblos once again, again being driven forth by his brother, and wandering from city to city. Then he disappears from the record. Perhaps he succeeded in reaching Egypt, and was welcomed at the court of his monarch. More likely, this brave Phoenician prince fell into Aziru's hands, and met death. With his passing, Egypt's last loyal vassal in Syria and Phoenicia left the scene, and the whole northern segment of the empire was thus lopped off.

In the southern part of the Levant, Palestine, the situation was equally chaotic. Even in the reign of Amenhotep III, there had been trouble there, stirred up by one Labayu of Shechem, in the central hill country of Canaan. Labayu had been raiding the land and caravans of his neighbors, and there had come to Akhnaten's father a letter from Biridiya, prince of Megiddo, denouncing Labayu:

Labayu has carried on hostilities against me, and we are not able to pluck the wool, and we are not able to go outside the gate in the presence of Labayu, since he learned that thou hast not given archers; and now his face is set to take Megiddo, but let the king protect his city, lest Labayu seize it. Verily, the city is destroyed by death from pestilence. Let the king give one hundred garrison troops to guard the city lest Labayu seize it. . . . He seeks to destroy Megiddo.

Labayu had defended himself with the glibness that must have been the despair of Pharaoh, trying to sort out the true from the false: "Behold, I am a faithful servant of the king, and I have not rebelled and I have not sinned, and I do not withhold my tribute, and I do not refuse the requests of my commissioner. Now they wickedly slander me, but let the king, my lord, not impute rebellion to me!" One of the accusations against Labayu was that his sons were friendly with the 'Apiru, that marauding tribe of bandits akin to the Khabiri who were raiding the cities of northern Syria under Aziru's encouragement. "I did not know that my son associates with the 'Apiru," Labayu tells Amenhotep III, virtuously promising to put a stop to such a friendship.

Despite this pledge of loyalty, Labayu fell into the hands of Biridiya of Megiddo, who planned to ship him to Amenhotep III and claim a reward. Biridiya turned the captive over to Zurata, prince of Acre, for shipment to Thebes, but Zurata, taking no chances with the wily Labayu, put him to death. This touched off a new rebellion, led by Labayu's two sons, who made war on those Palestinian princes loyal to Egypt.

Akhnaten, when he came to the throne, thus inherited a Palestinian province already in confusion and civil strife. Akhnaten's policy of ignoring all communications from his vassal princes soon fanned the spark of rebellion into a general conflagration. Palestine was split between loyal vassals and rebels, while the wandering 'Apiru attacked everyone in their path.

Thus we find Milkilu, prince of Gezer, telling Akhnaten,

"Let the king, my lord, protect his land from the hand of the 'Apiru." But soon Milkilu was overthrown, and Gezer, no longer loyal to Egypt, allied itself with such other rebel cities as Askalon, Lachish, and Megiddo.

The Palestinian counterpart of Ribaddi was Abdu-Heba, prince of Jerusalem, who struggled valiantly to defend his city against the 'Apiru, against the sons of Labayu, and against the rebel Palestinian princes. Jerusalem was the capital of south Palestine, in these pre-Israelite times, and was a rich prize for the rebels.

Evidently the rebel princes slandered Abdu-Heba in letters to Akhnaten, for we find him writing to Pharaoh attesting his loyalty. "Why should I commit transgression against the king, my lord?" he asks. He warns Akhnaten solemnly, "Let the king take care of his land! The lands of the king have all rebelled. . . . May it please the king to send me garrison troops. . . . Let the king turn his attention to the archers, and let the king, my lord, send out troops of archers, for the king has no lands left!"

This letter must not have drawn a reply, for soon Abdu-Heba was writing again:

The king's whole land, which has begun hostilities with me, will be lost. Behold the territory of Seir, as far as Carmel; its princes are wholly lost; and hostility prevails against me. . . . As long as ships were upon the sea the strong arm of the king occupied Naharin and Kash, but now the 'Apiru are occupying the king's cities. There remains not one prince to my lord, the king; every one is ruined. . . . Let the king take care of his land, and . . . let him send troops. . . . For if no troops come in this year, the whole territory of my lord the king will perish. . . . If there are no troops in this year, let the king send his officer to fetch me and his brothers, that we may die with our lord, the king.

Evidently Abdu-Heba was particularly friendly with the personal secretary of Akhnaten, because he adds a postscript specifically addressed to that scribe:

To the scribe of the king, my lord: thus Abdu-Heba, thy servant. At thy two feet I fall. Bring these words plainly before my lord the king. The whole land of my lord, the king, is going to ruin.

The loyalty of Abdu-Heba himself was called into question by another prince, Shuwardata of Hebron, an Egyptian ally who complained to Akhnaten, "Let the king, my lord, know that Abdu-Heba has taken the town from my hand. . . . Labayu is dead, who seized our towns, but behold, Abdu-Heba is another Labayu! He also seizes our towns! So let the king take thought for his servant." Soon, though, Shuwardata and Abdu-Heba must have composed their differences, for a later message from Shuwardata informs Akhnaten, "All my brethren have abandoned me, and it is I and Abdu-Heba who fight against the chief of the 'Apiru."

A final letter from Abdu-Heba sings a doleful chant of defeat. City after city has fallen to the rebels. Gaza, Gath-Carmel, Beth-Shan, Shechem and many more have gone over to the enemy. Even Puwure, the Egyptian commissioner in Palestine, has left Abdu-Heba and joined the rebels.

"Let my king hearken to Abdu-Heba, thy servant, and let him send archers to recover the royal land for the king!" These are the last words heard from Abdu-Heba. Perhaps he, too, defected to the enemy when he found himself the last loyal vassal of Akhnaten in Palestine.

If Akhnaten ever saw these pathetic letters, they must have caused him some pang of regret, since he was failing to aid allies of Egypt won by his ancestors. Yet there is no indication, in the few replies of Akhnaten's that survive, that he showed any great distress over the doings in Syria, Phoenicia, and Palestine. Now and then he sent a mild letter of rebuke to some rebel like Aziru or Labayu, and usually received a fervent pledge of loyalty in return. Labayu declared that if Pharaoh ordered him to drive a sword of bronze into his heart, he would do so. Aziru swore fealty to Akhnaten's god Aten, which must have pleased Pharaoh; the truly loyal vassals seem to have been unaware of Akhnaten's religion, and make frequent references to the "gods" of Egypt. When a loyal vassal did complain, Akhnaten, when he answered at all, would sometimes provide encouragement, but never anything tangible in the way of assistance. Thus when Yapahu, a prince of Gezer, takes up the familiar refrain, "Have concern for thy land," Akhnaten replies in a letter now lost, no doubt bidding Yapahu fight the good fight, and Yapahu sends a further letter, declaring, "Everything which the king, my lord, has said to me, I have heard most attentively. . . . Now I have heard the sweet breath of the king, and it goes out to me, and my heart is very serene."

The "sweet breath of the king" could win no battles for Yapahu, however. Palestine slipped away, as had Syria and Phoenicia. Once again, the Levant was a land of independent city-states, quarreling among themselves. With the control of Egypt withdrawn, petty chiefs and sheikhs and princes who had been bickering for generations were free to go for one another's throats once again; ancient blood-feuds could be revived; minor tribal leaders could dream of empire. The whole eastern shore of the Mediterranean was given over to strife.

In the seventeenth year of Akhnaten's reign, and the seventh year since the Hittite armies had marched to the border of Syria, the downfall of Egypt's empire was complete. Suppiluliumas, the Hittite king, concluded a treaty with Aziru. Aziru became a Hittite vassal, and the entire coast, from Byblos north, passed into Hittite hands. Suppiluliumas was now ready to turn once again to attack Mitanni, this time from a position of overwhelming strength.

A violent, bloody war would result. But Akhnaten, who by his neglect had given Syria to the Hittites, was destined not to live to see Mitanni's destruction. The seventeenth year of his reign was the last. As we will see, another Pharaoh was fated to preside over Egypt at the time of Hittite triumph.

No doubt there were those in the City of the Horizon of Aten who shared the agony of Ribaddi and Abdu-Heba and the other loyal vassals. General Horemheb was there, wearing an Atenist name and attending services faithfully, but how that tough soldier must have simmered with wrath at Pharaoh's inaction! From outlying districts of the north came Egyptian messengers, mooring their galleys at the quays of Akhetaten, hurrying to the king's minister Tutu with the latest communique from Byblos or

Jerusalem—but—as the Egyptologist Arthur Weigall wrote in the first book[1] devoted to Akhnaten's heresy, more than fifty years ago, "The townspeople smiled at their haste in this city of dreams; the court officials delayed the delivery of their letters, scoffing at the idea of urgency in the affairs of Asia; and finally these wretched documents, written—if ever letters were so written—with blood and with tears, were pigeon-holed in the city archives and utterly forgotten. . . . Instead of the brave music of the drums and bugles of the relieving army which these messengers had hoped to muster, there rang in their maddened ears only the ceaseless chants of the priestly ceremonies and the pattering love-songs of private festivals."

Akhnaten himself—"the lean, sad-eyed pharaoh, with his crooked head and his stooping shoulders," Weigall calls him—would talk only of Aten. The empire was breaking up, Lebanon and Syria were falling into the hands of enemies, the blood spilled by the armies of Thothmes III was going for naught, and still the priests chanted, still the incense spiralled upward in smoky clouds toward the gleaming Aten.

We can share Akhnaten's reluctance to take up the sword of his great-grandfather. Yet it is hard to sympathize with the heretic king in the face of the bewildered pleas of Egypt's vassals. For three generations, the princes of Syria and Palestine and Phoenicia had paid their tributes to Egypt, expecting that Egypt in turn would shield them from the hand of chaos. Now chaos had come, and where was Egypt?

In Akhetaten, men like Horemheb and Ay conferred privately, hoping to find some way to jolt Pharaoh from his dreams. In Thebes, doubtless, open outcry rose in the streets as news of the spreading breakup of the empire reached the people.

We are unable to reconstruct the events of the last five years of Akhnaten's reign with any clarity of detail. We know that in the twelfth year of his reign he still ruled in splendor, receiving costly tributes from overseas. Soon after came the death of his daughter, the first of a series of personal tragedies, and in the outer world came the rise of Itakama in Akhnaten's thir-

[1] Arthur Weigall, *The Life and Times of Akhnaton.*

teenth year, the fall of Simyra to Aziru that same year, then, a year later, the expulsion of Ribaddi from Byblos. In that fourteenth year, we hear the last protests of Abimilki of Tyre before he deserts to the enemy. In Palestine, Abdu-Heba disappears, and all is lost by the fifteenth or sixteenth year of Akhnaten's reign. By the seventeenth year, Aziru is openly in league with the Hittites, and Akhnaten has died.

Was the heretic Pharaoh a victim of his own people? Was Akhnaten put out of the way lest Egypt itself fall the way its foreign empire had? We can only turn to the sketchy evidence, and try to form some picture of the final dark days at Akhetaten.

7

THE VENGEANCE OF AMON

The twelfth year of his reign marked the climax of Akhnaten's life. He ruled a serene land; Amon was overthrown; the sun was bright on Akhetaten. The ceremony of tribute, followed by the arrival of Queen Tiy at the City of the Horizon, were great moments for Akhnaten.

Then came the death of young Meketaten. From abroad came messengers with endless tales of woe. Perhaps Pharaoh was too absorbed in his private grief even to listen to the endless complaints of Ribaddi and Abdu-Heba. A sudden rift had split the royal family: Nefertiti, the beloved queen, had left Akhnaten's palace and withdrawn to a palace of her own, in the northern part of the city.

This is perhaps the most startling aspect of the entire Akhnaten story. No marriage could have been more harmonious. The murals of the tombs showed Akhnaten embracing Nefertiti, showed her always at his side, touching him, fondling him, smiling at him, dangling flowers playfully for him to sniff. The separation seems inexplicable.

There are several theories. The breakup of Akhnaten's marriage took place some time after the twelfth year of his reign, since the paintings of the tribute scene and of Queen Tiy's arrival show the royal couple as warm toward one another as ever. By the fourteenth year, the separation has definitely occurred. It has been suggested that Queen Tiy, taking up permanent residence at Akhetaten, displaced Nefertiti in a power struggle. The two royal women, mother and wife, faced each other in direct conflict—and Nefertiti was forced out.

It is possible. Queen Tiy, we know, was a powerful, strong-willed woman, capable of ruling Egypt herself after her husband had slipped into premature senility. Perhaps Akhnaten, too, had by this time become so much of a dreamer, so remote from reality, that he was unable to take Nefertiti's side against his mother. It may be that the king's health, always delicate, had given way completely. Akhnaten may have retired to a sickbed, unaware of the struggle taking place, while his mother and his wife contended for power.

One thing is certain: Nefertiti remained faithful to Aten. Her palace in the northern end of the city she named "The House of Aten," and she covered it with inscriptions linking herself and Akhnaten as though no break had occurred. Elsewhere in the city, Nefertiti's name was obliterated from many royal inscriptions, presumably at the order of Akhnaten—though it may have been Queen Tiy's doing. In one whole series of monuments, Nefertiti's name was erased and replaced with that of Meritaten, Akhnaten's eldest daughter, who evidently was now considered "first lady" of the realm after her mother's mysterious fall from favor.

The fact that Nefertiti never swerved from Atenism has given rise to a second theory explaining the breakup. This holds that in the last three or four years of his reign, Akhnaten weakened in his devotion to Atenism and began to make overtures of compromise to the party of Amon. Disgusted by this apostasy on his part, Nefertiti, even more fanatical than her husband, withdrew and set up her own household. Was Nefertiti the real driving force behind Akhnaten's heresy all along? Did Queen Tiy, seeing the empire breaking up, come down from Thebes to win her son back to reality? And did Akhnaten waver near the end, begin to negotiate with the leaders of Thebes, even at the expense of his marriage? Again, we can only suppose that toward the end of his life Akhnaten was too sick to make his own decisions, and that Queen Tiy, acting in her son's name, began to guide Egypt back toward the old religion over Nefertiti's bitter opposition.

The answers are shrouded in mystery. But one clue exists that leads us to think that Akhnaten did weaken toward the end, and that either he—or others acting in his name—did attempt to heal the breach between Pharaoh and Amon.

In the fifteenth year of his reign, Akhnaten took a co-regent. Just as he once had been raised to the throne at his father's side, so now did Akhnaten elevate a prince named Smenkhkare to join him as ruler of Egypt.

The identity of this prince is a puzzle. Nowhere does he appear on the tomb paintings of the first twelve years; nowhere is he mentioned earlier in the inscriptions of Akhnaten's reign. The first appearance of Smenkhkare is on the wall of an unfinished tomb at Akhetaten, showing him as the husband of Akhnaten's eldest daughter, Meritaten. An earlier panel in the same mural depicts the tribute ceremony of the twelfth year, so this scene must date from the thirteenth or fourteenth year, at the earliest. The tribute scene shows Meritaten as unmarried; out of nowhere comes a husband for Pharaoh's daughter.

Who was Smenkhkare?

There is some evidence that he may actually have been Akhnaten's son—not by Nefertiti, for we know she bore only daughters, but by some secondary wife. A mummy found in 1907, and now thought to be Smenkhkare's, shows a remarkable physical resemblance to the portraits we have of Akhnaten. There is the same elongated head, the same strange swelling of the thighs. Indeed, Smenkhkare's mummy was long thought to be that of Akhnaten himself, because of this resemblance. But it is the mummy of a man in his mid-twenties. Was he the eldest son of Akhnaten?

It was a familiar event in the Eighteenth Dynasty for the king's eldest daughter by his chief wife to marry a son born to some secondary wife. Akhnaten may well have arranged the marriage of Meritaten and her half-brother to give Smenkhkare an unquestioned claim to the throne—and then raised him to the co-regency to complete the designation of Smenkhkare as his heir.

When Smenkhkare became co-regent, Akhnaten bestowed new names on him: that of Ankh-kheperu-re—which is similar to Akhnaten's own throne name of Nefer-kheperu-re—and also that of Nefer-nefru-aten. The latter had been one of Nefertiti's names. By transferring it from the fallen Nefertiti to the newly favored Smenkhkare, Akhnaten was apparently intending to show that from now on it would be Smenkhkare, not Nefertiti, who would sit by Akhnaten's side on the double throne.

If Smenkhkare really was Akhnaten's son, however, it is strange that no mention of him appeared anywhere in Akhnaten's official inscriptions. Yet even this may have been a traditional omission, since Akhnaten himself is nowhere to be found in the inscriptions of Amenhotep III. It may have been customary for a king to depict only his daughters.

A letter from Dushratta of Mitanni to Akhnaten offers a slim bit of evidence that Akhnaten did have sons. The letter declared:

"To Naphuria [Akhnaten], the King of Egypt, my brother, my son-in-law, who loves me and whom I love, has spoken thus Dushratta, the King of Mitanni, thy father-in-law, who loves thee, thy brother: I am in health. Mayst thou be in health! To thy houses, to Tiy, thy mother, the mistress of Egypt, to Tadukhepa, my daughter, thy wife, to thy other wives, *to thy sons and daughters,* to thy great ones, to thy chariots, to thy horses, to thy warriors, to thy land and to everything that belongs to thee, may there be health in a very high degree."

Now, this reference to Akhnaten's "sons and daughters" may be a purely conventional one, since Dushratta had earlier written to Amenhotep III using a nearly identical salutation.[1] Or perhaps Dushratta may have had specific knowledge of specific sons. Smenkhkare may well have been Akhnaten's eldest child, born while his father was still Prince Amenhotep, and not even yet co-regent with Amenhotep III.

[1] See p. 38.

There is another, and more plausible possibility: that Smenkhkare was Akhnaten's brother, and not his son. That would account for the strong physical resemblance. And, though Akhnaten was some twenty years older than Smenkhkare, we know that Queen Tiy had given birth to a daughter early in Akhnaten's reign—when Smenkhkare was five or ten years old. He might well have been a younger son of Amenhotep III and Queen Tiy, and his absence from the official records can be accounted for by the same tradition that kept the crown prince himself, Amenhotep IV, from appearing in the inscriptions.

Son or brother, Smenkhkare came to the throne in the fifteenth year of Akhnaten's reign, and took to wife Meritaten, Pharaoh's daughter. There is good reason to think that Smenkhkare was chosen to play the role of ambassador to Thebes. In the third year of Smenkhkare's co-regency, his name was scribbled on the wall of a Theban tomb, as though implying that the co-regent had visited Thebes that year. And several portraits of Smenkhkare show him in the guise of Osiris, certainly indicating that he was no Atenist fanatic.

It may be, then, that Akhnaten—or Queen Tiy, acting in her son's name—despatched Smenkhkare to Thebes with an olive branch. It was his task to bring about a reconciliation of the forces that had split Egypt for the past dozen years. Possibly the Thebans were willing to recognize Smenkhkare as sole Pharaoh, in place of the despised heretic Akhnaten. And Nefertiti, her place on the throne and even one of her names usurped by this prince, withdrew to her own palace on the outskirts of Akhetaten, embittered by the failure of the noble experiment in monotheism.

All this is conjecture, of course. The only facts we have are that Nefertiti fell into apparent disgrace no later than the fourteenth year of Akhnaten's reign, and that an obscure prince named Smenkhkare became co-regent with Akhnaten in the following year.

There was another event of the fifteenth year: Akhnaten took his daughter Ankhesenpaaten to wife.

There was precedent for that. Amenhotep III had also married one of his daughters in the closing years of his reign. In Akhnaten's case, it must have been a marriage in name only, for the little princess, his third daughter, could hardly have been much more than seven or eight years old. Why the marriage? Perhaps Akhnaten felt the need to bolster his own position on the throne, now that Nefertiti had been banished from the palace. The princess carried the right to the throne; by marrying her, Akhnaten could maintain his crown against other claimants.

The story of the heretic Pharaoh fizzles away into anticlimax and mystery, after the fifteenth year. We know that the co-regency with Smenkhkare lasted three years, and during those years Nefertiti lived as an outcast in Akhetaten. Queen Tiy's role is unknown; she may even have died during those years.

Then, abruptly, the stage is swept clean. Both Pharaohs are gone virtually simultaneously, in the seventeenth year of Akhnaten's reign and the third of his co-regency with Smenkhkare. Smenkhkare and Meritaten both disappear into oblivion. Akhnaten too dies. We hear no more of Queen Tiy, nor of Nefertiti. In that fateful year—the same year when Syria finally and officially fell into Hittite hands, and Suppiluliumas poised himself for new conquests—the whole cast of the Akhnaten drama vanishes from the scene.

What happened?

There is no positive answer to that question—only maddening silence. It is tempting to think that a conspiracy of patriotic Egyptians did them all in, lest the land taste Hittite strength. General Horemheb, perhaps, and Ay, and a group of influential Thebans, may have risen in a swift coup to put an end to the heresy that had so badly weakened Egypt. Did men with daggers break into the royal palace at Akhetaten, where Akhnaten, emaciated and haggard, still dragged himself through the rituals of his religion despite the numbing knowledge that it had failed? Did Smenkhkare and his royal wife fall to assassins, too, poisoned perhaps while at Thebes? Did the grim messengers come for lovely Nefertiti, most devout of all Aten's worshippers?

The end may have been less dramatic. Akhnaten's father and grandfather had both died in early middle age, and Akhnaten, in the seventeenth year of his reign, was probably past forty-five. The slender thread of his health may simply have snapped of its own accord. The weight of events may have been too much for Akhnaten, battered down by the death of his daughter, the split with Nefertiti, then perhaps the death of Queen Tiy, the growing rebellion all about him, the doleful news coming from beyond Egypt's borders. Faced with the knowledge that the sunlit religion he had created had been rejected by Egypt, confronted with the awareness that his dreams had ended in failure, Akhnaten may have collapsed at last. As Arthur Weigall wrote, "In the imagination there seems to ring across the years a cry of complete despair, and one can picture the emaciated figure of this 'beautiful child of the Aten' fall forward upon the painted palace-floor and lie still amidst the red poppies and the dainty butterflies there depicted."

However it had happened, Akhnaten was dead in the seventeenth year of his reign, and the co-regent Smenkhkare perished almost at the same time. What became of Akhnaten's body, we do not know. He was not put to rest, as had been his wish, in the lonely rock-tomb east of Akhetaten. Probably not for him were the elaborate ceremonies of mummification, the age-old rituals of burial. His body went hastily to an unknown grave; perhaps it was even torn to pieces by the vengeful priests of Amon, thus, to their way of thinking, depriving Akhnaten of immortality. As for Smenkhkare, he was hurriedly mummified and cast into a small, crude tomb in Thebes.

A new king came to Egypt's throne—a boy who, through an irony of history, would win, thousands of years after his death, a notoriety out of all proportion to his real importance. His name was Tutankhamen.

He could not have been much older than ten or eleven when Akhnaten died, and perhaps that was all that saved his life when the heresy collapsed. He appears on the scene just as suddenly and just as mysteriously as his predecessor Smenkhkare, and quite possibly was that shadowy prince's younger brother, a son of Akhnaten and the same nameless secondary wife.

But it is also possible that he was the last child of Amenhotep III and Queen Tiy. He was born a year or two before Amenhotep III's death, and only a short while after the birth of Beketaten, Queen Tiy's last known daughter. Tutankhamen may thus have been the third and last of Amenhotep III's long-headed sons to wear the double crown of Egypt.

He was born with the name Tutankhaten, and as Tutankhaten he was known all through the succeeding years of Akhnaten's heresy. When Nefertiti retired to her northern palace, Tutankhaten went with her. So, too, did Nefertiti's daughter, Ankhesenpaaten. Though the princess was officially Akhnaten's wife, she remained with her mother. She was a year or so younger than Tutankhaten, who was either her uncle or her half-brother, and the two children played together at the palace, bewildered by the sudden tensions in what had once been so tranquil a city.

Another who spent time with Nefertiti at the northern palace was her father, Ay, now a stout man of middle age. Once, he had been Akhnaten's closest confidant, but in the last years of his reign Akhnaten had ceased to heed Ay. When Nefertiti fell from grace, so, too, did the "Divine Father." Ay remained with his daughter for a while, conferring, perhaps, about the deteriorating state of things. Then he may have departed for Thebes, to look after young Smenkhkare. Ay was playing a double game at that point, outwardly loyal to his daughter's god, Aten, but quietly scheming with the Thebans for a restoration of the old religion.

After the mysterious series of events that removed both co-regents and their wives from the picture, Ay stepped forward as the king-maker of Egypt.

Who would wear the crown? Why, none other than Tutankhaten, of course! He was the last surviving prince of Amenhotep III's line, and Ay did not care to bring about a change of dynasty. It was important to keep the loyalty of the traditional-minded Egyptians during the difficult period of readjustment that lay ahead. The boy Tutankhaten would make a useful puppet as Ay guided the country back to Amonism. Swiftly, Tutankhaten found himself married to his playmate, Ankhesen-paaten. Boy and girl, ten-year-old king and nine-year-old queen, moved bewilderedly through the age-old rituals of anointing a monarch.

Of course, Tutankhaten and Ankhesenpaaten were tainted with heresy. Even their very names bore the now hated word "Aten." Ay found this no drawback. He explained that they were mere children, without theological partiality. Naturally, they had been forced by Akhnaten and Nefertiti to worship the heretical deity; as for their names, they had not chosen them themselves. To symbolize the change of gods, the young king and queen dropped their heretical names. Tutankhaten now became Tutankh*amen*. Ankhesenpaaten was renamed Ankhesen-*amen*.

The city in the desert was abandoned. Hardly was the boy-pharaoh on the throne than Akhetaten was officially stripped of its rank as capital city, and the court returned to Thebes. Only the poor remained at Akhetaten, and a few minor nobles. They were not long in following their new king. The exodus from Akhnaten's city was swift. Archaeologists have found the bones of Akhnaten's dogs in the royal kennels; the poor beasts were simply left behind to starve. Oxen were abandoned in the sheds of the king's farm. The elaborate, handsomely painted tombs in the hills remained empty. Akhnaten's loyal followers, Meryre and Huya and May and the others, seemingly reconverted to Amonism, returned to Thebes with Tutankhamen, and lived happily ever after.

Desert sands blew across the City of the Horizon of the Disk as it stood desolate and dead. Owls and hyenas moved in to take up habitations in the fine villas. Jackals howled in the temples of Aten and in the royal palace itself.

Akhnaten's dream was at an end.

The people of Egypt felt no grief at the downfall of the heretic. For the seventeen years of his reign they had known only aston-ishment and puzzlement, as Akhnaten had moved from one unpredictable act to another. At the outset of his reign, Akhnaten had captured the imagination of the people with his vigor, his freshness, his novelty. But that appeal had quickly worn off, and Akhnaten had forfeited the love of his people.

The heresy had been a time of dislocation and confusion for Egypt. Temples had been closed; priests forced to become beggars; holy places defiled. Traditional feast days had ceased to be times of celebration. And, as Breasted put it,[2]

> The great comforter and friend, Osiris, the champion of the dead in every danger, was banished, and no man dared so much as utter his name. . . . Groups of muttering priests, nursing implacable hatred, must have mingled their curses with the execration of whole communities of discontented tradesmen—bakers who no longer drew a livelihood from the sale of ceremonial cakes at the temple feasts; craftsmen who no longer sold amulets of the old gods at the temple gateway; hack sculptors whose statues of Osiris lay under piles of dust in many a tumbled-down studio; cemetery stone-cutters who found their tawdry tombstones with scenes from the Book of the Dead banished from the necropolis; scribes whose rolls of the same book, filled with the names of the old gods, or even if they bore the word god in the plural, were anathema; . . . shepherds who no longer dared to place a loaf and a jar of water under yonder tree, hoping thus to escape the anger of the goddess who dwelt in it, and who might afflict the household with sickness in her wrath. . . .

Aten had not captured the imagination of Egypt's millions. An abstract deity, formless and faceless, could not take the place of warm-hearted Isis and pathetic Osiris, of benevolent Ptah who built the universe, of Khnum, the goat-headed potter worshipped at the city of Elephantine, of the jackal-god Wepwat of Abydos, the crocodile Sobek of Ombos, even of fierce Set, the god-slayer. Re had been a hero, a mighty falcon-headed warrior to whom men could bend the knee in awe; but Akhnaten had not permitted men to worship the sun itself, only the divine heat that resided in it. To prevent his religion from becoming mere sun-worship, Akhnaten had provided that Aten be worshipped only at sunrise and sunset, and not during the day itself, when the blazing orb might distract his followers from

[2] Breasted, *The Dawn of Conscience.*

138

the true deity. A religion without mythology, without images, without personified gods with whom a man could identify, was able to make no headway in the minds and hearts of Egyptians. Akhnaten's insistence on serving as sole mediator between Aten and mankind had further weakened the strength of his creed. In the City of the Horizon of Aten, men had worshipped Pharaoh, not Aten, and with Pharaoh's death the religion crumbled.

There were no complaints, then, as Atenism was relegated to oblivion and Amon was restored to his place atop the pantheon. Amon, though he had hardly been a beloved god, was at least a god of triumph who could stir men's souls. Armies marching in Amon's name had planted the banner of Egypt on foreign shores. Amon had brought foreign gold in abundance to Egypt. What had Aten done? He had lost the empire, that was all.

There was at first no attempt to wipe out the memory of Aten. He was no longer worshipped, and his city was deserted, but Aten's name remained on many inscriptions, and the symbol of the solar disk radiating hands still was used as an ornament by artisans. Tutankhamen's throne itself displayed the Aten symbol, while he and his young queen were portrayed with the fluidity of line characteristic of the heretic's preferred style of art. On some rings and articles of jewelry, symbols of Aten and Amon appeared side by side in peaceful coexistence. Ay did not decree any violent transition back to the old official god. He was content to let Egypt gradually return to Amon, knowing that Aten had never taken root beyond the fevered brains of Akhnaten and Nefertiti. Pharaoh's vineyard in the Delta was allowed to retain the name of "Domain of Aten"; from inscriptions on wine jars found in Tutankhamen's tomb, we know that the Aten vineyard produced wine for twenty-one years, which means that if the vineyard received its name in the third or fourth year of Akhnaten's reign, as seems likely, it continued to bear the name of heresy for the first six or seven years of Tutankhamen's reign.

The real ruler, beyond doubt, was Ay. The "Divine Father" gave the orders and wielded the royal seal; Tutankhamen simply acquiesced. Ay's role is made clear by the art of Tutankhamen's reign. A scene embossed on gold foil shows Tutankhamen slaying a Libyan enemy, while Ay looks on approvingly, holding his ostrich-feather fan of office in his right hand. The scene of Pharaoh slaying an enemy had long been traditional in Egypt—but it had always been a divinity who watched, not a courtier. Ay, putting himself in Amon's place, implied his supreme rank in the kingdom.

The immediate task of the new regime was the restoration of the official state religion of Amon—no simple job, since Akhnaten had closed Amon's temples, scattered Amon's priests, shattered the images of Amon, and obliterated every inscription or document that mentioned the Theban god.

An inscription at Karnak tells how the restoration was accomplished, during the reign of Tutankhamen and under the benign guidance of Ay. The inscription declares that when Tutankhamen came to the throne, "the temples of the gods and goddesses from Elephantine to the marshes of the Delta" had fallen into ruin. "Their shrines had become desolate, had become mounds overgrown with weeds. Their sanctuaries were as if they had never been. Their halls were a footpath. The land was topsy-turvy, and the gods turned their backs upon this land."

Maat—truth and justice—had departed from Egypt during the time of heresy, Tutankhamen says. Egypt "was passed by and sick." The gods looked away. "If one prayed to a god to seek counsel from him, he would never come. If one made supplication to a goddess similarly, she would never come at all. Their hearts were hurt in their bodies, so they did damage to what had been made."

Tutankhamen set all this to rights: "The good ruler, performing benefactions for his father [Amon] and all the gods . . . has made what was ruined to endure as a monument for the ages of eternity, and he has expelled deceit throughout the Two Lands, and justice was set up . . . as in its first time."

Amon was soothed by new and grand images: "His majesty deliberated plans with his heart, searching for any beneficial deed, seeking out acts of service for his father Amon, and fashioning his august image of genuine fine gold. He surpassed what

140

had been done previously. He fashioned his father Amon upon thirteen carrying-poles, his holy image being of fine gold, lapis lazuli, and every august costly stone, whereas the majesty of this august god had been upon eleven carrying-poles." The other gods, too, were honored, Pharaoh "building their sanctuaries anew as monuments for the ages of eternity, established with possessions forever, setting for them divine offerings as a regular daily observance, and provisioning their food-offerings upon earth." Akhnaten's *arriviste* priesthood returned to obscurity, and the old families were restored to their high places: "He [Tutankhamen] has inducted priests and prophets from the children of the nobles of their towns, each the son of a known man, whose own name was known." The temples received an indemnity for the shabby treatment toward them during the time of heresy: "All the property of the temples has been doubled and tripled and quadrupled in silver, gold, lapis lazuli, every kind of august costly stone, royal linen, white linen, fine linen, olive oil, gum, fat . . . incense, myrrh, without limit to any good thing. His majesty (Life! Prosperity! Health!) has built their barques upon the river of new cedar from the terraces. . . . They make the river shine."

And, Tutankhamen concludes, "The hearts of the gods and goddesses who are in this land are in joy; the possessors of shrines are rejoicing; the regions are in jubilee and exultation throughout the land: the good times have come!"

The old gods had been restored. Amon was again supreme. Akhnaten's experiment in bringing both government and religion under Pharaoh's direct control had ended. From now on, the priests of Amon would grow steadily more powerful, as though determined never again to let such a disaster befall them, and ultimately they would come to control the kingship.

Restoring the empire was a more difficult matter than restoring Amon. Army morale was low; Syria, Phoenicia, and Palestine were held by independent princes or by Hittites; the whole achievement of Thothmes III had to be repeated, and there was no leader of Thothmes III's caliber in the land. Horemheb, at the head of the army, found it a sufficient challenge simply to

141

guard the homeland itself. His troops manned the borders, maintaining them against a possible invasion. Recapturing the lost provinces was beyond hope now.

During this time, refugees flocked out of Palestine, arriving hungry and desperate at Egypt's borders. The tomb of Horemheb at Memphis shows these displaced persons, gaunt and haggard, begging the general for asylum, and an inscription relates:

"The barbarians have taken their land, their dwellings have been destroyed, their town devastated and their crops burnt. Their country has been so hungry that they lived in the mountains like goats. Now they come to beg the Powerful [Horemheb] to send his victorious sword to protect them, saying: 'We few Asians who do not know how we may survive, have come to seek refuge in the land of Pharaoh as we did in the time of the fathers of his father, since the beginning.' "

To the south, Nubia, which had made itself nearly independent under Akhnaten, returned more peacefully to the Egyptian fold. Tutankhamen appointed Huya as Viceroy of the Nubian land of Kush; it was the same Huya whose tomb at Akhetaten showed us the visit of Queen Tiy. Huya made a smooth transition from Atenism to Amonism, and built a new tomb for himself at Thebes, whose murals show Tutankhamen receiving the rich tribute of Nubia while Huya beams in self-satisfaction.

While Horemheb, on the borders of Palestine, drilled Egypt's long-neglected army and tried to prepare it for a campaign against the defiant Aziru, the Hittites were gathering strength for a final assault on Mitanni. Suppiluliumas was careful to remain on good diplomatic terms with the new young Pharaoh; he sent congratulations to Tutankhamen when he took the throne, and bestowed on him an iron dagger, its hilt fashioned of gold and crystal and diamonds, and several iron awls and chisels. The gifts must have been examined in awe at the Theban court; the Hittites had mastered the art of forging iron, tempering it to a toughness and a sharpness that far excelled that of Egypt's finest bronze weapons. More clearly than any belligerent words, Suppiluliumas' gifts to Pharaoh spoke of Hittite strength.

Mitanni would soon feel that strength. Suppiluliumas had

carved northern Syria into a number of kingdoms, and had placed some of his many sons at their heads. A Hittite army under Prince Telipinus was besieging the Mitanni capital of Carchemish, which was holding out valiantly.

It was the year 1353, the ninth year of Tutankhamen's reign. But the boy-king's brief course had been run. Still short of his twentieth birthday, Tutankhamen died at Thebes, and the line of Amenhotep was extinct. The young Pharaoh and his girl-queen had brought no children into the world.

While the priests embarked on the seventy-day ritual of mummification, Egypt lay paralyzed, her throne vacant, with no heir to claim it. There had been eleven kings and a queen in the Eighteenth Dynasty, and always there had been a prince of the royal blood who could step forward to inherit the rule. Not now. Tutankhamen's unexpected, sudden death had left Egypt's succession broken.

The key to the situation was Queen Ankhesenamen. Hardly eighteen, she had already been married twice, first to her father Akhnaten, then to Tutankhamen. The right to the throne resided with her. Her next husband would be Egypt's new king.

Who would be her choice?

The two most powerful men in the realm were Horemheb and Ay. But Horemheb was a commoner, from Lower Egypt at that, and a fierce man of war. Ankhesenamen could hardly relish the thought of making him Pharaoh. On the other hand, Ay, the sly, potbellied turncoat who had managed to survive not only the transition from Amon to Aten but the restoration of Amon, was Ankhesenamen's own grandfather. He, too, was a commoner, despite his close family connections with the throne.

In her desperation, the young queen attempted to turn to a foreigner.

The man of the hour was Suppiluliumas, the mighty Hittite king, whose armies were then gnawing and rending the remnants of Mitanni. It was obvious that the Hittites would turn against Egypt next. Would it not be better to form an alliance through marriage with the Hittites, and spare Egypt an inevitable defeat? By marrying a Hittite prince, Ankhesenamen would have

143

a young husband of noble birth, and Egypt would be saved from chaos.

Somehow the widowed queen managed to slip a messenger past the watchful Ay. Off to Carchemish the courier sped. Suppiluliumas was there, encamped beneath the walls of the Mitanni city, laying siege to the powerful fortress.

When word reached him that a letter had come from Egypt, the Hittite king must have imagined that the Egyptians were protesting against his occupation of their Syrian provinces. How great his surprise must have been when he read what Ankhesenamen had written:

My husband has died, and I have no sons. It is said that you have many sons. If you will give me a son of yours, he could be my husband. I will on no account take one of my subjects and make him a husband and honor him. Such a thing would be abhorrent to me.

The startled Suppiluliumas knew that Ankhesenamen's new husband would become Egypt's king. It seemed that she was handing him the land of the Nile for the asking. It was too good to be true. More likely, Egypt simply wanted him to send to Thebes a Hittite prince who could be held as a hostage against further invasion of Egyptian territory.

The Hittites deliberated, examining the proposition from every aspect. "Since the most ancient times such a thing has never happened before," Suppiluliumas pointed out. Unable to take the queen's letter at face value, the Hittite king selected his chamberlain, Hattu-Zittish, and sent him to Egypt, telling him, "Go, bring back reliable tidings. Perhaps they already have a new king. Perhaps they only mean to mock and deride me."

Hattu-Zittish departed for Thebes, arriving in the midst of Tutankhamen's funeral. While he was gone, Suppiluliumas conquered Carchemish, and returned to his native land for the winter. In the spring, Hattu-Zittish returned from Egypt, bearing a new message from Ankhesenamen:

"Why do you say I wish to deceive you?" she asked. "If I had a son, why would I write to a foreigner to publish my distress and that of my country? You insult me by speaking this way. He who was my husband is dead, and I have no son. Must I then take one of my subjects and marry him? Everyone says you have many sons. Give me one of them that he may become my husband and rule over Egypt."

The Hittite envoy confirmed all that Ankhesenamen had written. Egypt was indeed kingless, and there were no royal heirs. A Hittite prince sent at this time would become Pharaoh.

Suppiluliumas selected one of his sons and sent him to Egypt. But he had waited too long. Egypt did have a king now, and the new ruler intercepted the Hittite prince and had him put to death. Suppiluliumas had missed his chance to join his crown with that of Egypt.

The new Pharaoh was Ay, the "Divine Father."

He had travelled a long journey in his time. Priest and vizier, counsellor and planner, he had served at the court of Amenhotep III, had risen to great eminence in the reign of Akhnaten, had been the power behind the throne when Tutankhamen reigned, and now, portly and middle-aged, had himself taken the highest rank, bedecking himself with the white crown of Upper Egypt and the red crown of Lower Egypt. We can never know the details of the political in-fighting that put Ay and not Horemheb on the throne after Tutankhamen; perhaps it was simply Horemheb's absence on the Palestinian frontier that gave Ay his chance. He seized the opportunity eagerly. Young Ankhesenamen, daughter of Ay's daughter Nefertiti, was joined to him in marriage, and it was Ay, as Pharaoh, who supervised the funeral of Tutankhamen.

That funeral was carried out, we know, with stunning pomp and splendor. Magnificent and exquisite works of art in dazzling abundance were sealed with the boy-king into his rock tomb in the Valley of the Tombs of the Kings, where his ancestors had been buried for hundreds of years until Akhnaten interrupted the custom. Two thousand separate objects formed the burial treasure of Tutankhamen, the finest craftsmanship Egypt had to offer. If this puppet monarch went to the grave amid such opulence, what were the burials of the really great Pharaohs like?

What bounty went to proclaim the eternal glory of the all-conquering Thothmes III, or the beloved Amenhotep III? We will never know, for the graves of the kings all were rifled in antiquity—all but that of Tutankhamen, which survived almost untouched until 1922 A.D.

Into the royal tomb went a fantastic treasure. Ay was not particular about its source; many of the works of art were in the heretical style, and many, indeed, openly displayed the symbol of Aten. Nor did Ay hesitate to rob the dead to honor the dead. He had the tomb of Smenkhkare, nine years dead, invaded and partly stripped of its contents. The little golden sarcophagi that contained the intestines of the mummified king were transferred from Smenkhkare's tomb to Tutankhamen's by the simple process of scratching out Smenkhkare's name and replacing it with Tutankhamen's.

Smenkhkare, we think, had inclined toward Amon, and so this desecration of his tomb was undeserved in the time of Amon's restoration. But Smenkhkare had shared the throne with the hated Akhnaten. In the looting of Smenkhkare's tomb by Ay, we see the beginning of a campaign aimed against anyone at all associated with the dead heretic—a campaign that would ultimately engulf both Tutankhamen and Ay himself.

Smugly, pompously, the new Pharaoh conducted the services for Tutankhamen. The old burial rites had been revived; Tutankhamen was deemed to be Osiris, now, setting out on his journey toward solar rebirth. Symbolic wall-paintings in Tutankhamen's tomb show the dead king departing, sped on his way by the magical gestures of Ay, toward the other world where he would be welcomed by the "Lady of the Sky, Nut, mistress of the gods." Every aspect of the tomb, even the arrangement of the rooms, had its ritual and symbolic value in this ancient tale of rebirth which Akhnaten had attempted to suppress. The new Pharaoh—though he was three times as old as the dead one—would spring forth as Horus, the son of Osiris. The dead Pharaoh, Osiris now, would become one with Re and shine in the morning.

And so it happened. The sacred transfiguration took place,

and the tomb of Tutankhamen was sealed. Ay and his thrice-married queen returned to the great palace at Thebes. Once Ay had chanted the phrases of the Hymn to Aten in a now-forgotten city of the sun, and had thought so highly of that hymn that he had inscribed it on the walls of a tomb he would never use. "Thy dawning is beautiful in the horizon of heaven, O living Aten, beginning of life!" Ay had cried. He had boasted of his closeness to Akhnaten: "I was one favored of his lord every day, great in favor from year to year."

Akhnaten had been dead ten years, and Ay, Pharaoh himself, a living god in his own right, sang different hymns now, mocking the dead heretic:

> The sun of him who knew thee not has set, O Amon.
> But as for him who knows thee, he shines.
> The temple of him who assailed thee is in darkness,
> While the whole earth is in sunlight.
> Whoso putteth thee in his heart, O Amon,
> Lo, his sun hath risen!

We know little of Ay's four years of rule. It seems to have been a relaxed and uneventful time, marked chiefly by Horemheb's reorganization of the army. While Horemheb gathered strength far to the north, Ay at Thebes devoted his time chiefly to self-aggrandizement. He built a handsome funeral temple for himself, and ornamented it with two unfinished statues of Tutankhamen, simply removing the dead Pharaoh's name from the statues and having his own inscribed. It was an act that gained little for Ay, because soon afterward he was dead, and his successor usurped those same statues for his own benefit.

That successor, of course, was General Horemheb. No doubt there had been a period of anarchy upon Ay's death, and it was a simple matter for Horemheb to march southward from his encampment near Palestine and take possession of the throne, in 1350. For the second time in less than five years, Egypt acclaimed as Pharaoh a man of common birth.

Horemheb is the prototype of a figure familiar enough in our day: the hard-bitten career soldier who rises through the ranks and steps in at a time of national chaos to make himself dictator.

We have seen Spain's Franco and Cuba's Batista follow Horemheb's path, and a new Horemheb arises in Latin America practically every week.

The official biography of Horemheb, inscribed on a statue now in the Turin Museum, tells us that he came from an old feudal family of the city of Alabastronpolis, and attained royal favor through the kindness of his particular divine protector, Horus. He had held high military rank under Amenhotep III, and in the reign of Akhnaten had been at the head of the army, entrusted with many important missions. He had then been an Atenist, of course, and had exchanged his Horus-honoring name for that of Paatenemheb. Portraits of Horemheb dating from the Amarna era show him in the approved style, belly projecting, legs thickened.

In the reign of Tutankhamen, Horemheb had been unquestioned commander-in-chief of the royal armies, bearing such titles as "Greatest of the great, mightiest of the mighty, great lord of the people, king's-messenger at the head of his army to the South and the North." During Ay's reign, Horemheb had attained such power that an inscription refers to him as "hereditary prince of all this land," while upon Ay's death, we are told, "Now when many days had passed by, while the eldest son of Horus [Horemheb] was chief and hereditary prince in this whole land, behold the heart of this august god, Horus, lord of Alabastronpolis, desired to establish his son upon his eternal throne. . . . Horus proceeded with rejoicing to Thebes . . . and with his son in his embrace, to Karnak, to introduce him before Amon, to assign to him his office of king."

At the celebration of the great feast of Opet, Amon's priests, speaking as oracles of the god, decreed that Horemheb had been selected to reign. By way of making his claim legitimate, Horemheb took to wife the only surviving member of Akhnaten's family, Mutnedjmet, the sister of Nefertiti. She was hardly of royal blood, but she had been the sister-in-law of one Pharaoh, and the daughter of another (Ay), and this gave Horemheb a tenuous association with past royalty. Undoubtedly the tragic young Ankhesenamen had not survived her third husband, Ay, or else Horemheb would certainly have married her and thereby gained a genuine hold on the throne. (The two youngest daughters of Akhnaten vanish from the record late in their father's reign, as does Akhnaten's young sister, Princess Beketaten.)

Like most military dictators, Horemheb was rigidly conservative. Ay and Tutankhamen had tolerated Atenism, but not Horemheb. Now, more than a decade after Akhnaten's death, the persecution of the heretic's memory began in earnest.

Horemheb began by decreeing that Akhnaten had never been Pharaoh. For good measure, he blotted out the reigns of Smenkhkare, Tutankhamen, and Ay as well. The three of them had all had a hand in the Aten heresy. (So, too, had Horemheb —but no one dared mention that to the new king.)

It was declared that Horemheb had succeeded to the throne upon the death of Amenhotep III. An inscription of the next century, dated in the time of Rameses II, speaks of "the 59th year of Horemheb's reign." Yet we know that Horemheb was not made Pharaoh until about 1350, and ruled only about thirty years. The discrepancy is accounted for, though, if we add to those thirty years the four of Ay, the nine of Tutankhamen, and the seventeen of Akhnaten—which would bring Horemheb's inflated reign into at least its sixtieth year.

Having made the three previous Pharaohs what George Orwell would call "unpersons," Horemheb appropriated most of the monuments and inscriptions of their reigns. The statues of Tutankhamen which Ay had taken for his own use were re-engraved with Horemheb's name where Ay's had been. The commemorative inscription in which Tutankhamen had told of his restoration of Amon was altered to make Horemheb responsible. The temple of Aten at Thebes was hacked to pieces by Horemheb's artisans, and out of the more than ten thousand blocks of its stone there rose three new pylons in honor of Amon. Nor did the northerner Horemheb ignore the gods of Lower Egypt; Re and Ptah and Set were honored with new temples, often built with the stones of Akhnaten's temples of Aten.

Horemheb gave vent to his hatred of Akhnaten in the most

direct way possible to an Egyptian: he set out to obliterate Akhnaten's memory. Just as Akhnaten had sent agents throughout Egypt to remove the name of Amon from all inscriptions, so too, now, did the heretic and his god come under the chisel and the mallet. Wherever Akhnaten's name was found, or that of the Aten, the hatchets descended. Teams of workmen were sent to Akhetaten to demolish the abandoned city, though somehow they failed to destroy the murals of the tombs in the cliffs.

Those who had served Akhnaten were treated the same way. The tomb of Huya, at Thebes, was entered, and the name of Tutankhamen removed; Huya's own portraits were attacked. Ay's tomb was sacked. Mysteriously, Tutankhamen's resting place was spared. But little else escaped the vegeance of Amon, working through the will of Pharaoh Horemheb.

Why was he so vindictive? Why did he strike with such fury against a Pharaoh long dead, whose teachings had died with him? Did he fear a resurgence of Atenism? Hardly. There was no one left to carry on Akhnaten's dream; it had won no permanent followers even in the heretic's own lifetime, and was completely extinguished now. No one had tried to restore Atenism during the reigns of Tutankhamen or Ay. Now came a vicious campaign against the heretic. Why? Was Horemheb trying to wipe out the knowledge that he, himself, even as Ay and Huya and the others, had sung the praises of the new god? Was it his own Atenism that he hoped to obliterate?

It became illegal even to mention Akhnaten's name. He and his three hapless successors were stricken from the roll of kings, and thenceforward it was possible to refer to Akhnaten only as "that criminal of Akhetaten." Akhnaten had been excommunicated.

"It is not easy now," Arthur Weigall wrote,[3] "to realize the full meaning to the Egyptian of the excommunication of a soul: cut off from the comforts of human prayers; hungry, forlorn, and wholly desolate; forced at last to whine upon the outskirts of villages, to snivel upon the dung-heaps, to rake with shadowy fingers amidst the refuse of mean streets for fragments of de-

[3] Weigall, *The Life and Times of Akhnaton.*

cayed food with which to allay the pangs of hunger caused by the absence of funeral-offerings. To such a pitiful fate the priests of Amon consigned 'the first individual in history,' and as an outcast among outcasts, the men of Thebes bade us leave the great idealist, doomed, as they supposed, to the horrors of a life which will not end, to the misery of a death that brings no oblivion."

While the tough-minded Horemheb busied himself with the persecution of Akhnaten's memory, he was also engaged in an attempt to rebuild the empire Akhnaten had let slip. He appointed as vizier a comrade-in-arms, a general named Rameses, who led forays into southern Palestine, while Horemheb himself marched into the Sudan to put down a new rebellion there. Egypt was not yet strong enough to make any fresh bid for a Syrian empire, and Horemheb was content to come to an agreement with rugged old Suppiluliumas.

By this time, Mitanni had been dismembered. During the reign of Ay, King Dushratta had been murdered by a rival, who ruled as Artatama II. His son, Shutarna III, had been willing to become a puppet of the rising power of Assyria, and the result was the speedy partitioning of Mitanni, the Assyrians taking the eastern half and the Hittites the western.

Soon after Horemheb came to the throne, Suppiluliumas died, as well as the imperialist-minded Assur-uballit of Assyria. The new Hittite king, Mursilis II, had to look westward toward his homeland in Asia Minor, troubled by revolt, and for a moment the pressure was off Egypt. Mitanni was gone from the ranks of the nations, and thenceforth Assyria would be on the ascendant. But Horemheb's reign was a time of peace, of regrouping of strength. When he died, about 1319, he was succeeded by his vizier, Rameses I, with whom the Nineteenth Dynasty, a new empire-building age for Egypt, commenced. Rameses I ruled only a year; after his death came his son Seti I, who reconquered much of the lost Phoenician and Palestinian empire, reaching the Hittite frontier just north of Beirut and stopping there. And in the glorious sixty-six years of Rameses II, beginning in 1304, Egypt and the Hittites at last entered into the war that had been brewing for more than a century—but that story does not concern us here.

Although he had put the curse of Amon upon Akhnaten, and wiped out his name and his memory, Horemheb was unable completely to erase Atenism from the minds of Egyptians. Lingering traces of monotheism and revolutionary thought remained despite his best efforts.

Amon was more powerful than ever before, and his priesthood was rising toward that political domination it would achieve in a later century. Yet Amon had subtly changed. Gone was the "lord of fear," the remote, hidden god of terror. A Nineteenth Dynasty hymn to Amon speaks of him in phrases that might have been lifted directly from one of Akhnaten's own benedictions:

> Sole likeness, maker of what is,
> Sole and only one, maker of what exists.
> From whose eyes men issued,
> From whose mouth the gods came forth,
> Maker of herbs for the cattle,
> And the tree of life for mankind,
> Who maketh the sustenance of the fish in the stream,
> And the birds that traverse the sky,
> Who giveth breath to that which is in the egg,
> And maketh to live the son of the worm,
> Who maketh that on which the gnats live,
> The worms and the insects likewise,
> Who supplieth the needs of the mice in their holes,
> Who sustaineth alive the birds in every tree.
> Hail to thee, who hast made all these,
> Thou sole and only one, with many arms,
> Thou sleeper waking while all men sleep,
> Seeking good things for his cattle,
> Amon, enduring in all things, Atum-Harakhti.

And from another passage:

> . . . Maker of their sustenance,
> Who distinguished one color [race] from another;
> Who hears the prayer of him who is in captivity,
> Who is kindly of heart when one calls upon him,

152

Who saves the timid from the haughty,
Who separates the weak from the strong. . . .
Lord of sweetness, great in love,
At whose coming the people live.

The Amon hailed here as "lord of sweetness," who is addressed in another hymn of the same period as "the lord of the silent who cometh at the cry of the poor," the god of whom it is said, "When I cry to thee in my affliction, then thou comest and savest me," is hardly the austere, tribute-hungry god of the time of Thothmes III. Aten has somehow invaded Thebes, and Akhnaten's kindly deity has come to influence the role of Amon.

The abstract nature of Aten, too, found echoes in the new concept of Amon. A Nineteenth Dynasty hymn known as the Leyden Papyrus, addressed to Amon but distinctly Aten-tinged, refers to Amon as "The first to come into being in the earliest times; Amon, who came into being at the beginning, so that his mysterious nature is unknown. No god came into being before him; there was no other god with him, so that he might tell his form." A later verse testifies to Amon's abstractness: "Amon, concealing himself from the other gods, so that his very color is unknown. He is far from heaven, he is absent from the underworld, so that no gods know his true form. His image is not displayed in writings. . . ."

Akhnaten's monotheism is adopted in words startling to a Christian familiar with the doctrine of the Trinity. The Leyden Papyrus states:

All gods are three: Amon, Re, and Ptah, and there is no second to them. "Hidden" is his name as Amon, he is Re in face, and his body is Ptah. Their cities are on earth, abiding forever: Thebes, Heliopolis, and Memphis unto eternity.

The text does not say, "There is no *fourth* to them." Amon, Re, and Ptah are one, a trinity, and there is no god *second* to them. Nowhere else in Egyptian literature, except in the hymns of Akhnaten himself, is the monotheistic idea phrased so directly.

The kindly, light-filled teachings of Akhnaten, then, had their influence despite the terrible persecution visited upon their

153

originator by Horemheb. Even the daring style of art fostered by Akhnaten continued to exist, though in a diluted form. The name of the Aten, however, reverted to its original meaning as that of the solar disk, sacred only as the abode of Re. In the reign of Seti I we find an inscription at Karnak declaring, "Re made for him his boundary as far as the limits of that which Aten illuminates," but this pertains to the disk and is not meant as a reference to Akhnaten's Sole God. An inscription of Rameses II also makes passing mention of Aten. Then we hear of him no more. As for the tormented heretic Pharaoh himself, his name faded from the memory of man, and, excommunicated and nameless, his wandering *ka* roved the sandy wastelands. As Weigall put it,

Over the hills of the west, up the stairs of the moon, and down into the caverns under the world, the poor twittering shadow was hunted and chased by the relentless magic of the men whom he had tried to reform. There was no place for his memory upon earth, and in the under-world the priests denied him a stone upon which to lay his head.

Amon had exacted his vengeance upon the shade of Akhnaten.

8

FROM EGYPT'S SANDS

And so Akhnaten's memory was lost. Centuries went by; great Rameses II died at last, and lesser men came to Egypt's throne, a string of Twentieth Dynasty kings who called themselves Rameses, too. After the eleventh Rameses had become one with Osiris, Egypt split in half, a nobleman from the Delta city of Tanis establishing a dynasty of the north while priests of Amon ruled Upper Egypt and Nubia. Then foreigners from the desert country of Libya took control of Egypt, and kings with barbarous names like Sheshonk, Osorkon, Takelot, and Pedibast ruled Egypt. After the Libyans came a dynasty of Nubians, then a native dynasty in the Delta. Finally, the Persian conquest of Egypt ended her independence forever, in 525 B.C. Four puppet dynasties controlled by Persians were followed by the sons of Ptolemy, a Macedonian Greek who inherited part of the world-empire of Alexander the Great.

With each wave of invaders, more of Egypt's splendid past was submerged and forgotten. The Pharaohs of the Twenty-sixth Dynasty, last independent Egyptians to rule, did make a deliberate and conscious effort to revive past glories, and we might almost call such kings as Psamettik I, who excavated and restored the monuments of his remote predecessors, archaeologists of a sort. Then came darkness.

It is not surprising that the name of Akhnaten was forgotten in those years of turmoil and oppression. When Herodotus, that splendid story-teller and credulous historian, visited Egypt about 450 B.C., he took down all he could learn about Egyptian history, but nowhere in his distorted and jumbled account of the Pharaohs do we find mention of anyone who might possibly have been Akhnaten.

Yet the ghost of a memory of the heretic king did endure. About 250 B.C., the Egyptian historian Manetho wrote (in Greek) a history of Egypt and made unmistakable reference to the interlude of heresy.

Manetho's works did not survive, except where they were quoted by other historians of antiquity. Thus the ancient Jewish historian Josephus quoted a long passage of Manetho which tells how a certain Pharaoh named Amenophis (the Greek form of Amenhotep) wished to hold communion with the gods. He asked the advice of a wise man, Amenophis-son-of-Papis, who told him that he first must clear Egypt of "all impure persons." Whereupon 80,000 "unclean" people were brought together and sent to certain quarries on the east bank of the Nile, where they might live apart from other Egyptians.

Amenophis-son-of-Papis foresaw a time when these unclean people would rise up and gain control of Egypt for thirteen years. This so distressed him, says Manetho via Josephus, that the wise old man took his life, leaving a letter of warning to the king.

Soon after, a group of these "unclean" people settled in the Delta city of Avaris, the old Hyksos capital. There, under the leadership of a certain priest of Heliopolis, they refused to worship the old gods, and declared war on the rest of Egypt, allying themselves with wandering Semites out of Syria. King Amenophis thereupon sent his five-year-old son Rameses into hiding at Memphis, and himself fled to Ethiopia, where he remained in exile for thirteen years. During this time the unclean Egyptians and their Syrian allies destroyed the images of the old gods, slaughtered the sacred animals, and forbade all traditional worship. At the end of the thirteen years, Amenophis returned from exile, overthrew the sacrilegious ones, and drove them from Egypt.

What Manetho tells is apparently a confused and hazy story

of Akhnaten's heresy, as seen from the viewpoint of its opponents. Pharaoh Amenophis is evidently Amenhotep III; Amenophis-son-of-Papis undoubtedly is Amenhotep-son-of-Hapi, an actual historical figure of Amenhotep III's reign, who served as court adviser and died—not by his own hand—at a great old age.

The 80,000 "unclean" people must be the worshippers of the Aten, who did indeed remove themselves to a certain quarry on the east bank of the Nile late in the reign of Amenhotep III, when the city of Akhetaten was founded. From Akhnaten's own inscriptions we know that the first break with Amon occurred in the fourth year of his rule, so that the heresy's time of greatest power was exactly thirteen years, matching the figure provided by Manetho.

The next part of the story—the persecution of the old gods of Egypt by the "unclean ones"—we know to be accurate. Of course, Amenhotep III died before this began, but Manetho's inaccuracy can be excused, since Horemheb had struck from the records the names of the four Pharaohs who had ruled between Amenhotep III and himself. It might have seemed, to Manetho ten centuries later, that all these events had taken place during the reign of Amenhotep III, when actually many Pharaohs were involved.

The statement that Amenophis went into exile and sent his five-year-old son Rameses into hiding is, of course, corrupt. None of the Pharaohs involved in the actual story ever went into exile, nor was Rameses the son of Amenhotep III. (He was not related to any of the others, though he did succeed Horemheb, whom Manetho here has combined with Amenhotep III.) As for the statement that the "unclean" Egyptians allied themselves with Syrians against the rest of Egypt, we can interpret this as a blurred version of the uprising of Aziru and other rebels in Syria during the time of the heresy.

In Manetho, then, is a distinct reference to the Amarna era, which at least gets the duration of the heresy right even if most of the other details are inaccurate. Akhnaten is nowhere mentioned in Manetho's story, however.

The next important historical source is Diodorus Siculus, a

Greek of Sicilian birth who visited Egypt about 60 B.C. His *Bibliotheca Historica,* "Historical Library," was an attempt to write the history of the entire known world from earliest times down to his own. Of its forty books, less than a third have survived, but the Egyptian section was among those preserved.

Diodorus' account of Egyptian history is as cloudy as Herodotus', but he affords one useful fragment of information. He mentions a king called Mendes, "who never undertook any warlike design," and observes that "After the death of this Mendes, and five generations spent (during which time there was an interregnum), the Egyptians chose one Cetes, of an ignoble extraction, to be their king. . . . This fell out in the time of the Trojan war."

Was Mendes Amenhotep III, who also "never undertook any warlike design"? And was this king "of an ignoble extraction," who ruled after an interregnum, Horemheb? Diodorus tells us that Cetes was succeeded by his son, Remphis. Rameses, perhaps?

That fleeting mention of an interregnum is the only hint in Diodorus that there had been such a thing as the heresy of Akhnaten, and it is hardly a satisfactory account. There the ancient record ends. A hazy story in Manetho, a tantalizing sentence in Diodorus Siculus, nothing more.

How, then, has it been possible to reconstruct the intricate story of the Amarna heresy?

The biography of Akhnaten and his family can be written today only because archaeologists have spent the last hundred years rolling back the mists of time. From Egypt's sands have come the clues on which our story is built. It has not been a simple task. Howard Carter, the archaeologist who found the tomb of Tutankhamen, confessed himself "perplexed by many difficulties and perforce by the lack of sufficient data." He observed that of the true histories of the ancient Egyptians, "we have but little which is trustworthy. . . . The few historical documents that we have are of a very miscellaneous character. An occasional weather-beaten inscription upon a cliff face, a scarab, or a piece of linen, a scrap of papyrus, or a potsherd, which chance has preserved and brought to light. . . . Searching those records, it is only here and there that the veil which shrouds those monarchs seems for an instant to be lifted, and we catch a glimpse of some amazing or puzzling fact."[1]

Even these fragmentary records held no meaning before the last century. Men puzzled over the hieroglyphics without knowing how to read them. Whole cities lay buried beneath desert sand. There was great interest in Egypt in the seventeenth and eighteenth centuries; learned men wrote extensive histories of the ancient era, but without exception those works were compilations of Herodotus, Josephus, Diodorus Siculus, Strabo, and other classical authors. There was no new information to offer.

Early in the nineteenth century, the flood of revelation began. Napoleon led an army to Egypt in 1798, and a year later one of his soldiers discovered the Rosetta Stone, a slab of black basalt which bore a hieroglyphic inscription and its equivalents in Greek and in demotic, or shorthand, hieroglyphics. By 1814, the English naturalist Thomas Young had made great strides toward translating the hieroglyphics, and less than ten years later the French linguist Jean-Francois Champollion could report that he had deciphered no less than 111 hieroglyphic symbols. Within a generation, hundreds of scholars could read the inscriptions of the Pharaohs. Champollion had given them the key that unlocked a treasure house of history.

The first history of ancient Egypt based on actual knowledge of Egyptian texts, rather than simply being a compilation of Greek and Roman works, was J. Gardner Wilkinson's *Manners and Customs of the Ancient Egyptians,* whose initial three volumes appeared in 1837. Wilkinson, son of an English theologian and antiquarian, had gone to Egypt for his health in 1821, and had remained there twelve years. His pioneering historical work brought him a knighthood in 1839; two more volumes of *Manners and Customs* followed soon after, and the book remained in print, a standard text, well on toward the end of the nineteenth century.

[1] Carter, *The Tomb of Tut-ankh-Amen,* Volume III.

What has this standard text to say about Akhnaten?

Not very much, it develops. Wilkinson assembles the various dynasty lists of Herodotus, Diodorus, and Manetho, and tries to bring some order out of their contradictions. Wilkinson's reading of Manetho's version of the Eighteenth Dynasty, for instance, begins properly with Amose, and includes such recognizable names as "Amenophis" (Amenhotep) and "Tuthmosis" (Thothmes). The second "Amenophis" in the list, given a reign of thirty-one years by Manetho, is described as "supposed to be the Memnon of the musical stone." This will do; Amenhotep III, whose colossi the Greeks attributed to Memnon, ruled thirty-odd years as sole king before the co-regency with Akhnaten. But the successor to "Amenophis" is given as "Horus," who ruled thirty-seven years—unmistakably Horemheb. Of Akhnaten, Smenkhkare, Tutankhamen, and Ay we hear nothing, as Horemheb intended.

Wilkinson next turns to the actual evidence of the recently translated monuments. He arranges the Eighteenth Dynasty kings in their proper order: "Amunoph I, Thothmes I, Thothmes II, Thothmes III, Amunoph II, Thothmes IV, Amunoph III." He even finds room for the reign of Hatshepsut, though in the wrong place. After "Amunoph III" he offers us "Amun-men," with a question mark, and then "Remeses I." A footnote supplies the information that "Amun-Toonh," brother of "Amunoph III," "is not admitted into the list of kings."

Here is a clue. And this is what Wilkinson offers a few pages later:

Amunoph III and his elder brother Amun-Toonh succeeded to the throne on the death of the 4th Thothmes; but as they were both young, the office of regent and tutor during their minority was confided to their mother, the queen Maut-m-shoi. . . . They appear to have ruled with equal authority and in perfect harmony, till some event caused the secession of Amun-Toonh, who left to Amunoph the undivided possession of the throne, and retired from Egypt. So anxious was the younger brother to obliterate every recollection of his having ruled conjointly with him, that he not only prevented the mention of his name, in the lists of kings, but caused it to be erased from all the monuments of Upper and Lower Egypt.

Already, the first stumbling translations of the hieroglyphics have brought us far from the uncertainties of Diodorus Siculus. Wilkinson in 1837 is aware that a co-regent had ruled with Amenhotep III and that his name had later been blotted from the records, though Akhnaten masquerades here as "Amun-Toonh" and is wrongly identified as Amenhotep III's elder brother. The reason for his secession, Wilkinson admits, "it is now difficult to determine."

By the time Wilkinson's fourth volume appears, in 1840, a little more light has been shed. He is aware now of a change in religion somehow centering around Tell el-Amarna, but his interpretation of Atenism is off-base:

"Even the alteration which took place in the name of Amun, and the introduction of the worship of the Sun with rays, represented at Tel-el-Amarna, and some other places, about the time of the 18th Dynasty, cannot be looked upon as changes in the religion."

Wilkinson seems here to think that the substitution of "Aten" for "Amon" was nothing more than a spelling change. But he does not even know the spelling of the new form, for it has been obliterated by a second change: "The alteration to which I allude . . . has been remarked by me on many of the oldest monuments of Egypt, where the hieroglyphics or phonetic name of Amun-re have been continually substituted for others, the combinations of which I could never discover, being most carefully erased, and the name of Amun, or Amun-re, placed in their stead." And he gives credit to Horemheb unknowingly: "Wherever the name of Amun occurs, the substitution has been so systematically made, that nothing short of a general order to that effect, sent to every part of Egypt, and executed with the most scrupulous care, can account for it." He notes that all the substitutions evidently were made during or just after the reign of "Amunoph III"—Akhnaten's father.

Soon after, Wilkinson became aware of a deity he calls "Atin-re," which he finds represented in the inscriptions of the king "who was noted for the peculiar worship of the Sun represented at the grottoes of Tel-el-Amarna," these inscriptions "being always so systematically erased, some may argue the animosity of the people against a King, who had made an unwelcome foreign innovation in the religion of the country, or at least in the mode of worshipping that Deity."

In 1843, Wilkinson brought out the two volumes of his new work, *Modern Egypt and Thebes,* as guidebooks for tourists who wished to visit the monuments of Egypt. Here we see that knowledge of Akhnaten has advanced another notch. Wilkinson tells how he discovered the grottoes, or tombs, at Amarna in 1824, finding in them "sculptures of a very peculiar style. . . . The king and queen, frequently attended by their children, are . . . represented praying to the Sun, whose rays, terminating in human hands, give them the sign of life, in token of his accepting the offerings placed before him." He observes that the royal names at Amarna have been defaced, but here and there he finds mention of the king's name surviving. He translates the name of this king as "Atinre-Bakhan."

Wilkinson suggests that the novel art styles of Amarna "indicate the introduction of a new form of worship, by a foreign usurper." Contemplating the evidence, he concludes that "Atinre-Bakhan" ruled before Thothmes IV, who was succeeded by "Amunoph III" and then by "Horus." The whole line of them, Wilkinson thinks, were "foreign princes," and "their omission in the lists of kings, the erasure of their names, the destruction of their monuments . . . prove them to have been looked upon with hatred in the country." Wilkinson thereupon suggests that "Atinre-Bakhan" and his family belonged to the Hyksos line, which gets him farther from the truth than ever— but at least he now has a name for the heretic king. *"Atin*re-Bakhan," corrupt reading though it is, is still closer to the truth than Wilkinson's earlier "Amun-Toonh." At least it mentions Aten.

The same year Wilkinson's *Modern Egypt and Thebes* appeared, the first systematic archaeological work was undertaken at Tell el-Amarna. (The name, by the way, is a synthetic one. It seems to mean "Mound of Amarna," from the Arabic word *tell,* "mound." But this is not the case. The name was coined by Europeans in the nineteenth century from two sources: the name of the modern village just north of the site, el-Till, and the "Beni Amran," or "Amarna," the tribe of Bedouins who inhabited the region.)

The pioneering archaeologist at Amarna was Richard Lepsius, born in 1810 in Germany. He had been a lecturer in philology and comparative languages at the University of Berlin. At the urging of the famous scientist Alexander von Humboldt, King Friedrich Wilhelm IV of Prussia put up funds for a German expedition to Egypt, and Lepsius was chosen to head it.

It was the best-equipped expedition that had yet gone to Egypt, except for Napoleon's original 1798 entourage. Lepsius had generous funds, and all the time he needed—three full years, from 1843 to 1845. He took with him a capable staff, including an architect, several draftsmen, and even an expert in that startling new technique, photography. This was to be no plunder-hunting sally; Lepsius intended to make a careful survey of the Egyptian antiquities, with the methodical precision that would be a specialty of German archaeologists thenceforward.

They spent six months on Memphis, the Old Kingdom capital, and seven months on Thebes. Then they moved on to Tell el-Amarna. Lepsius and his men measured, photographed, sketched, and dug. They made accurate plans of the ruins of Akhnaten's city, including the outlines of the streets and private buildings, the royal palace and the temple of Aten, and of the rock tombs. They transcribed wall inscriptions overlooked by Horemheb's wreckers.

On his return to Germany, Lepsius began to publish the twelve spectacular volumes of his *Monuments of Egypt and Ethiopia,* containing only plates of the monuments and inscriptions he had copied. This mammoth work was not completed until 1859, and the accompanying text volumes did not appear until much later. Volume III of Lepsius' *Monuments* contained twenty-one plates of the Amarna tombs, along with many inscriptions of Akhnaten's reign. These plates formed the foundation for all study of the Amarna period over the next fifty years.

Lepsius was also responsible for two landmarks in Egyptian

history: his *Egyptian Chronology,* published in 1849, and the *Book of Egyptian Kings* (1858). In these, he was able to supplement the vague and incorrect king-lists of Manetho and Diodorus Siculus with newly discovered information. The Royal Tablet of Karnak, discovered in 1843, provided a list of Egyptian kings from early times down to the Eighteenth Dynasty. The Royal Tablet of Sakkara, found in a tomb, listed fifty-eight kings down to Rameses II. The Royal List of Abydos, most useful of all, listed seventy-six kings through the early Nineteenth Dynasty. The name of Akhnaten was missing from all of these lists, of course, thanks to the diligence of Horemheb. But they helped to provide a sound historical structure for ancient Egypt.

The work of Lepsius spurred the Egyptologists on. More inscriptions were translated; the methods of translation themselves were improved; new correlations between separate inscriptions were made. There was an enormous advance in Egyptological understanding in the middle years of the nineteenth century.

Much of Wilkinson's standard book thus became obsolete. The German scholar Henry Brugsch undertook to replace it, and in 1877 published his *A History of Egypt Under the Pharaohs, Derived Entirely from the Monuments,* which quickly went into several editions and a number of translations.

The hazy guesses of Wilkinson are now replaced by relatively accurate information, drawn from Lepsius' published plates. Brugsch is aware that Akhnaten was the son of Amenhotep III, not, as Wilkinson had it, the elder brother. He dates Akhnaten's accession at 1466 B.C.—about a century too early—and, though he correctly reads Akhnaten's birth-name and coronation-name as "Nofer-Kheper-Ra Ua-En-Ra Amenhotep IV," he interprets the later name of the heretic as "Khu-n-Aten."

Brugsch has the essence of the story. He knows that Amenhotep III bypassed the women of Egypt and chose as his wife a girl neither of royal blood nor of Egyptian descent, and declares, "the son of the unfortunate marriage had to pay the penalty of his father's fault. In the eyes of the priestly corporation of the imperial temple at Thebes, who jealously watched over the letter of the law regarding the succession to the throne, the young king was an unlawful ruler." Perhaps this is so; it is an aspect of the story not much examined today. And, Brugsch says, "In the house of his mother Thi [Tiy], daughter of the foreigner, beloved by his father, hated by the priests, the young prince had willingly received the teaching about the one God of Light; and what the mouth of his mother had earnestly impressed upon his childish mind in tender youth became a firm faith when he arrived at man's estate."

After discussing, accurately enough, Amenhotep IV's quarrel with the priests of Amon, his change of name to—as Brugsch had it—"Khu-n-Aten, that is, 'splendor of the sun's disk,' " and the building of the new city, Brugsch goes astray in a footnote. The tomb of Ramose at Thebes, unknown to Lepsius, had been discovered by a native in 1860, entered by the German Egyptologist Ebers in 1872, and further explored by the Englishman Villiers Stuart in 1879—and a portrait on this tomb wall helped to confuse everything for a while.

The Vizier Ramose, it will be remembered, converted to Atenism after he had already begun to decorate his tomb. Alongside a relief of Amenhotep IV in the conventional style, Ramose, after his conversion, placed a new and realistic portrait of the king in the thin-necked, heavy-bellied style. The earlier portrait was labelled "Amenhotep IV," the later one, "Akhnaten."

Villiers Stuart concluded from this that Amenhotep IV and Akhnaten, whom he called "Khunaten," were separate individuals. His theory, repeated by Brugsch, was that "Khunaten was a foreigner who held some office at the court of Amunoph [Amenhotep] IV, and that he married his master's daughter, and eventually reigned in her right; that on first coming to the throne he adopted his father-in-law's [name], and called himself Amunoph [Amenhotep] as a matter of policy, but eventually dropped that name for the one he is best known by."

This erroneous distinction between Amenhotep IV and Akhnaten was still perplexing Egyptologists twenty years later, when Gaston Maspero published the second volume of his encyclopedic history of the ancient world, *The Struggle of the Nations.* Maspero, born in Paris in 1846, had served as director-general of Egypt's Antiquities Department, and the three ponderous volumes he wrote at the end of the last century formed a summary of all knowledge of the ancient world that had then been gleaned through archaeology. Maspero notes that early archaeologists had identified the puzzling Pharaoh as "Bakhen" or "Bakhnan," and had mistakenly placed him in the Hyksos dynasties—a nod here at Wilkinson.

Lepsius, Maspero adds, had placed him between "Amenothes III" and "Harmhabi," and had known that he had afterwards taken "the name of Bakhnaten, which is now read Khunaten or Khuniaton. His singular aspect made it difficult to decide at first whether a man or a woman was represented." The French archaeologist Mariette, Maspero tells us, "while pronouncing him to be a man, thought that he had perhaps been taken prisoner in the Sudan and mutilated, which would have explained his effeminate appearance, almost like that of an eunuch." Maspero next cites Villiers Stuart's attempt "to prove that Amenothes IV and Khuniaton were two distinct persons," and the theory of the Frenchman Lefebure that "Khuniaton was a queen," but, says Maspero, "they have hitherto been rejected by Egyptologists."

Maspero himself comes down clearly against Villiers Stuart. Aside from the spelling of the names, there is little in Maspero's 1897 account of the Amarna period that we can object to. "Amenothes IV," he says, was the son of "Amenothes III," and after a quarrel with the priests of Amon changed his name to "Khuniatonu," built a new city north of Thebes, and, accompanied by his wife, "Nofrititi," devoted himself to the worship of the new solar deity "Atonu" until his death in the seventeenth or eighteenth year of his reign. The names of his successors Maspero gives as "Saakeri" (Smenkhkare) and Tutankhamen, followed by "Ai" (Ay) and then "Harmhabi" (Horemheb).

The old Brugsch-Maspero reading, "Khu-n-Aten" or "Khuniatonu," was soon heard no more. British Egyptologists had been interpreting the heretic's name as "Akhenaten," "Akhnaten," or "Akhenaton" since the 1890's, and those are the preferred readings today, although James Henry Breasted of the University of

Chicago put his considerable influence behind the reading, "Ikhnaton."

Maspero could afford to be much more definite in dismissing the Villiers Stuart theory than Brugsch. For between the time Brugsch wrote and the time Maspero did, an extraordinary archaeological find, explaining a great deal about the reign of Akhnaten, had come to light. It was perhaps one of the most important discoveries in the history of archaeology.

The Tell el-Amarna letters—the archives of Akhnaten—had been discovered.

The story of the Amarna letters begins in 1887. An Arab woman had been digging at Tell el-Amarna for *sebakh,* a nitrogenous earth used as fertilizer, when she stumbled across a large box full of pieces of clay. The clay tablets "resembled nothing so much as stale dog-biscuits," as one writer put it, but the woman saw that they had markings on both sides. Perhaps they were *antikas*—antiquities—which could be sold for a few piasters to a dealer.

Egypt was then a hotbed of antiquity-smuggling. Under British guidance, the Egyptians had set up a reorganized government a few years before, and were valiantly trying to halt the wholesale export of their archaeological treasures for the private profit of dealers in antiquities. Under the terms of the British protectorate, the French were placed in charge of supervising archaeology in Egypt, and a Department of Antiquities was established to maintain control over the numerous free-lance excavators. Nothing was to be taken from Egypt without the express permission of the Department of Antiquities, a law honored more in the breach than otherwise. The first head of the Department of Antiquities had been Auguste Mariette; after his death in 1881, Gaston Maspero took the post, but in June, 1886, returned to his professorial duties in Paris. Maspero's successor was a pupil of his named Grebaut, a man temperamentally unsuited for the delicate diplomacy required of him.

It was during Grebaut's regime that the peasant woman found the clay tablets at Amarna. To increase their value, she and her friends cut them into pieces, and then took the fragments to

Luxor for sale. The tablets were carried in sacks, and about half of them were ground to powder during the jouncing journey.

Egyptian antiquity dealers in Luxor bought what remained and offered them for sale on the "black market." The dealers recognized that the tablets were similar to other clay tablets found by the thousands in Mesopotamia. For more than two thousand years, the Mesopotamian lands of Assyria, Babylonia, and Sumer had made use of clay tablets on which to write, in the wedge-shaped characters known as cuneiform, and these tablets were popular among collectors of Near Eastern antiquities. No one had ever found cuneiform tablets in Egypt before; the Egyptians had written on papyrus or on slate.

The battered tablets found their way into many hands. Jules Oppert, a ranking expert on Sumerian cuneiform, examined some in Paris and pronounced them forgeries. Grebaut of the Department of Antiquities saw a few, but said nothing about them. They did not seem to him to be Egyptian, and he was concerned only with Egyptian antiquities. The dealers peddled some of the strange tablets to tourists, and those tablets were never heard of again.

One dealer, Abd-el-Haj of Gizeh, after losing a sale to a museum official who decided the tablets were fakes, sold them to the Viennese collector Theodor Graf, and, luckily, Graf sold his collection, numbering about 160 tablets, to the Berlin Museum. German scholars, puzzling over the tablets, realized their importance and sent word to their agents to buy up all that came on the market.

Now began a curious cloak-and-dagger chase. Not only the Germans were after the tablets, but also the British Museum. In the summer of 1887, the British Museum had been about to despatch an agent to Mesopotamia, to deal with the theft of tablets from the Assyrian site of Kuyunjik. When rumors reached the museum that a new supply of tablets had come on the market—in Egypt, of all places!—the agent was authorized to go first to Luxor and investigate the situation. If the tablets were of any value, he was to obtain some before the Germans acquired them all.

On December 7, 1887, the representative of the British Museum left London. He was a thirty-year-old scholar named Ernest Alfred Wallis Budge, who would later become head of the British Museum's department of Egyptian and Assyrian antiquities, and one of the great authorities in the field. Then, he was simply a young and ambitious archaeologist who had had a brief taste of field work and who was eager to make a mark in the world.

Delayed by gales and high seas, Budge reached Cairo on December 19, and was greeted by the disturbing news that the popular Maspero had left Egypt some months before, to be replaced by the blustering, unlikeable Grebaut. Grebaut was belatedly showing some interest in the Amarna tablets, now that the Germans were after them, and a network of spies and informers was keeping watch over all archaeologists in Egypt lest they sneak something out of the country without permission.

Budge got his first taste of this as he travelled south from Cairo by rail. At the station nearest Amarna, a Frenchman travelling with Budge left the train and tried to buy some tablets from the Egyptians on the platform, who could always be depended upon to have some antiquity for sale. "As he left the station," Budge tells us, "some of the police from the train followed him."

Budge himself saw no tablets. He purchased mummies and manuscripts, and chafed at the restrictions Grebaut imposed on him. Egypt was then virtually a British possession, and Budge, as an Englishman, clearly resented the interference of this French official. On his return journey from the southern city of Aswan, he stopped off at the village of Hajji Kandil, near Amarna, and there, at last, he saw some of the celebrated tablets.

"In shape and form, and color and material," he wrote, "the tablets were unlike any I had ever seen. . . . The writing on all of them was of a most unusual character and puzzled me for hours. By degrees I came to the conclusion that the tablets were certainly not forgeries, and that they were neither royal annals nor historical inscriptions in the ordinary sense of the word, nor business or commercial documents. Whilst I was examining the

169

half-dozen tablets brought to me a second man from Hajji Kandil arrived with seventy-six more of the tablets, some of them quite large. On the largest and best written of the second lot of tablets I was able to make out the words 'A-na Ni-ib-mu-a-ri-ya,' *i.e.*, 'To Nib-muariya,' and on another the words '[A]-na Ni-im-mu-ri-ya shar matu Mi-is-ri,' *i.e.*, 'to Nimmuriya, king of the land of Egypt.' . . . I felt certain that the tablets were both genuine and of very great historical importance."[2]

Budge bought the eighty-two tablets on the spot, and offered to buy any others the men might have. But the rest, he learned, belonged to "dealers who were in treaty with an agent of the Berlin Museum in Cairo." Among these was a large one, about twenty inches long. The man taking it to Cairo for sale hid it under his clothing, but as he boarded the train it slipped out and fell on the track, breaking in pieces. Word of this reached Grebaut, who telegraphed police officials near Amarna, ordering them to arrest anyone found trafficking in cuneiform tablets.

Grebaut now set out in earnest to acquire tablets, coming down from Cairo himself. Meanwhile, a private collector in Cairo, who had paid one hundred Egyptian pounds for four small tablets, showed them to an English professor visiting there. The Englishman, though he mistranslated and misunderstood the tablets, wired an account of their discovery to an English newspaper. The price of tablets immediately shot up.

Budge and his eighty-two tablets reached Luxor, near the ancient site of Thebes, before Grebaut did. He stored his cases of antiquities in a private house, which was immediately sealed and guarded by police awaiting Grebaut's arrival. Budge induced a group of gardeners to dig from without, under the garden wall and into the house, while the police on duty were distracted by cognac and boiled mutton. The antiquities were spirited out.

The next day, Grebaut arrived in Luxor. Budge sidestepped him and got his tablets aboard a steamer bound for Cairo, not without being arrested by a zealous policeman. He talked his way out of that and made his departure.

[2] E. A. Wallis Budge, *By Nile and Tigris*, Volume I.

At the town of Kana, he left the steamer and took a train for Cairo. The train was behind schedule, arriving early in the morning instead of late the previous night, and Budge found himself alone, with baggage and boxes of papyri and tablets, without transportation, at a terminal far from town. Two British officers out for an early morning ride passed him, and, he tells us, "as they did so one of them hailed me in a cheery voice, and asked me why I was sitting there at that time of the morning. I recognized the voice as that of an officer of whom I had seen a great deal the year before in Aswan, and I quickly told him why I was there, and about the contents of my bags and boxes, and my wish to get into the town as soon as possible. After a short talk with his brother officer . . . my friend dismounted and went to the police . . . and told them to carry my bags and boxes into Cairo for me."

Grebaut's own henchmen thus helped Budge get the Amarna tablets into Cairo, past the customs inspection booth on the Nile bridge. The customs men had been warned by Grebaut to seize any antiquities in private luggage, but they asked no questions, "assuming that the police were carrying into the town goods belonging to the British Government, as indeed they were!"

Having foiled Grebaut, Budge repacked his precious tablets carefully and set out for Baghdad to fulfill the next part of his mission. A lengthy sea voyage brought him to Mesopotamia. On his arrival in Baghdad, he proposed to store the tablets aboard the British vessel *Comet* while carrying out his work in Mesopotamia on behalf of the British Museum. While loading the box aboard the ship, Budge ran into difficulties with Baghdad customs officials, who "jumped to the conclusion that I was trying to smuggle into Baghdad a case of whiskey, and this they determined to frustrate at all costs." A wild melee followed, in which the box holding the Amarna tablets nearly fell into the Tigris. The arrival of a high customs official luckily put an end to the struggle, and the tablets boarded the *Comet* safely.

Budge now proceeded to his Mesopotamian tasks, and obtained twenty-four more boxes of tablets, these from Assyrian sites. In the course of collecting them, he managed to antagonize the local dealers in antiquities, and they conspired with the Turkish authorities in Baghdad against him. The plan was, Budge writes, that "the dealers were to sell me as many tablets as possible, and were to tell the authorities how many they had sold. Then, when I was about to leave Baghdad, I was to be arrested and all my possessions searched, and the tablets were to be confiscated, and handed back to the dealers for a consideration."

Budge eluded this trap as deftly as he had sidestepped Grebaut's. The *Comet,* a merchant ship, was temporarily designated as part of an official British mail convoy, and was exempted from customs inspection. Off the tablets went, as property of the British Government, from Baghdad to Basrah, thence to Bombay, and finally to London. Budge justified his not-quite-legal maneuvers by pointing out that if he had not smuggled the twenty-five boxes of tablets out of Egypt and Mesopotamia, someone else would have done it. "Had I not come to a decision at once, and taken the eighty-two [Amarna] tablets when I had the chance of getting them," he writes, "they would certainly have gone to the Berlin Museum, or into the possession of some private collector, or anywhere except to the Government Museum of Egyptian Antiquities, Cairo."

Today, the Amarna tablets are scattered all over the world. Many of them are in Berlin. The British Museum, thanks to Budge's light-fingered ways, has a fine collection of them. Some drifted to Paris, to Russia, to Chicago, to New York. Often, a single tablet that had been cut in fragments by unscrupulous dealers ended shared by several museums.

By 1890, however, scholars in many parts of the world began to publish their translations of these invaluable documents. First came the texts of the Berlin tablets, published by Hugo Winckler as *Der Thontafelfund von El Amarna.* Two years later, Budge and C. Bezold published the tablets held by the British Museum, and, beginning in 1907, the Norwegian Assyriologist J. A. Knudtzon compiled and collated all known tablets for his *Die El-Amarna-Tafeln.* These and several later editions have placed

172

the texts of all the extant Amarna tablets in the hands of students, though the tablets themselves are widely disseminated.

There are some 377 known tablets today. Of these, about 300 were written by scribes in Palestine, Phoenicia, and Syria. Most of the others come from Mitanni, though there are some Hittite letters.

All the tablets are in Akkadian, the language of Assyria and Babylonia. It may seem odd at first that letters to an Egyptian king should be written in a language other than Egyptian; but Akkadian was the diplomatic language of the Near East, just as French was in Europe until quite recently. It was the one language that was understood and written everywhere, and even the kings of proud Egypt bowed to the custom and did their diplomatic corresponding in Akkadian.

Most of the letters are addressed to Akhnaten. A number of them, addressed to Amenhotep III, date from the last years of that king's reign, and apparently were transferred from Thebes to Akhetaten when Akhnaten moved his court and archives there. A handful of the Amarna letters are addressed to Tutankhamen, and one or two may possibly be addressed to Smenkhkare.

Because the letters were written in Akkadian, the scribes had some difficulty with the names of the Pharaohs. In the course of transliterating them from Egyptian to Akkadian, some odd distortions crept in. As was customary, the kings were addressed by their coronation-names. Thus Amenhotep III, whose coronation-name was Neb-maat-re, is called "Nimmuria." Akhnaten (Nefer-kheperu-re) becomes "Naphuria" or "Napkhuria." Tutankhamen (Neb-kheperu-re) is addressed as "Nibphuria" or "Niphuria."

The letters are such a treasury of information that we can only lament the loss of more than half their number through ignorance and carelessness after their discovery. Here are the letters of Ribaddi, Abdu-Heba, Aziru, and the other Syrian, Phoenician, and Palestinian princelings whose strife forms such a melancholy counterpoint to the latter years of Akhnaten's reign. Here is correspondence from Dushratta of Mitanni, from several

173

kings of Babylonia, from the Hittite monarch Suppiluliumas, providing invaluable data on the relationships of those kingdoms in the Amarna period. It would have been impossible to write whole chapters of Egypt's history without the aid of the clay tablets found in the dusty ruin of Akhnaten's archives building.

The finding, and subsequent publication, of the Amarna tablets aroused new interest in the excavation of Tell el-Amarna itself. No archaeologist had worked there in almost fifty years, not since Lepsius' visit in 1844. Two wealthy English hobbyists, Jesse Haworth and Martyn Kennard, subsidized a new investigation of Amarna, beginning in November, 1891, and lasting to the end of March, 1892, under the direction of William Matthew Flinders Petrie.

Flinders Petrie is one of the great men of Egyptology, perhaps the greatest archaeologist ever to work in the Nile Valley. Born in 1853, he did his first excavating in his native England, and came to Egypt in 1881. The methodical and careful Petrie was the forerunner of the modern school of archaeologists. When only eight, he had declared, "The earth ought to be pared away inch by inch to see all that is in it and how it lies," and that became his working credo. When he arrived in Egypt, excavation techniques were crude and careless, and more data was being destroyed than recovered. Petrie changed all that.

Sponsored at first by the Egypt Exploration Fund, a philanthropic British organization, Petrie worked at the Gizeh pyramids and at many other sites in Egypt before turning to the city of Akhnaten. A wiry, colorful figure, he was something of a legend in the field. As James Henry Breasted's son wrote of Petrie, "His clothes confirmed his universal reputation for being not merely careless but deliberately slovenly and dirty. He was thoroughly unkempt, clad in ragged, dirty shirt and trousers, worn-out sandals and no socks. It was one of his numerous idiosyncrasies to prefer that his assistants should emulate his own carelessness, and to pride himself on his own and his staff's Spartan ability to 'rough it' in the field. He served a table so excruciatingly bad that only persons of iron constitutions could survive it, and even they had been known on occasion stealthily to leave his camp in order to assuage their hunger by sharing the comparatively luxurious beans and unleavened bread of the fellahin."[3]

For all his eccentricities, Petrie was a brilliant and meticulous archaeologist. In his six months at Amarna he worked mainly in the royal palace, finding a rich assortment of small antiquities. The most strenuous of his labors were directed toward uncovering the painted pavement of Akhnaten's palace, one of the finest examples of Amarna art. It covered about 250 square feet, and showed scenes of natural life in soft, brilliant colors. Small calves cavorted and gambolled through flowering reeds and low shrubs, while fish played in a swiftly flowing stream, and huge lotus flowers swayed in the current. As though startled by the playful lambs, great water birds came fluttering up out of the shrubbery, their wings beating the air.

To preserve this magnificent scene, Petrie covered the entire surface with a transparent solution, rolling the preservative on with one finger, because no brush was delicate enough for the task. He set up gangplanks and walkways so that visitors could see the pavement from above without damaging it—building the path himself, for he could not trust the local workmen. Petrie's efforts went for nothing; in 1912, tribesmen of the village of Hajji Kandil, vexed because their neighbors in the village of el-Till were getting a greater share of tourist tips than they were, broke into the palace one night and hacked Petrie's pavement to powder. Nothing remains of it except the drawings and paintings Petrie made of it after he had restored it, and a small section of the original which he was able to raise and ship to the Ashmolean Museum at Oxford.

Between 1907 and 1914 German archaeologists under Ludwig Borchardt worked at Tell el-Amarna, and, like all other expeditions in Egypt since the late nineteenth century, obtained permission of the Egyptian Department of Antiquities to excavate only by agreeing to submit all finds to the head of the department. It was he who would decide which objects were

[3] Charles Breasted, *Pioneer to the Past.*

important enough to remain in the Cairo Museum, and which could be taken out of Egypt.

In 1912, Borchardt came across the best known single object of Amarna art: the famous head of Queen Nefertiti. He found it in the studio of an Amarna sculptor named Thothmes, who had evidently been still at work on it when Nefertiti fell from favor, for the painted limestone head is unfinished; it lacks the left eye. Near it, Borchardt found a shattered statue of Akhnaten. It is as though Horemheb's agents, bursting into the abandoned studio, destroyed the image of the heretic king, but, perhaps moved by the beauty of the Nefertiti head, left it unharmed.

The magnificent head, painted in blue, red, yellow, green, white, black, and flesh color, is one of the triumphs of ancient art. Long-necked, sharp of chin and nose, Nefertiti wears an immense headdress with grace, and her secret smile is aristocratic and mysterious. She looks across the ages at us in timeless beauty, and it is easy to see how she must have captivated Akhnaten and all others who beheld her.

She captivated Borchardt and his fellow archaeologists, too, to such an extent that they determined to smuggle her out of Egypt. At the end of the season's work, there came a day of reckoning when the director-general of the Department of Antiquities, at that time Pierre Lacau, was supposed to visit Tell el-Amarna and set aside those objects to be retained by Egypt.

Lacau heard from Borchardt that nothing of any significance had been found in the 1912 season, and so, instead of making the journey from Cairo himself, he sent a young assistant. The Germans showed him a few baskets of broken pottery and some sandstone fragments. There was nothing there worth retaining, and the inspector, not realizing that he had been gulled, signed the papers permitting Borchardt to take out of Egypt the finds of that season.

Soon, World War I put an end to archaeology for the duration. After the war, the superb head of Nefertiti appeared on display in the Berlin Museum, listed as a "recent acquisition." It received widespread attention, and the Egyptian government rather testily asked how it had been obtained. Under pressure, the Germans admitted that it had been found at Amarna in the 1912 season. How, then, had it failed to catch the eye of the director-general of the Department of Antiquities? Because, it was explained, the head had been in fragments, and not until it had been reassembled in Berlin had anyone realized its beauty.

This was an unlikely story, since the head showed no sign of having been shattered and repaired. Egypt's King Fuad asked that Nefertiti be returned to Egypt; the request was politely declined; diplomatic conferences followed, and there very nearly was a formal break in relations between Germany and Egypt. Nefertiti remained in Germany, and no German excavations in Egypt were permitted for many years after the dispute. The regulations governing the export of antiquities from Egypt were considerably toughened in 1924 as a direct result of the Nefertiti incident, which is one reason why the treasures of Tutankhamen, discovered at about that time, remain in Egyptian possession today.

During World War II, the bust of Nefertiti was stored in a salt mine for safe keeping. American soldiers found it there in 1945, and—over Egyptian protests—returned it to Berlin. Akhnaten's queen still adorns the Berlin Museum today; Egyptians must content themselves with the full-color reproduction that appears on their highest-value postage stamps.

The German expedition to Amarna aroused irritation in other quarters, too. No formal excavation report ever appeared, only some preliminary statements. Thus most of the scholarly value of the work was never made available, drawing this scathing comment from the most recent archaeologist to work there:

Thanks to the fact that the Germans have only published their results in a most inadequate preliminary form, the objects which they found can only be regarded as so much loot from random excavations and the scientific knowledge acquired during the course of the work must be considered as lost.[4]

In the winter of 1920–21, the Egypt Exploration Society, successor to the Egypt Exploration Fund, sent a new expedition to

[4] J. D. S. Pendlebury, *Tell el-Amarna.*

Amarna under the direction of T. E. Peet. In 1922, Peet was joined by Leonard Woolley, who worked there several years before transferring his activities to the ancient Sumerian city of Ur "of the Chaldees," supposed birthplace of Abraham. The Peet-Woolley expedition produced a detailed account of its work, *The City of Akhenaten,* but the results were meager; they could be appreciated only by a specialist. Some years later, the late Henri Frankfort and the late J. D. S. Pendlebury conducted further excavations at Amarna, publishing their findings as Volume II of *The City of Akhenaten* in 1933. A third volume, in 1950, offered more of the results of the Frankfort-Pendlebury expedition, but, again, little was found of interest to a layman. In more recent years, Tell el-Amarna has been neglected by Egyptologists, who are devoting their energies to the urgent task of exploring the valley of the Nile in Nubia before the waters of the new Aswan High Dam submerge the sites forever.

In the early years of this century, when the discovery of the Tell el-Amarna tablets had created new interest in Akhnaten and the Atenist heresy, other archaeologists searched for relevant sites elsewhere in Egypt and Nubia. Thus, in January, 1907, James Henry Breasted visited Dulgo, in Nubia, and examined a ruined temple previously seen by Lepsius. Lepsius had noted that the three standing columns which were all that remained of the temple bore inscriptions of the Nineteenth Dynasty Pharaoh Seti I. But Breasted, quoted in the biography of him written by his son, tells how, looking more closely, he "noticed also that on all three columns a deeply cut sun-disk penetrated through and interrupted Seti's inscriptions. . . . I worked on, when suddenly behind the form of Amon on the column I saw dimly through the rough chisel marks of intentional expungement the lines of the well-known figure of the great heretic. A dozen other unexplained peculiarities in the reliefs of Seti I were now immediately explained, and I could discern the figure of Ikhnaton on each of the columns, worshiping the sun-disk. This meant much: it meant the first discovery of a temple of the great reformer in Nubia; it meant the sudden extension of his sun-worship temple 500 miles farther south; it meant the possibility

178

of identifying this place with the Nubian city founded by Ikhnaton and known as Gem-Aton. . . ."[5]

Even more significant discoveries, though, would soon be made far to the north. They would be the most important Amarna-era finds of our century, but they came to light, not at Akhnaten's own city, but at Thebes—the city of Amon.

Since the time of Thothmes I, the kings of Egypt had gone to their final repose in the Valley of the Tombs of the Kings, outside Thebes, where chambers hewn in the rock received them. King after king was buried there, until Akhnaten interrupted the custom. After the interlude of heresy, the tradition was revived. Tutankhamen was buried there, and Ay, and Smenkhkare, and the kings of the Nineteenth and Twentieth Dynasties.

Fabulous treasures had accompanied the Pharaohs to their graves, and hardly did a king go to his rest than the tomb-robbers began their raids. Guards were posted in the Valley, but guards could be bribed, and in the increasingly demoralized days of the Twentieth Dynasty even high officials of the Theban government were willing to take part in the thefts, as existing documents reveal. To thwart the robbers, the priests of the mortuary temples shifted the royal mummies from place to place, to little avail. The elaborate curses inscribed in the mortuary temples proved no discouragement; Amenhotep III had called the flaming wrath of Amon down on desecrators of his tomb in flamboyant phrases,[6] but his tomb was robbed just the same, during the Nineteenth Dynasty.

By Twentieth Dynasty times, nearly all the tombs had been robbed again and again, and the Pharaohs had abandoned the whole idea of building their graves in the Valley. The royal mummies, stripped now of their funeral finery, were unceremoniously stored in bundles; thirteen monarchs were transferred to the tomb of Amenhotep II and allowed to remain there. Only one tomb seems to have gone nearly untouched—that of Tutankhamen. It had been broken into soon after the boy-

[5] Charles Breasted, *Pioneer to the Past.*
[6] See p. 42.

pharaoh's death, but little had been stolen, and the priests had sealed the tomb again. After that, it remained undisturbed.

Why was this one tomb spared? Probably the fact that Horemheb had deleted Tutankhamen's name from the roster of kings had helped; no one remembered Tutankhamen, and no one went looking for his grave. Then, too, it was in a low-lying part of the Valley, and its entrance may quickly have been hidden by shifting sands. Later, workmen building the tomb of Rameses VI had erected huts right over the site of Tutankhamen's tomb, further concealing it.

The other tombs stood open and empty. When European tourists began to visit Egypt in the eighteenth century, they made a point of visiting the royal tombs. Early in the nineteenth century the Italian giant Giovanni Battista Belzoni, who ransacked Egypt in his own energetic way, hunted for a sealed tomb in the Valley, but reported, "I exerted all my humble abilities in endeavoring to find another tomb, but could not succeed."

In 1898, a French archaeologist, Loret, came across several forgotten tombs in the Valley. One of them was that of Amenhotep II, which yielded its thirteen royal mummies, among them that of Akhnaten's father. Loret also found the tombs of Thothmes I and Thothmes III. But all had been plundered in antiquity. Nothing but the looted mummies remained.

In 1902 a wealthy American named Theodore M. Davis came to explore the Valley of the Tombs of the Kings. No archaeologist himself, but only an enthusiast, Davis hired a team of professional archaeologists to do the actual digging for him. Among them was a young man named Howard Carter, who had learned his trade under Flinders Petrie and shared that pioneer's careful, meticulous approach.

Within a year, Carter and Davis had found the tomb of Thothmes IV, and soon afterward that of Queen Hatshepsut, both having been entered in antiquity. In 1904, Carter withdrew, and Davis' new archaeologist, J. M. Quibell, took his place. In 1905, Quibell and another archaeologist, Arthur Weigall, excavated the tomb of Yuya and Tuya, the parents of Queen Tiy. The following year, they were joined by Edward R.

Ayrton, and new discoveries resulted. As Weigall, who was then director-general of the Egyptian Department of Antiquities, explains, Davis paid for the excavations, the Egyptian government bore all other working costs; Quibell and Ayrton did the actual work, Weigall supervising on behalf of the Egyptian government. "We all united to give him [Davis] the credit of the discoveries, the work being deemed worthy of every encouragement, in spite of the fact that the promoter was himself an amateur, and that the greatest tact had to be used in order to impose proper supervision on his work," Weigall wrote.

In January, 1907, this team, "having exhausted the surrounding sites," as Davis tells us, began work in a small area where "there was no sign of the probability of a tomb." Limestone chips, dumped by workmen who had built the surrounding tombs of Seti I and Rameses I, II, III, and IX, covered the spot. "It seemed to be a hopeless excavation, resulting in a waste of time and money. Nevertheless, it had to be cleared whatever the result."[7]

After several days of work, Davis and his co-workers found themselves on a rough stairway leading downward to a door blocked with stones. Clearing these away, they entered, only to find more stones blocking the passageway to within four feet of the roof. Lying atop these stones, as if thrown there in discard, were two wooden doors with copper hinges. "The upper faces of the doors," Davis wrote, "were covered with gold foil marked with the name and titles of Queen Tiyi [Tiy]: It is quite impossible to describe the surprise and joy of finding the tomb of the great queen and her household gods, which for 3,000 years had never been discovered."

Within the tomb itself, which Davis reached by crawling down the passageway for seventy feet, were the remaining pieces of the gold-covered shrine to which the two doors belonged. The shrine had evidently been taken apart, but it had proved impossible to remove it. One panel of the shrine showed Queen Tiy, wearing a thin tunic, worshipping beneath the rays of Aten.

[7] Theodore M. Davis, *The Tomb of Queen Tiyi.*

The figure of Akhnaten had once been beside her, but had been hacked out of the gold foil. The name of Akhnaten, too, had been hammered out. Here and there on the shrine the name of Amenhotep III had been inscribed, but it had been erased and replaced by his coronation name, Neb-maat-re. So the tomb had been visited twice, once by Akhnaten's men to purge it of references to Amon, and later by the agents of Horemheb, wiping out the name of Akhnaten himself.

Elsewhere amid the rubbish and disorder of the tomb, Davis found four exquisite canopic jars—the alabaster jars used for preserving the internal organs of a mummified person. Once, the jars had borne inscriptions, but they had been carefully chiseled away.

Not far from the dismembered shrine and the canopic jars, Davis found a coffin made of wood, covered with gold foil and inlaid with semiprecious stones. In his account, we learn that "the coffin had either been dropped or had fallen from some height, for the side had burst, exposing the head and the neck of the mummy. On the head plainly appeared a gold crown encircling the head, as doubtless it was worn in life by a probable queen. Presently we cleared the mummy from the coffin and found that it was a smallish person, with delicate head and hands. The mouth was partly open, showing a perfect set of upper and lower teeth. The body was enclosed in mummy-cloth of fine texture, but all of the cloth covering the body was of a very dark color. Naturally it ought to be a much brighter color. Rather suspecting injury from the evident dampness I gently touched one of the front teeth, and alas! it fell into dust, thereby showing that the mummy could not be preserved. We then cleared the entire mummy, and found that from the clasped hands to the feet, the body was covered with pure gold sheets, called gold foil, but nearly all so thick that when taken in the hands, they would stand alone without bending. These sheets covered the body from side to side."

Obviously the tomb had never been robbed, since so much gold remained in it. Yet the tomb was in disorder, and had clearly been visited by someone long ago. Akhnaten's name

182

could still be seen on the gold foil of the coffin, though an attempt had been made to erase it; gold ribbons encircled the body, and the forbidden name had been cut out of them. The coffin still bore the inscription, "The beautiful child of Aten, who lives here forever and forever, and is true in the sight of earth and sky."

That was mysterious enough, but the disorder could be explained as having been caused by Horemheb's agents when they launched their attack against the name of Akhnaten. More puzzling, why had Queen Tiy—if this were really her tomb, as the inscriptions indicated—been buried so meanly? The tomb was rough-hewn and damp, its walls unadorned. A woman of Queen Tiy's importance would have merited a far more imposing sepulchre.

Davis cautiously unwrapped the mummy, and two surgeons who happened to be in the Valley at the time examined it. Davis writes that "they reported that the pelvis was evidently that of a woman. Therefore, everyone interested in the question accepted the sex, and supposed that the body was doubtless that of Queen Tiyi."

That early verdict was swiftly reversed by Dr. G. Elliot Smith, a celebrated British anatomist who had devoted much of his career to the study of mummies. "Alas!" wrote Davis, "Dr. Smith declared the sex to be male. It is only fair to state that the surgeons were deceived by the abnormal pelvis and the conditions of the examination."

A man's body—in Queen Tiy's tomb?

The furniture in the cell bore Queen Tiy's name and titles. Yet the body, it now was declared, could only be that of Akhnaten!

Gaston Maspero, called in to study the evidence, offered the opinion that Ay, or someone else favorably disposed toward Akhnaten, had secretly removed his body from Akhetaten and hidden it in an obscure cell at Thebes to spare it from the fury of the priests of Amon. "First of all," Maspero noted, "it must be clearly understood that the vault discovered by Davis is not a real tomb; it is a rough cell in a rock which has been used as a secret burying-place for a member of the family of the so-called Heretic Kings, when the reaction in favor of Amon triumphed. . . ." Tomb furniture, presumably belonging to Queen Tiy, had been appropriated for the burial of Akhnaten. "Such being the facts," Maspero went on, "how are we to reconcile them and explain satisfactorily the presence of Akhnaten's body amidst Tiy's furniture?" He suggested that "the hiders wanted the people to believe that the body they were burying was Tiy's in order to prevent any harm being done to the king by some fanatical devotee of Amon." But he added, "I must confess that I look on this explanation as being too far-fetched to hold good."

More probable, Maspero thought, was that "the mummies of the dead members of Khuniatonu's [Akhnaten's] family must have been taken out of their tombs and brought over to Thebes all together. . . . Once there, they must have been kept quietly for a few days in some remote chapel. . . . When the time came for each to be taken to the hiding place which had been prepared for them in the Biban el-Moluk [Valley of the Tombs of the Kings] the men who had charge of these secret funerals mixed the coffins, and put the son where the mother ought to have been."

While this sort of speculation was current, the coffin was being pieced together in the Cairo Museum, and now an inscription engraved on the gold foil beneath the mummy's feet was discovered. It proved to be a kind of epitaph, which could be interpreted either as a prayer to Aten, or simply as a private expression of love and grief for the departed one:

I breathe the sweet breath which comes forth from thy mouth. I behold thy beauty every day. It is my desire that I may hear thy sweet voice, even the north wind, that my limbs may be rejuvenated with life through love of thee. Give me thy hands, holding thy spirit, that I may receive it and may live by it. Call thou upon my name unto eternity, and it never shall fail.

The mummy itself underwent further examination. Dr. Smith reported that the skeleton was that "of a young man who, judged by the ordinary European standards of ossification, must have attained an age of about 25 or 26 years at the time of his death."

184

It was a jarring note. Akhnaten had unquestionably ruled seventeen years. He had founded the city of Akhetaten in the sixth year of his reign. He was the father of six daughters, at least one of whom had been born before the sixth year of his reign. If he had died at 26, he must have been only 15 when Princess Meritaten was born, perhaps even younger. That was biologically possible, but what seemed wholly unlikely was the notion that Akhnaten had been hardly into his teens when he led the revolt against Amon. Possibly, some archaeologists and historians suggested, Dr. Smith had underestimated the mummy's age on death? "It is highly improbable that he could have attained thirty years if he had been normal," Dr. Smith replied.

But the mummy was not that of a normal man. The pelvis was unusually broad, which had led to the original false identification of the mummy as a female. The skull was misshapen and elongated, showing, according to Dr. Smith, "in an unmistakable manner the distortion characteristic of a condition of hydrocephalus," an affliction in which fluid accumulates in the skull, causing insanity and death. This was a slip on the part of the great anatomist, for, as other doctors soon pointed out, the *back* of the mummy's skull was distorted, while in hydrocephalus it is the frontal part of the cranium that is distended. None the less, the mummy showed definite deformities—and those deformities matched those in the many portraits of Akhnaten.

Here and there in the rubbish on the floor of the tomb were bricks stamped with the name of Akhnaten, and this was offered as proof that the mummy was indeed his. The seal of Tutankhamen was also found stamped into the cement, as though that young king had ordered the burial of his predecessor. Arthur Weigall, reviewing the evidence, expressed the belief that the tomb had originally been Queen Tiy's, and was entered first by agents of Akhnaten, who removed the name of Amenhotep III, substituted Neb-maat-re (Amenhotep's coronation name), and sealed it again. Next, after Tutankhamen had become Pharaoh and the capital had been shifted to Thebes, Akhnaten's body was brought to the tomb and allowed to rest by his mother's side, and again the tomb was sealed. Finally, in Horemheb's day, Weigall declared, "when Akhnaten's memory came to be hated, the priests removed the mummy of Tiy from the tomb which had been polluted by the presence of 'that criminal,' as Akhnaten now was called, erased the king's name, and left him the solitary and nameless occupant of the sepulchre."

Weigall was emphatic that the mummy was Akhnaten's. Brushing aside the mummy's youthfulness with the assertion that Akhnaten had obviously been precocious, he summed up by saying, "The mummy lay in the coffin of Akhnaten, was enclosed in bands inscribed with Akhnaten's name and was accompanied by the canopic jars of Akhnaten. It was that of a man of Akhnaten's age, the facial structure corresponds to the portraits of Akhnaten, and it has physical characteristics similar to those of Akhnaten's father and grandfather. How, then, can one possibly doubt its identity?"

At least one expert did doubt. He was Kurt Sethe of Germany, who offered the opinion that the mummy was not Akhnaten's. To which Weigall replied, "It is evident that all the facts were not marshalled before him when he set himself to question an identification which surely is not open to doubt."

Weigall wrote those lines in June, 1922. He was highly respected, a dean of his profession, and few cared to challenge him. Yet his conclusions were rickety indeed.

Why, for instance, had the priests simply removed Queen Tiy's mummy, to guard it from "pollution," without taking the obvious step of destroying the body of Akhnaten? Why was Queen Tiy buried in such a crude cell in the first place? Where was her mummy now? Above all, could Akhnaten really have accomplished what he did when only a boy?

Later workers, pondering the mysteries of the 1907 Davis find, have discarded Weigall's conclusions entirely. Dr. Douglas E. Derry of Cairo re-examined the controversial mummy, exploded Smith's hydrocephalus opinion, and argued that the man had been no older than twenty-three at his death. Smith, reconsidering, admitted "that the anatomical evidence seemed to point to an age of about 23." If the mummy were Akhnaten, then, he had become Pharaoh at the age of 6, had formulated his heresy before he was 9, had become a father at 10 or 11, and had ordered the construction of Akhetaten when he was 12. Hardly!

Nor was the tomb Queen Tiy's. Although the sarcophagus itself had been intended for a woman, the original occupant of the tomb, or at least the one for whom its furniture had been designed, was now felt to be Princess Meritaten. Queen Tiy, no doubt, had gone to a more splendid burial elsewhere in the Valley, probably at the side of her husband, and her mummy disappeared during the looting of Amenhotep III's tomb. As for the mysterious mummy, that, it finally was decided, belonged to Smenkhkare, the shadowy co-regent of Akhnaten and husband of Meritaten, who had been, perhaps, Akhnaten's son, but more likely his brother. Having died at Thebes, murdered, it may be, in the same year of Akhnaten's death, Smenkhkare was hastily packed into a tomb that had been made ready for some royal princess. After his three brief years of joint rule, he went to his rest in a poor and shabby cell. And, nine years later when his brother Tutankhamen also died, Smenkhkare's tomb was rifled of its treasures to ornament the tomb of Tutankhamen—the final outrage.

Thus—again in anticlimax—there ended the strange story of "Akhnaten's mummy," not Akhnaten's at all. Where the heretic lies remains a mystery, and probably will so remain through all eternity.

The final chapter in the rediscovery of the royal family of Amarna was written in November, 1922, only a few months after Arthur Weigall dogmatically stated that the mummy of the 1907 tomb could only be that of Akhnaten. It was then that the most spectacular single find in all of archaeological history came from the Valley of the Tombs of the Kings: the tomb of Tutankhamen.

"Curiously enough, for all the splendor of his burial, Tutankhamen was a ruler of little importance," wrote Howard Carter, the discoverer of the tomb. "In the present state of our knowledge we might say with truth that the one outstanding feature of his life was the fact that he died and was buried."

He died, we know, after a reign of nine years, when still less than twenty, and was buried with the pomp and majesty befitting the mightiest of kings. Ay, who had put him on the throne, superintended his funeral, and had himself portrayed on the walls of the tomb administering the final rites to Tutankhamen—the only known instance in all of Egyptian history when a succeeding Pharaoh was depicted in a former ruler's tomb.

The story of the discovery has often been told, and need not be repeated in detail here.[8] In brief, Howard Carter, who had worked for Theodore Davis in the Valley of the Tombs of the Kings, shifted his employ in 1907 to another wealthy amateur archaeologist, Lord Carnarvon. When Theodore Davis withdrew from the Valley in 1914, convinced that no further undiscovered tombs remained, Carter and Carnarvon took over the concession. War delayed them, and not until late in 1917 did they begin work in earnest. Their goal was the tomb of Tutankhamen, its location unknown. Theodore Davis had found a few fragments of cups and boxes bearing Tutankhamen's name and seal in a cache in the Valley, not far from the tomb then thought to be that of Queen Tiy. Carter and Carnarvon felt that Tutankhamen's tomb could not be far off.

Extensive searching produced no results, and by 1922 they were ready to abandon the quest. Then, on November 1 of that year, Carter's workmen uncovered a step in the ground, under the site of an old hut. A staircase leading downward was revealed, and a sealed doorway.

It was Tutankhamen's tomb. The tomb had been entered in antiquity, but the thieves seemingly had been apprehended in the act, and got away with little. Priests had closed the tomb again with Tutankhamen's seal. Eagerly, Carter removed the doorway, cleared a rubble-filled passageway that led to an inner door, and made a small opening in that door, inserting a candle.

"Can you see anything?" Carnarvon asked him.

"Yes, wonderful things!"

Tutankhamen's tomb consisted of several chambers packed with treasures of art—thrones, statues, couches, caskets, vases,

---

[8] I have already dealt with it in *Empires in the Dust* (Chilton, 1963), pp. 39–50.

even overturned chariots. Hampered by bureaucratic complications, a swarm of sightseers, and the sudden death of Lord Carnarvon, Carter spent the next few years removing, preserving, and cataloguing the jumble of wonders in the tomb before he reached the coffin itself.

Tutankhamen had been laid to rest at the heart of a puzzle-box of concentric coffins and shrines, some of wood and some of solid gold. Covering the mummy's face was a golden mask portraying the young Pharaoh as he probably looked: a gentle, sensitive, handsome boy. The mummy itself, badly decayed except for the face and feet, underwent elaborate examination when Carter removed it. "The face," he wrote, "was refined and cultured, the features well-formed, especially the clearly marked lips." Dr. Douglas E. Derry reported that the age of Tutankhamen at death had been about eighteen years. The skull showed elongation of the same sort found in the 1907 mummy, and there could be little doubt of a family relationship. Carter and Derry believed that Tutankhamen was Akhnaten's son, and the younger brother of Smenkhkare.

Today, it seems clear from an examination of their mummies that Tutankhamen and Smenkhkare were certainly brothers. Whether they were sons of Akhnaten, or of Amenhotep III, remains an open matter.

With the finding of Tutankhamen's tomb in 1922, the archaeological side of the Amarna story ends for us, since nothing of significance has been discovered since. Exactly a hundred years passed between the time Champollion cracked the hieroglyphic code and the day Howard Carter stared in awe at the golden treasure of Tutankhamen. Within that span, Horemheb's work was undone, and the rebellious Akhnaten returned from the land of the forgotten.

9

AKHNATEN AND MOSES

The religious revolution fostered by Akhnaten cast its brilliant glow over Egypt for less than a dozen years, then sputtered into darkness. But was Akhnaten forgotten? In name, yes, certainly. Did his teachings, though, perish with him?

He taught that there was only one god, a universal god of warmth and forgiveness, an unseen god of whom no images could be made. He cast out demons and hobgoblins, offering instead a creed of simplicity and purity. Truth, justice, order—Maat—were the highest ideals of Akhnaten, he who called himself "living in truth."

We have seen that some of these teachings filtered into the religion of Amon. But the effect was shortlived. Egypt soon slipped back into polytheism and ritualistic magic, and it was as though Akhnaten had never been.

Yet elsewhere in the Near East, the monotheistic idea persisted. A stubborn, self-willed tribe of desert nomads called the Hebrews let it be known that they were the chosen people of Yahweh, the only God, abstract and immanent, a god of justice and truth who would tolerate no idols. Furthermore, these Hebrews preserved a tradition of once having dwelled in Egypt, and of having been led forth by a great lawgiver named Moses, who walked with Yahweh and conversed with him. Moses, the tradition said, had been a foundling, raised in Pharaoh's own palace as an Egyptian. He had joined his own people only as a young man, and had led them forth out of unjust Egypt to Canaan, where they could serve the true god in peace. The date of this exodus from Egypt, according to the Hebrew writings, could be placed within a century or so of the time that we know Akhnaten ruled in Egypt.

Did Moses learn monotheism from Akhnaten, and transmit it to the Hebrews?

Do three of the modern world's greatest faiths—Judaism, Christianity, and Islam—stem directly from the mind of a tormented religious fanatic who once occupied the throne of Egypt?

A persistent line of thought says yes. Moses, it is asserted, was a disciple of Akhnaten. After the downfall of Atenism, Moses attached himself to the Hebrews, who happened to be dwelling in Egypt, and led them forth to Canaan to avoid the persecution then being meted out to all adherents of the monotheistic Pharaoh. And it was upon Akhnaten's teachings that the religion of Moses was founded—a foundation later to be used by Jesus, and still later by Mohammed.

The earliest known statement of this idea comes from Manetho, as quoted by Josephus in *Contra Apion,* about 80 A.D. Manetho, it will be recalled, told a distorted but recognizable version of the Amarna heresy, in which he stated that at one point a group of heretics settled in Avaris, the old Hyksos capital in the Delta, and, *led by a certain priest of Heliopolis,* refused to worship the old gods of Egypt.

The name of that priest of Heliopolis, Manetho tells us, was —Moses.

Manetho, of course, was writing a thousand years after the event, and his reference to Moses may well have been a gratuitous attempt to link the Egyptian historical tradition with the Judaic. But Heliopolis is the Biblical city of On, at whose university Moses, by Hebraic tradition, is said to have been educated "in all the wisdom of the Egyptians." Since Heliopolis was the center of the solar cult of Re, out of which Atenism developed, the wisdom Moses would have learned there could well have been the monotheistic solar worship that theologians of

191

Heliopolis had pondered since the days of the Old Kingdom.

These are uncertain speculations. More to the point, because it cannot be argued away at all, is the startling resemblance between the "long hymn" to Aten found in Ay's tomb at Amarna, and Psalm 104 of the Old Testament.

James Henry Breasted was the first to point out the kinship, in his *History of Egypt,* published in 1905, and many have made the same observation since then. What Breasted did was to pair lines from his translation of the Aten hymn with various lines of the Psalm, to this effect:

THE ATEN HYMN	PSALM 104
When thou settest in the western horizon of heaven, The world is in darkness like the dead. . . . Every lion cometh forth from his den. . . .	Thou makest darkness and it is night, Wherein all the beasts of the forest do creep forth. The young lions roar after their prey, and seek their meat from God.
When thou risest in the horizon. . . . The darkness is banished. . . . Then in all the world, they do their work.	The sun ariseth, they gather themselves together, and lay them down in their dens. Man goeth forth unto his work and to his labour until the evening.
All trees and plants flourish, The birds flutter in their marshes, Their wings uplifted in adoration to thee, All the sheep dance upon their feet. . . .	The trees of the Lord are full of sap. . . . Where the birds make their nests. . . . The high hills are a refuge for the wild goats. . . .
The barques sail upstream and downstream alike. Every highway is open because thou hast dawned. The fish in the river leap up before thee, And thy rays are in the midst of the great green sea.	So this is the great and wide sea, wherein are things creeping innumerable, both small and great beasts. There go the ships: there is that leviathan, whom thou hast made to play therein.

How manifold are all thy works!
They are hidden from before
us,
O thou sole God, whose powers no other possesseth.
Thou didst create the earth according to thy desire.

Thou hast set a Nile in heaven,
That it may fall for them,
Making floods upon the moun-
tains, like the great sea;
And watering their fields among
their towns.

Thou makest the seasons, in
order to create all thy
works. . . .
Thou hast made the distant
heaven to rise therein. . . .
Dawning, shining afar off and
returning.

The world is in thy hand,
Even as thou hast made them.
When thou hast risen, they live;
When thou settest, they
die. . . .
By thee man liveth.

O Lord, how manifold are thy
works!
in wisdom hast thou made
them all: the earth is full of
thy riches.

He watereth the hills from his
chambers: the earth is satisfied with the fruit of thy
works.
He causeth the grass to grow
for the cattle, and herb for
the service of man: that he
may bring forth food out of
the earth. . . .

He appointed the moon for
seasons: the sun knoweth
his going down.

These wait all upon thee; that
thou mayest give them their
meat in due season.
That thou givest them they
gather: thou openest thine
hand, they are filled with
good.
Thou hidest thy face, they are
troubled: thou takest away
their breath, they die, and
return to their dust.

This can be no coincidence. The unknown Hebrew psalmist
must have known Akhnaten's hymn well, for he adapted many
passages from it, and quoted several outright.

It does not necessarily follow from this, of course, that Moses
carried the text of the hymn with him out of Egypt, and that
it was handed down through the generations of the Hebrews
until the Psalms were finally written down, some six or seven

hundred years after the time of Akhnaten. We know that Akhnaten attempted to make Atenism a universal religion. Quite likely, the text of the hymn was inscribed at the Atenist temples in Syria, and passed into general circulation among the Syrians, Phoenicians, and Canaanites. It may have come into Hebrew possession much later, when the Hebrews entered Canaan and displaced the earlier population.

There are many other Old Testament quotations from Egyptian literature; the compilers of the Hebrew Scriptures leaned heavily, for instance, on such a well-known Egyptian work as "The Wisdom of Amenemope," a late Egyptian text written after 1000 B.C. Much of this work was absorbed into the Book of Proverbs, although, to be sure, at least one commentator has argued that the Hebrew text was written earlier. One example should suffice:

AMENEMOPE	PROVERBS
Incline thine ears to hear my sayings,	Bow down thine ear, and hear the words of the wise,
And apply thine heart to their comprehension.	and apply thine heart unto my knowledge.
For it is a profitable thing to put them in thy heart,	For it is a pleasant thing if thou keep them within thee;
But woe to him who transgresses them.	they shall withal be fitted in thy lips.
(*Amenemope III, 9–12*)	(*Prov. 22:17–18*)

In examining the evidence of a connection between Akhnaten and the Hebrew religion, our chief source of information is the Old Testament. But this, unfortunately, is anything but a true historical record. Before we can admit it as evidence, we must understand the origins of the text we now have.

Biblical scholars have demonstrated, through careful study of the text, that the Old Testament is actually a composite of a number of versions, edited and spliced over a period of hundreds of years to suit the needs of the Hebrew community. Changing theological views led to alterations in the earlier versions, but these alterations were not always carried out consistently or thoroughly, and traces of the original text show through, like the writings on a palimpsest.

The earliest source of the Bible is called the J text, for Jahvistic, since its author referred to God by the name of Jahveh (Yahweh). This, it is thought, was assembled in the time of King David—about 1000 B.C. Upon the death of David's son Solomon, the Kingdom of Israel split into two rival and hostile kingdoms, Judah and Israel, and a new Biblical text was set down by a priest of the northern kingdom, which still bore the old name of Israel. This second text is known as the E text, because the name of God is given as Elohim.

In 722 B.C., the northern kingdom was sacked and destroyed by the Assyrians, and its ten tribes were carried away into exile. A priest of Judah drew from the J text and the E text such passages as suited his purpose, added emendations of his own, and combined the whole into what scholars term the JE text. This comprised the first four books of the Pentateuch. In the seventh century, a time of backsliding and moral decay in Judah, a fifth book, Deuteronomy, was "discovered" at Jerusalem and added to the canon, and the entire text once again revised. The Babylonian Captivity of Judah followed; after the return from Babylon, the text was edited again, in the rewriting known as the Priestly Code. The final editing took place about 400 B.C., in the time of the prophet Ezra, and since then no substantial changes have been made.

What we have, then, is a compilation of five differing texts— J, E, JE, the Deuteronomist, and the Priestly—as edited by a sixth priest some six hundred years after the first passages were set down. Much of the contradiction and mystery of the Pentateuch is simply the result of careless editing; for example, the enigmatic statement, "And Enoch walked with God, and he was not; for God took him" is all that survives of what no doubt was an extensive myth in David's time. Such submerged references are our only clues to an oral tradition that was pruned from the final written version of Genesis.

The so-called Five Books of Moses are credited to his authorship—even though the death of Moses is related in the text he supposedly wrote! We know now that the Pentateuch did not begin to take form until several hundred years after Moses' death, and that its content was altered many times to reflect changes in the official Jewish concept of the religion.

With this in mind, we can turn to the Old Testament and try to relate it to the story of Akhnaten.

What, first of all, are the points of similarity between Aten and the god of the Old Testament?

We are in difficulties at once. For the god of the Hebrews underwent changes during the hundreds of years that the Old Testament was taking shape. In the late chapters of Isaiah, we find a god of love and warmth, who tempers justice with mercy. "For a small moment have I forsaken thee," the Lord declares, "but with great mercies will I gather thee. In a little wrath I hid my face from thee for a moment; but with everlasting kindness will I have mercy on thee, saith the Lord thy Redeemer."

This God of Isaiah, who promises, "Ye shall go out with joy, and be led forth with peace," is not unlike the warm-hearted Aten, who thoughtfully puts "a Nile in heaven . . . for the strangers," who makes "all trees and plants flourish," who looks after the chicken crying in the egg-shell, who "fillest every land with . . . beauty," who banishes darkness and fear. The compassionate, redeeming God of Isaiah is a god of love, akin to Aten, and looking forward to the God of whom Jesus taught.

But the latter chapters of Isaiah were written during the Babylonian Captivity of the Jews, six centuries before Christ, and seven hundred years after Akhnaten's day. The Old Testament preserves certain traces of a very different sort of God in its earlier books. "The Lord is a man of war," we read in Exodus. "He hath triumphed gloriously: the horse and his rider hath he thrown into the sea." Moses asks, "Who is like unto thee, O Lord, among the gods? who is like thee, glorious in holiness, fearful in praises, doing wonders? Thou stretchedst out thy right hand, the earth swallowed them."

The deeds of this martial god ring through the early books of the Bible. The Lord has armies, and sends the "captain of the Lord's host," "with his sword drawn in his hand," to visit Joshua, and Joshua "fell on his face to the earth, and did worship." The Lord has chariots and weapons; the Lord is mighty in battle. Is this the god of Akhnaten? Of Jesus? Of Isaiah?

The priestly editors of the Pentateuch failed to cover another slip, while letting these warlike passages stand. Isaiah knows only one god, and he is so pure a monotheist that he admits of the existence of no other gods: "Ye are my witnesses, saith the Lord . . . before me there was no God formed, neither shall there be after me. I, even I, am the Lord."

But here is Moses praising Yahweh by declaring, "Who is like unto thee, O Lord, *among the gods*." And here is Joshua, bowing the knee before a messenger from heaven who, though not God, is certainly divine. How can this be? The Lord is not the only god, but merely the greatest of the gods? The God of Exodus is not the Sole God of Isaiah, of Akhnaten.

Then, too, Akhnaten's god was abstract. A symbol represented him, but there were no representations, no statuettes, no visualizations whatever. Aten was the heat which dwelleth in the sun's disk, and heat is an abstract concept.

The God of the Jews is similarly abstract. There are no graven images to be made of him, no hints of his appearance, and, in the late days of the Biblical era, no temple, no altar, nothing tangible connected with him: "The heaven is my throne, and the earth is my footstool: where is the house that ye build unto me?" God is everywhere, immanent, intangible, infusing everything, just as the Aten, symbolized by reaching hands, entered into every aspect of life: "Thy rays, they encompass the lands, even all thou hast made."

When we turn to the Pentateuch, we see a much more tangible deity. True, one of the commandments brought down from Sinai by Moses forbids the making of graven images—not merely images of God, but "any likeness of anything that is in heaven above, or that is in the earth beneath, or that is in the water under the earth." But we can take this as a later insertion, added by an editor eager to stamp out the worship of idols. For in the first chapter of Genesis, we learn that God said, "Let us make man in our image, after our likeness." In the third chapter, God is corporeal enough to go "walking in the garden in the cool of the day: and Adam and his wife hid themselves from the presence of the Lord God." Angels of the Lord go among men— Akhnaten would have tolerated no angels in his creed—and they are solid enough angels, who will wrestle with a man until the breaking of the day, and put the hollow of a man's thigh out of joint. The Lord holds conversations with men, turning rods to serpents when necessary to win a debating point. All this is evidence enough that the early Israelites believed in a god very much different from that of the later prophets—who, nevertheless, could not quite bring themselves to expunge from the record the legends of the earlier days when God had shape and form and voice.

Akhnaten's god was universal—not only the god of Egypt, but of Syria, of Nubia, of all the world. He did not merely look after one people in one particular place. He could put a Nile in heaven for the strangers; he "divided the peoples"; he cared for all the earth, and it was Akhnaten's dream that all the earth would worship him.

Yahweh, the god of the Pentateuch, is quite different. He has a local sovereignty in a land of his own choosing, over a people with whom he has a special covenant relationship. The oldest texts of the Bible recognized that neighboring people, the Amorites, the Hittites, the Philistines, and the rest, had gods of their own. It was not argued that these gods had no existence. They existed, the Baals and Dagons of the gentiles, but their gods were less mighty than Yahweh. And the Amorites and Philistines were welcome to keep their gods. Yahweh belonged to the Hebrews, and the Hebrews to Yahweh, chosen on both sides. Not until Isaiah is there an open statement of God's universality and uniqueness. In Isaiah we see that Israel has been chosen, not as God's only people, but as the bringers of light, who will carry the word of God to the unbelievers: "I the Lord have called thee in righteousness, and will hold thine hand, and will keep thee, and give thee for a covenant of the people, for a light of the Gentiles; to open the blind eyes, to bring out the prisoners from the prison, and them that sit in darkness out of the prison

198

house. I am the Lord; that is my name: and my glory I will not give to another, neither my praise to graven images."

It is this monotheistic God of Isaiah—"I am the first, and I am the last; and beside me there is no God"—who has chosen Israel as a servant, to spread enlightenment. "Listen, O isles, unto me; and hearken, ye people, from far."

So, then, emerges the concept in Isaiah of the "suffering servant" unheeded by the heathen, the Messiah, the rejected prophet, whom Isaiah describes in words that would later be applied to Jesus, and which can equally well be turned toward Akhnaten:

"He is despised and rejected of men; a man of sorrows, and acquainted with grief: and we hid as it were our faces from him; he was despised, and we esteemed him not.

"Surely he hath borne our griefs, and carried our sorrows: yet we did esteem him stricken, smitten of God, and afflicted.

"But he was wounded for our transgressions, he was bruised for our iniquities: the chastisement of our peace was upon him; and with his stripes we are healed.

"All we like sheep have gone astray; we have turned every one to his own way; and the Lord hath laid on him the iniquity of us all."

The god of Akhnaten, loving, universal, intangible, a sole god, has much in common with the god of Amos and Isaiah and Hosea. But Akhnaten died in the middle of the fourteenth century before Christ; Amos preached about 700 B.C.; Isaiah, the "second" Isaiah of the later chapters, wrote more than a century and a half after Amos. If Akhnaten transmitted his beliefs to his disciple Moses, who taught them to the Hebrews, why do they appear not to have been followed for six centuries? Why, belatedly, does a definite strand of Atenism appear in Judaism after the destruction of the northern kingdom in 722 B.C.? Is it simply a coincidence, a rebirth of Akhnaten's great idea without any direct link? Could it be that the Jews evolved an abstract, monotheistic, loving god independently over the centuries, with no knowledge of Akhnaten's teachings?

199

But, then, how did Akhnaten's hymn to the Aten get into the Book of Psalms?

Let us retrace the history of the Hebrews, as best we can under the clouded circumstances of the chronicles we have.

The Old Testament would have us believe that the Hebrews held converse with God from Adam's time onward, that early patriarchs such as Noah were favored by God, that God selected one Abram, who lived in Ur of the Chaldees, and, changing his name to Abraham, covenanted with him, saying, "Get thee out of thy country, from thy kindred, unto a land that I will shew thee: And I will make of thee a great nation."

Whereupon Abraham led his people into the land of Canaan, in which his descendants prospered until famine drove them into Egypt in the days of Joseph, several hundred years later. Joseph was favored by Pharaoh, and the Hebrews "were fruitful" in Egypt, "and increased abundantly, and multiplied, and waxed exceeding mighty." But then "there arose up a new king over Egypt, which knew not Joseph," and afflicted the children of Israel with persecutions and slavery, until Moses led them forth. It was Moses who renewed the ancient covenant of Abraham, and brought new laws to the Hebrews, and took them back to Canaan. The final editors of the Pentateuch would have us think that the Jewish religion was fully fixed in Moses' time, and that subsequent backslidings into polytheism and idolatry were only interludes of moral decay.

This concept, of a covenant with one unchanging god, going back to Abraham and before, is, we are now aware, the result of much mending and patching and doctoring of the record. The actual picture is quite different.

The Hebrews, most scholars believe, were one of the many nomadic desert tribes who inhabited the Near East about 2000 B.C. While the pyramids were rising in Egypt and the cities of Sumer were attaining greatness in Mesopotamia, these wandering shepherds roamed from place to place. They spoke a language of the linguistic family we call Semitic, which made them linguistically, though not necessarily otherwise, related to such

200

peoples as the Canaanites, the Assyrians, the Edomites, the Amorites, and many others.

In the period around 2000 B.C., the Hebrews—known to their neighbors as Habiru, or Khabiri, or 'Apiru—lived in southern Mesopotamia. Led by one Abraham, probably an actual sheikh of the tribe, they migrated westward into northern Syria, and then drifted downward into Canaan, or Palestine. This migration was part of a general movement of Semitic peoples which, as we have seen, reached its climax when the desert princes known as the Hyksos conquered Egypt herself, about 1700 B.C.

With Egypt in the hands of the Hyksos, the Hebrews continued their migration southward into the land of the Nile, where they found a friendly welcome. The Hyksos, themselves Semitic-speaking, were the same sort of people as the Hebrews in most respects, and many Hebrews attained to high positions under the Hyksos Pharaohs—as we see in the story of Joseph.

The religion of the Hebrews had undergone evolution during these three or four hundred years of migration. As desert-dwellers, they had begun with a simple animism—that is, the idea that supernatural beings are everywhere, abiding in rocks and stones and trees which are therefore sacred. The early Hebrews felt themselves surrounded by gods and demons: raging spirits of the sandstorm, kindly spirits of the sun, friendly oracles living in groves of trees, benevolent spirits of wells and oases, grim demons of heat and thirst. Any spirit possessing supernatural power was called an *el,* and spirits in general were known by the plural word, *elohim.*

There were many *elohim.* As the desert tribes evolved past the stage of animism, they came to give specific names and characters to the *elohim,* making them gods, and so entering into a theistic period. Like other tribes, the Hebrews recognized a number of gods at first—a storm god, a sun god, a wind god, a fertility god, a goddess of motherhood, an entire pantheon. The names of the gods were usually titles of respect: Moloch or Melek, meaning "King"; Adonai or Adonis, "Lord"; Baal, "Possessor of the Land"; and so forth. Head of the pantheon was El,

"God"—not sole god, not then, but simply first among many.

Gradually there came a consolidation of the many gods into one. The linguistic evidence remains: for *Elohim,* which became the Hebrew name for God, is a plural word, "the gods." Despite this trend toward monotheism, the Hebrews, like the Egyptians, continued to worship a variety of gods. Most particularly they worshipped Baal, the year-god, whose death and rebirth symbolized the annual agricultural miracle of spring, and Asherah, the Mother Goddess, depicted as the consort of El and also as the sister-wife of Baal. The situation was roughly parallel to Egypt's, where a creator-god, Atum-Re, held the position El did among the Hebrews, while Osiris and Isis were the nearly exact equivalents of Baal and Asherah.

At some point a Hebrew patriarch, perhaps Abraham, came to place all his faith in a single protective deity, one *el* out of the many, whom he may have called El-Shaddai, "the El of the Mountains."[1] His tribe, the Hebrews, now devoted themselves to the worship of El-Shaddai, without, however, neglecting Baal and Asherah.

In Egypt, after the overthrow of the Hyksos, the Hebrews suffered grievously. No longer did their kinsmen rule. Native Egyptians were supreme again, and enslavement was the fate of any Semites who failed to make their escape when the Eighteenth Dynasty arose. It was against this background that Moses emerged. Moses, like Abraham, made a covenant with a god.

But it was not the same god.

The account in Exodus has it that Moses, after being cast away by his Hebrew mother, was found in the rushes of the Nile by the daughter of Pharaoh, and raised in the palace. But when Moses was grown, he came upon an Egyptian smiting one of the Hebrews, and slew the Egyptian in his anger. Fleeing Egypt after the murder, Moses journeyed eastward beyond the Red Sea to the land of Midian, where he entered the household of a Midianite priest named Jethro, and took one of his seven daughters to wife.

While in Midian, Moses encountered Yahweh.

[1] The King James Version translates "El-Shaddai" as "God Almighty."

He had taken Jethro's flocks to pasture, and "came to the mountain of God, even to Horeb. And the angel of the Lord appeared unto him in a flame of fire out of the midst of a bush: and he looked, and behold, the bush burned with fire, and the bush was not consumed."

The deity in the burning bush declares, "I am the God of thy father, the God of Abraham." He explains, "I appeared unto Abraham . . . by the name of God Almighty [El-Shaddai] but by my name Jehovah [Yahweh] was I not known to [him]." He tells Moses that "I am come down to deliver them out of the hand of the Egyptians, and to bring them up out of that land unto a good land and a large, unto a land flowing with milk and honey; unto the place of the Canaanites."

The god of Moses is accompanied by entirely different imagery than the god of Abraham. Abraham's god dwells somewhere in the desert, and manifests himself impersonally and distantly. Moses' god is a god of fire and smoke, a rumbling, thundering deity who dwells on the wild slopes of a desolate mountain. The message of Moses was that the Hebrews were to replace the covenant of the desert-god El-Shaddai, or Elohim, with that of the volcano-god Yahweh.

Moses returns from Midian brimming over with his idea of the new god, and preaches Yahweh to the Hebrews. Yahweh is stern, vindictive, fierce, no agricultural deity like El-Shaddai, but the spirit of an active volcano. The Hebrews, following Moses out of Egypt, see Yahweh as a pillar of cloud by day, a pillar of fire at night. Yahweh speaks in the voice of a trumpet, above the thunder and lightnings, and when he appears on his mountain "the smoke thereof ascended as the smoke of a furnace, and the whole mount quaked greatly." The volcano imagery survived even into Isaiah's day, long after Yahweh's volcanic origin had been forgotten: "Behold the name of Yahweh cometh from afar, his anger burneth, and violently the smoke riseth on high: his lips are full of indignation, and his tongue is a devouring fire." There were no active volcanoes in Mesopotamia, where Abraham dedicated himself to El-Shaddai, nor in Egypt. But Moses would have had ample opportunity to see—

and be terrified by—a volcano in Midian, in northern Syria.

It is this Yahweh, this belligerent, proud, jealous god out of the volcano, whom Moses brought to the Hebrews. But Yahweh is certainly not Akhnaten's god. Does this defeat the idea that Jewish monotheism stems from the Amarna heresy?

Determining the date of the Exodus may help clarify things.

The Biblical tradition, as given in Kings I, sixth chapter, is that 480 years elapsed between the Exodus and the building of Solomon's temple at Jerusalem. The building of the temple is dated fairly reliably at about 980 B.C., which would place the time of the Exodus at roughly 1460 B.C. Akhnaten's heresy, we know, flourished circa 1360, a full century later.

On the other hand, in the first chapter of Exodus we learn that during the Egyptian oppression of the Hebrews, they were forced to build "for Pharaoh treasure cities, Pithom and Raamses." By the historical evidence, these cities were built under Rameses II, who reigned for 66 years beginning in 1304. By this tradition, the Hebrews were still in Egypt long after Akhnaten's death in 1361.

The archaeological record, as opposed to the Biblical, is not much more helpful. From the inscriptions of Amenhotep II, who was Pharaoh forty years before Akhnaten's birth, we find that several thousand members of a tribe called the 'Apiru were brought back as captives from a campaign in Syria and Canaan. The Tell el-Amarna letters tell us again and again of a tribe of marauders called variously the Khabiri and the 'Apiru who are attacking the cities of Syria and Canaan.

There can be little doubt that "Khabiri" and " 'Apiru" and "Hebrew" all have the same etymology. But we cannot therefore assume that the Israelite invasion of Canaan, led by Joshua, was already under way in the time of Amenhotep II, and reached a peak of activity during the latter years of Akhnaten. It may simply have been that the Hebrews of Abraham split and went their several ways, one branch going into Egypt, the rest continuing to roam in Syria and Canaan. Modern historians generally distinguish between the Biblical Hebrews, whom they prefer to call Israelites, and these other 'Apiru who caused so much trouble earlier in Canaan. Indeed, much of later Jewish history is hard to interpret unless this assumption is made.

The one clear archaeological clue comes from an inscription of the fifth year of Pharaoh Merneptah, the successor of Rameses II. In that year—about 1234—Merneptah led a military campaign into Canaan, and caused to be set up at Thebes (using a slab borrowed from Amenhotep III's mortuary temple for the purpose) a long victory hymn which ended with these lines:

The kings are overthrown, saying: "Salaam!"
Not one holds up his head among the Nine Bows.
Wasted is Tehenu,
Kheta is pacified,
Plundered is Pekanan,
Carried off is Askalon,
Seized upon is Gezer,
Yenoam is made as a thing not existing.
Israel is desolated, his seed is not;
Palestine has become a widow for Egypt.
All lands are united, they are pacified;
Everyone that is turbulent is bound by King Merneptah, given life
      like Re, every day.

This is the earliest known reference to "Israel." Clearly, by the reign of Merneptah, Israel was well established in Canaan. From this—and from the reference to the treasure cities of Pithom and Raamses—it is usually concluded that Rameses II (1304–1238) was the Pharaoh of the Exodus. The date of the actual migration, then, would be about 1260 or 1270.

By one reckoning, the Exodus occurred a century before Akhnaten, by another, a century after him. And the god whom Moses preached was a fiery volcano-god bearing little resemblance to Aten. It would seem from this that the link between Akhnaten and Moses supplied by Manetho was false, and that the later pure monotheism of the Jews was an independent invention, arrived at after they had shaken off the concept of the vengeful, personified god of Moses, who was only the most mighty "among the gods," and not sole god of the universe.

Then, in 1939, a startling and original little volume called

205

Moses and Monotheism revived the idea that Akhnaten's teachings had been transmitted to the Jews. The author was no archaeologist nor any Biblical scholar, but rather the founder of psychoanalysis, Sigmund Freud.

Freud maintained that Moses indeed had been a disciple of Akhnaten's—moreover, that Moses himself had been an Egyptian!

Freud dismissed the tale of Moses' abandonment and discovery as mere myth-making. The concept of the foundling leader, he pointed out, was a standard myth. Not only Moses but the great Assyrian king Sargon of Akkad, Cyrus of Persia, Romulus and Remus of Rome, and even Oedipus of Greek Thebes, had all been cast away in infancy and raised by others. Freud was willing to accept the idea that Moses had been raised by an Egyptian mother, as indeed the Bible said—but felt that the story of his birth to a woman of the Hebrew tribe of Levites was a later editorial change, designed to unite the great lawgiver with his adopted people.

The very name of Moses, Freud observed, was Egyptian. That had earlier been pointed out by Breasted, who wrote, "It is simply the Egyptian word 'mose' meaning 'child,' and is an abridgement of a fuller form of such names as 'Amen-mose' meaning 'Amon-a-child' or 'Ptah-mose,' meaning 'Ptah-a-child,' these forms themselves being likewise abbreviations for the complete form 'Amon-(has given)-a-child' or 'Ptah-(has given)-a-child.' The abbreviation 'child' early became a convenient rapid form for the cumbrous full name, and the name Mose, 'child,' is not uncommon on the Egyptian monuments. The father of Moses without doubt prefixed to his son's name that of an Egyptian god like Amon or Ptah, and this divine name was gradually lost in current usage, till the boy was called 'Mose.' (The final *s* is an addition drawn from the Greek translation of the Old Testament. It is not in the Hebrew which has 'mosheh.')"[2]

Furthermore, Moses is traditionally credited with having introduced the Hebrews to the custom of circumcision, which had

[2] James H. Breasted, *The Dawn of Conscience*.

206

been common practice in Egypt for thousands of years. If Moses had been a Jew, Freud asks, "What sense could there be in his forcing upon them [the Israelites] a burdensome custom which, so to speak, made them into Egyptians and was bound to keep awake their memory of Egypt, whereas his intention could only have had the opposite aim; namely, that his people should become strangers to the country of bondage." Freud concluded that Moses had given the Jews a new religion as well as a new custom. The custom, it is known, was Egyptian. So too, Freud feels, was the religion.

(The Bible is a contradictory witness here. Exodus has Moses introducing circumcision to the Israelites. Genesis indicates that circumcision was practiced in Abraham's time. Again, a case of faulty editing of the interwoven texts.)

The religion which Moses gave the Israelites, Freud says, was none other than that of Akhnaten. He pictures Moses as one of Akhnaten's disciples. "He held high rank and was a convinced adherent of the Aten religion, but, in contradistinction to the brooding king, he [Moses] was forceful and passionate. For this man the death of Ikhnaton and the abolishing of his religion meant the end of all his hopes. Only proscribed or recanting could he remain in Egypt. If he were governor of a border province he might well have come into touch with a certain Semitic tribe which had immigrated several generations before. In his disappointment and loneliness he turned to those strangers and sought in them for a compensation of what he had lost. He chose them for his people and tried to realize his own ideals through them. After he had left Egypt with them, accompanied by his immediate followers, he hallowed them by the custom of circumcision, gave them laws, and introduced them to the Aten religion, which the Egyptians had just discarded. Perhaps the rules the man Moses imposed on his Jews were even harder than those of his master and teacher Ikhnaton; perhaps he also relinquished the connection with the sun-god of On [Heliopolis], to whom the latter had still adhered."

This is simply Manetho's old story brought up to date. It can be attacked on two main grounds: that the Exodus took place a century after Akhnaten's death, and that the Yahweh religion of Moses was not very much like the creed of Akhnaten.

Freud meets both these objections with one astonishing hypothesis. There was not one Moses, he suggests, but two!

The earlier Moses, Freud says, lived about 1350, and was an Egyptian who taught the Aten religion to the persecuted Israelites after Akhnaten's death. The second Moses was a Midianite who lived a few generations later, the son-in-law of Jethro, who, while tending his flocks, encountered a volcano in eruption and conceived the worship of Yahweh, "an uncanny, bloodthirsty demon who walks by night and shuns the light of day."

There is, of course, no Biblical proof of this. Yet certain lingering contradictions in the Scriptural text as we have it raise an interesting point. Moses is usually described as being hot-tempered, violent, impulsive; he smote an Egyptian dead, smashed the tablets of the Law in his anger. Yet in some places he is described as patient, "meek," gentle. Freud asserts, "I think we are justified in separating the two persons from each other and assuming that the Egyptian Moses never was in [Midian] and had never heard the name of Jahve, whereas the Midianite Moses never set foot in Egypt and knew nothing of Aton. In order to make the two people into one, tradition or legend had to bring the Egyptian Moses to Midian."

Freud's reconstruction moves a step further when he suggests that the first, Egyptian, Moses met a violent death at the hands of his adopted people in the wilderness. For this remarkable idea, Freud was indebted to the German scholar Ernst Sellin, who in 1922 claimed to have found some passages in the Book of Hosea pointing to the murder of Moses. These passages were obscure, as though later editors had covered up Hosea's revelation of the grim event, and Sellin's interpretation is by no means accepted widely by Biblical students today.

What Freud suggests is that the Egyptian Moses, a stubborn, passionate man, forced upon the Israelites a religion they could no more accept than had the Egyptians. Atenism was too pure a creed, too austere, too abstract. The Jews wanted something more tangible: a god they could see and fear. The teachings of the original Moses, Freud argues, met the same fate as those of Akhnaten. "In both cases . . . those who felt themselves kept in tutelage, or who felt dispossessed, revolted and threw off the burden of a religion that had been forced on them. But while the tame Egyptians waited until fate had removed the sacred person of their Pharaoh, the savage Semites took their destiny into their own hands and did away with their tyrant."

A period of confusion among the Israelites followed, Freud maintains. Moses, though he had been stern and unlovable, had been a great leader. No one appeared to fill his place for several generations—and then there came from Midian the true leader of the Exodus, the other Moses, with his religion of Yahweh. This less lofty religion met eager acceptance. The Israelites, who had earlier cast out Abraham's El–Shaddai for Aten, now offered themselves to the volcano-demon Yahweh, and under his banner marched into Canaan and conquered it. There could be no conquest in the name of gentle Aten, but Yahweh was "a man of war," who could spur his newly adopted people onward.

In Canaan, the Israelites met with a new difficulty. A religion even more acceptable than that of Yahweh was practiced there—that of Baal and Asherah. The Canaanites, being farmers, had no need of a blustering warrior-god like Yahweh. The deities best suited to their needs were those of fertility: the Mother Goddess, Asherah, and the reviving year-god, Baal.

The situation was complicated by the fact that many of these Canaanites were cousins of the Israelites. They were the 'Apiru or Khabiri who had marched victoriously through Canaan in Akhnaten's day. Now they held possession. The Israelites, at last reunited with this other branch of their ancient tribe, found themselves troubled by intermarriage and by the temptation to give up Yahweh for Baal.

Thus hundreds of pages of the Old Testament tell a sad tale of the encroachments of Baal. In Judges, we read how the Jews were warned by an angel, "Ye shall make no league with the inhabitants of this land [Canaan]; ye shall throw down their altars: but ye have not obeyed my voice: why have ye done this?" We hear how "the children of Israel dwelt among the Canaanites, Hittites, and Amorites. . . . And they took their daughters to be their wives, and gave their daughters to their sons, and served their gods." We are told, "The children of Israel did evil in the sight of the Lord, and forgat the Lord their God, and served Baalim and the groves."

Yahweh, the god of Moses, though he had not been so rarefied and advanced a concept as the god of Akhnaten, was nevertheless preferable to fertility cults. During the years in Canaan the Jews slid backward into polytheism, while prophets angrily urged a return to the religion of Moses. They saw that the exalted figure of Yahweh was giving way to a mere local nature god.

One of the most vehement of the prophets was Hosea, in the eighth century before Christ. According to Sellin's theory, Hosea declared that the evils that had befallen Israel were punishment for having murdered Moses—but later scriptural editors, Sellin said, deleted all but a few phantom references to this idea, since —as in Freud's view—Moses the Egyptian and Moses the Midianite had officially become one man. Hosea declared:

"They [the Israelites] sacrifice upon the tops of the mountains, and burn incense upon the hills, under oaks and poplars and elms, because the shadow thereof is good. . . . For Israel slideth back as a backsliding heifer. . . ."

The prophets predicted tragedy, and tragedy came. The Kingdom of Israel was destroyed by the Assyrians. The Kingdom of Judah was pillaged by the Babylonians. The Jews were carried into captivity. The temple at Jerusalem was destroyed. The very Ark of the Covenant, the symbol of Yahweh that supposedly had been with the Jews from the days of Moses, disappeared.

It was at this dark moment in Israel that the great change occurred. Cut off from their ancestral lands, exiled, lacking temple and altar, the Jews renounced Baal and such gods forever. They returned to the god of Moses.

But not Yahweh—not the petty, firebreathing, vindictive local deity who had come out of Midian. The god to whom the Jews were returning was a universal, invisible, abstract, infinite and

210

infinitely wise being: a deity much like the one Akhnaten had proclaimed hundreds of years before in Egypt.

We are at the crux of the matter now. Did this God of latter-day Judaism evolve out of Yahweh to meet the new needs of the homeless, downtrodden Jews, without any connection with Akhnaten's teachings? Or did the message which the first Moses brought out of Egypt lie dormant among the Jews for eight hundred years until a time of need?

Ernst Sellin wrote, "Therefore we have to picture the true religion of Moses, the belief he proclaimed in one ethical god, as being from now on, as a matter of course, the possession of a small circle within the people. We cannot expect to find it from the start in the official cult, in the general belief of the people. All we can expect is that here and there a spark flies up from the spiritual fire he had kindled, that his ideas have not died out, but have quietly influenced beliefs and customs until, sooner or later, under the influence of special events . . . they broke forth again more strongly and gained dominance with the broad mass of the people."[3]

And Freud sums the debate up with these words:

The Jewish people had abandoned the Aton religion which Moses had given them and had turned to the worship of another god [Yahweh] who differed little from the Baalim of the neighboring tribes. All the efforts of later distorting influences failed to hide this humiliating fact. Yet the religion of Moses did not disappear without leaving any trace; a kind of memory of it had survived, a tradition perhaps obscured and distorted. It was this tradition of a great past that continued to work in the background, until it slowly gained more and more power over the mind of the people and at last succeeded in transforming the God Jahve into the Mosaic God and in waking to a new life the religion which Moses had instituted centuries before and which had later been forsaken.

Did it happen that way? Did Moses bring Akhnaten's religion out of Egypt, and did it lie dormant for centuries? Does the presence of Akhnaten's great hymn in the body of the Old Testament mean that Atenism lingered in the minds of the Jews during the centuries of backsliding, and finally triumphed?

[3] Ernst Sellin, *Mose und seine Bedeutung.*

So Freud said. Others think that Akhnaten's religion died with him, and was independently redeveloped by the Jews eight centuries later. I offer no final conclusion here. We can only speculate. It would be strange indeed if Judaism, and its two modern descendants, Christianity and Islam, owe their existence to the mind of a deformed, dreaming Egyptian whose own people obliterated even to his very name, thirty-four centuries ago.

10

AKHNATEN AND THE VERDICT OF HISTORY

Akhnaten certainly must have been controversial in his own day, and controversial he remains. No other Egyptian monarch has been the subject of such discussion, so many words—and the words aimed at Akhnaten have not always been complimentary.

"He possessed a determined will and very definite religious convictions and a fearless nature," wrote E. A. Wallis Budge. "But with all these gifts he lacked a practical knowledge of men and things. He never realized the true nature of the duties which as king he owed to his country and people, and he never understood the realities of life. He never learnt the kingcraft of the Pharaohs, and he failed to see that only a warrior could hold what warriors had won for him."[1] In another place Budge called Akhnaten "a religious fanatic, arrogant and obstinate, but earnest and sincere in his seeking after God." He spoke of him as a "religious megalomaniac," who, "being a king, was able to inflict untold misery on his country during the seventeen years of his reign. He spent the revenues of his country on the cult of his god, and in satisfying his craving for beauty in shape and form, and for ecstatic religious emotion."

Another historian spoke of Akhnaten as an "unbalanced genius," one who "possessed the mind and outlook of a fanatic,"

[1] E. A. Wallis Budge, *Tutankhamen*.

and yet another wondered if he "was not really half insane." Was he "the mad Pharaoh, an inbred neurotic," as one writer has it? These are harsh words, but they have the ring of truth. Akhnaten let Egypt crumble. He allowed his calling as a prophet to obscure his responsibilities as a king.

A serious charge against Akhnaten's religion is its lack of ethical content. "Here is no subtle or complicated theology but simply an adoration of the physical sun," wrote T. E. Peet, one of the excavators of Akhetaten. His colleague J. D. S. Pendlebury observed, "So much has been written about Akhnaten in the character of Christ before his time that it must be pointed out that Atenism was in no sense a way of life but merely an exercise in theology." Pendlebury wrote, "The Aten is purely a creative god. He has made all things living and provided for their wants, but there his work ends. There is no feeling that he will reward good or punish evil. There is no sense of sin or even of right or wrong." Budge declared, "I cannot find in them [the Amarna hymns] a single expression that contains any spiritual teaching, or any exhortation to purity of life, or any word of consciousness of sin, or any evidence of belief in a resurrection and a life beyond the grave."

All this is, of course, undeniable. Yet even Budge is willing to admit that the ethical texts of Atenism may have perished in the reaction that followed his death. James Henry Breasted, a partisan of Akhnaten's who called him a "god-intoxicated man," "the first *individual* in history," "a lovely idealist . . . ecstatic in his sense of the beauty of the eternal and universal light," was positive that there must have been more substance to Atenism than what we know from "a few accidental scraps and fragments" that survived the otherwise clean sweep of Horemheb. Akhnaten, Breasted wrote, was "the first prophet in history"— with which no one can disagree—and "the most remarkable of all pharaohs," which is also unquestionable. But was he, as Arthur Weigall put it, so lofty that "he may be ranked in degree of time and . . . perhaps also in degree of genius, as the world's first idealist"?

One psychoanalyst of the Freudian school had less regard for

Akhnaten than Freud himself. This was Karl Abraham, who wrote an essay on Akhnaten in 1912 maintaining that the whole mainspring of Akhnaten's movement was the Oedipus complex. Centering his investigation on the vindictive way Akhnaten ordered the destruction of all inscriptions containing his father's name, Abraham wrote, "His libido became fixed in an unusually strong degree on his mother, and his attitude towards his father became equally strongly negative. . . . His strongest hatred was directed against his father whom he could not reach because he was no more among the living," and whom he attacked, therefore, by destroying his name and thus his soul.

Even Abraham was willing to concede the importance of Akhnaten's religious ideas, however they had arisen: "He was thus a forerunner of Mosaic monotheism," he wrote, though his emphasis on the loving nature of God placed him "closer to the Christian concept than to the Mosaic."

Akhnaten's position as the first monotheist has come under attack also. John A. Wilson of the University of Chicago wrote, "Was this monotheism? If so, was it the world's first ancestral monotheism, and did it come down to us through the Hebrews? Our own answer to each question is in the negative. . . . Our modern Jewish, Christian, and Moslem faiths express the doctrine that there is one—and only one—God and that all ethical and religious values derive from that God. In application of this definition to the Amarna religion, we see that there were at least two gods [Aten and Akhnaten himself], that the Aton was concerned strictly with creating and maintaining life, and that ethics and religion derived from the pharaoh. . . ."

To this can be replied that we are at so great a distance in time from Akhnaten that we cannot be sure how seriously he regarded his divine nature. Wilson to the contrary, it seems just as likely that Akhnaten's claim of godhood was purely formal, deriving from his rank as king, and that Aten was sole god in his belief. After all, if historians of the future were to look back at our modern religions after they had been extinct for thousands of years, would they regard *them* as monotheistic? They might say that the Christians had three main gods—the Trinity; a

Mother Goddess—Mary; and a host of lesser gods—the saints and angels. They might say that Islam had two gods, Allah and Mohammed. They might say that the Jews had no god at all, but simply an elaborate system of ritualistic observances. We are in a poor position to pass judgment on the purity of Akhnaten's monotheism.

Budge is willing to admit that Akhnaten was a monotheist, but not that he was the *first* monotheist. Cutting through the dense pack of Egyptian deities to the underlying philosophy, Budge declared categorically, "A study of ancient Egyptian religious texts will convince the reader that the Egyptians believed in One God who was self-existent, immortal, invisible, eternal, omniscient, almighty, and inscrutable." In Budge's view, "It is certain that from the earliest times one of the greatest tendencies of the Egyptian religion was towards monotheism," although "a kind of polytheism existed in Egypt side by side with monotheism from very early times." He saw Akhnaten as the logical summit of the ancient monotheistic trend, not as an innovator.

Again, it would seem, an injustice has been done. Certainly Akhnaten drew his inspiration from the ancient solar philosophy of Heliopolis (and from such Asian doctrines as happened to be circulating among the women of Mitanni at the royal court). His great accomplishment was not the invention of these doctrines, for which he can hardly claim credit, but the imposition of them upon all of Egypt, the abolition of the cluster of other gods, and the purification of the solar creed into something far transcending anything dreamed of at Heliopolis.

The bitterest attack of all against Akhnaten's importance came from the archaeologist, Pendlebury, who said, simply, that Akhnaten did not matter at all. "The trend of events," he wrote, "would have been the same had Akhnaten been but a sack of sawdust."

This is an oft-heard theme of modern history: that there is no such thing as a great man, that what governs history is the impersonal interplay of events, that no man is indispensable to the scheme of things. Had there never been a Napoleon, there would still have been an attempt to build a European empire early in the nineteenth century. Had there never been a Charlemagne, an Alexander, a Caesar, a Hitler, a William the Conqueror, the argument runs, things would have worked out much the same anyway.

This line of thinking is a reaction against the excessive hero-worship of nineteenth-century historians, and, perhaps, it grows out of the awareness of the vast and imponderable forces that shape our own troubled times. Yet completely to discard the "great man theory of history" seems a mistake, to me. Certainly economics, agriculture, climate, technology, and population pressures all play their parts in bringing events to pass. It is futile to look, as historians once did, for any single cause of events, when every event is the climax of a constellation of forces.

Yet to dispense with the catalyst, with the man who brings the mixture to a boil, is to carry the process too far. Now and again in history, certain unique individuals have arisen, capable of seizing the reins of action, of giving unity and direction to the inchoate forces at work in the world. These are the great men of history.

"The great man," Freud wrote, "influences his contemporaries in two ways: through his personality and through the idea for which he stands."

Akhnaten—no sack of sawdust—stood for a great idea, beyond question. Fool and fanatic, dreamer and madman he may have been, but we cannot deprive him of his solitary greatness in the ancient world. Nor can we deny the force of his personality. Through persecution and oblivion, the smiling, mysterious figure of the Amarna murals beckons to us across the ages, and, while historians quarrel over his merits, no one can deny the power of the fascination this rebel Pharaoh exerts even today.

217

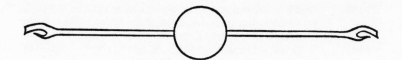

CHRONOLOGY

Note: all dates are Before Christ, and all dates are approximate. Those marked with question marks are even less certain than the others.

1555	Amose I founds the Eighteenth Dynasty.
1406	Accession of Amenhotep III. Marriage to Queen Tiy.
1400?	Birth of Akhnaten (Prince Amenhotep IV).
1397	Amenhotep III marries Gilukhepa of Mitanni.
1389?	Dushratta becomes King of Mitanni.
1386	Suppiluliumas becomes King of the Hittites.
1384?	Birth of Smenkhkare, son of Amenhotep III (?).
1377	Thirty-year jubilee of Amenhotep III. Amenhotep IV becomes co-regent. Some time earlier, Amenhotep IV has married Nefertiti, daughter of Ay (?).
1374	Suppiluliumas invades Mitanni and is repulsed.
1374?	Birth of Amenhotep IV's first daughter, Meritaten.
1374?	Birth of Beketaten, last daughter of Amenhotep III and Queen Tiy.
1373	Amenhotep IV begins openly to challenge the priests of Amon.
1372	Sixth year of Amenhotep IV. He changes his name to Akhnaten and orders construction of new capital, Akhetaten. Birth of second daughter, Meketaten.
1371	Tadukhepa of Mitanni comes to Thebes as a wife for Amenhotep III. But she becomes a secondary wife of Akhnaten.
1371?	Birth of Tutankhaten, son of Amenhotep III (?).
1370	Eighth year of Akhnaten. He moves permanently to the new city. Birth of third daughter, Ankhesenpaaten.

219

1369	Death of Amenhotep III. Akhnaten proclaims abolition of all Egyptian gods but Aten. Ribaddi of Byblos, under pressure from enemies, asks Akhnaten for military aid.
1368?	Birth of Akhnaten's fourth daughter, Neferneferuaten. Suppululiumas again attacks Mitanni.
1367?	Birth of Akhnaten's fifth daughter, Neferneferure. Fall of Tyre.
1366?	Birth of Akhnaten's sixth daughter, Setepenre. Fall of Simyra. Twelfth year of Akhnaten's reign. Ceremony of tribute is held. Queen Tiy visits Akhetaten and perhaps takes up permanent residence. At end of year, Meketaten, Akhnaten's second daughter, dies. Suppululiumas's forces cross the Euphrates and harry Mitanni. Aziru is summoned to Egypt but refuses to come.
1365?	Betrothal of Akhnaten's daughter Meritaten to her uncle (?) Smenkhkare. Friction between Akhnaten and Nefertiti. Betrothal of Akhnaten's daughter Ankhesenpaaten to Akhnaten. Aziru and Itakama form an alliance against Ribaddi.
1364	Fourteenth year of Aknaten's reign. Akhnaten and Nefertiti separate. She goes to live in north palace, taking with her Ankhesenpaaten and the young prince Tutankhaten, brother (?) of Akhnaten. Smenkhkare and Meritaten are married. Ribaddi is driven from Byblos by his brother.
1363	Akhnaten makes Smenkhkare co-regent.
1362	Smenkhkare visits Thebes, perhaps to restore relations with the priests of Amon.
1361	Seventeenth year of Akhnaten's reign. Aziru openly allied with the Hittites. End of Egypt's empire in Syria, Phoenicia, and Canaan. Akhnaten dies. Smenkhkare and presumably Meritaten also die. Tutankhaten is married to Ankhesenpaaten and becomes Pharaoh. They change their names to Tutankhamen and Ankhesenamen.
1360?	Tutankhamen and his court return to Thebes.
1359?	Final abandonment of Akhetaten.
1353	Tutankhamen dies in the ninth year of his reign. Suppululiumas is besieging the Mitanni capital. Ankhesenamen writes to him asking for a Hittite prince as her husband. The prince is intercepted en route. Ay becomes Pharaoh, marrying Ankhesenamen.
1352	Dushratta of Mitanni is murdered. Collapse of Mitanni.
1350	Death of Ay. Horemheb becomes Pharaoh. Persecution of Akhnaten's memory. Horemheb marries Nefertiti's sister Mutnedjmet.

1348	Death of Suppiluliumas. Mursilis II the new Hittite king. Temporary end of hostilities in Near East.
1319	Death of Horemheb. The new king is Rameses I, founder of the Nineteenth Dynasty, who dies after one year of rule.
1318	Seti I is king.
1304	Accession of Rameses II, "the Great." He rules 66 years. Persecution of the Israelites.
1260???	The Israelites leave Egypt.
1238	Death of Rameses II, accession of Merneptah.

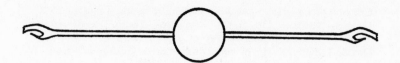

BIBLIOGRAPHY

ALDRED, CYRIL. *The Egyptians*. Thames & Hudson, London. 1961.
BIBBY, GEOFFREY. *Four Thousand Years Ago*. Knopf, New York. 1962.
BREASTED, CHARLES. *Pioneer to the Past: The Story of James H. Breasted*. Scribners, New York. 1943.
BREASTED, JAMES HENRY. *Ancient Records of Egypt*, Volumes I, II, III. University of Chicago Press, Chicago. 1906.
——. *The Dawn of Conscience*. Scribners, New York. 1933.
——. *Development of Religion and Thought in Ancient Egypt*. Scribners, New York. 1912.
——. *A History of Egypt*. Second edition, Scribners, New York. 1933.
BRUGSCH, HENRY. *Egypt Under the Pharaohs*. Second edition, John Murray, London. 1881.
BUDGE, E. A. WALLIS. *Egyptian Magic*. London. 1900.
——. *Egyptian Religion*. London. 1900.
——. *By Nile and Tigris*. John Murray, London. 1920.
——. *Tutankhamen*. Hopkinson, London. 1923.
CAMBRIDGE ANCIENT HISTORY, Volumes I, II, III. Cambridge University Press, Cambridge. 1911–25.
CARTER, HOWARD. *The Tomb of Tut-Ankh-Amen*. Volume I, in collaboration with A. C. Mace, Cassell, London. 1923. Volume II, Cassell, London. 1927. Volume III, Cassell, London. 1933.
CERAM, C. W. *Gods, Graves, and Scholars*. Knopf, New York, 1951.
——. *The Secret of the Hittites*. Knopf, New York. 1956.
CHIERA, EDWARD. *They Wrote on Clay*. University of Chicago Press, Chicago. 1938.

COTTRELL, LEONARD. *The Lost Pharaohs*. Evans, London. 1950.

DAVIES, NORMAN DE GARIS. *The Rock Tombs of El Amarna*. Archaeological Survey of Egypt, London. 1903–08.

DAVIS, THEODORE M., in collaboration with Gaston Maspero. *The Tomb of Queen Tiyi*. London. 1910.

DESROCHES-NOBLECOURT, CHRISTIANE. *Tutankhamen*. New York Graphic Society, New York. 1963.

DIODORUS SICULUS. *The Historical Library*. Translated by G. Booth. Davis, London. 1814.

ERMAN, ADOLPH. *Life in Ancient Egypt*. Macmillan, London. 1894.

FRANKFORT, HENRI, and others. *Before Philosophy*. Penguin, Harmondsworth. 1949.

———— and J. D. S. PENDLEBURY. *The City of Akhenaten*, Volume II. London. 1933.

FREUD, SIGMUND. *Moses and Monotheism*. Knopf, New York. 1939.

GURNEY, O. R. *The Hittites*. Revised edition, Penguin, Harmondsworth. 1961.

HILPRECHT, H. V., editor. *Explorations in Bible Lands During the 19th Century*. Holman, Philadelphia. 1903.

JAMES, E. O. *The Ancient Gods*. Putnam, New York. 1960.

JONES, ERNEST. *The Life and Work of Sigmund Freud*, Volume III. Basic Books, New York. 1957.

KING, L. W. and HALL, H. R. *Egypt and Western Asia in the Light of Recent Discoveries*. S.P.C.K., London. 1907.

KITCHEN, K. A. *Suppiluliuma and the Amarna Pharaohs: a study in relative chronology*. Liverpool University Press, Liverpool. 1962.

MASPERO, GASTON. *The Struggle of the Nations*. Appleton, New York. 1897.

NOSS, JOHN B. *Man's Religions*. Macmillan, New York, 1949.

PEET, T. E., and others. *The City of Akhenaten*, Volume I. London. 1923.

PENDLEBURY, J. D. S. and others. *The City of Akhenaten*, Volume III. London, 1950, 1951.

————. *Tell el Amarna*. Lovat Dickson, London. 1935.

PETRIE, W. M. FLINDERS. *Syria and Egypt from the Tell el Amarna Letters*. Methuen, London. 1898.

————. *Tell el-Amarna*. London. 1894.

PRITCHARD, JAMES B., editor. *Ancient Near Eastern Texts*. Second edition, Princeton University Press, Princeton. 1955.

RUNDLE CLARK, R. T. *Myth and Symbol in Ancient Egypt*. Thames & Hudson, London. 1959.

SILVERBERG, ROBERT. *Empires in the Dust*. Chilton, Philadelphia. 1963.

SMITH, HOMER W. *Man and His Gods*. Little, Brown, Boston. 1952.

STEINDORFF, GEORG. *The Religion of the Ancient Egyptians.* New York. 1905.

VELIKOVSKY, IMMANUEL. *Oedipus and Akhnaton.* Doubleday, New York. 1960.

WEIGALL, ARTHUR. *The Life and Times of Akhnaton.* Revised edition, Putnam, New York. 1922.

————. *Tutankhamen and Other Essays.* Thornton Butterworth, London. 1923.

WILKINSON, J. GARDNER. *Manners and Customs of the Ancient Egyptians.* Third edition, John Murray, London. 1847.

————. *Modern Egypt and Thebes.* John Murray, London. 1843.

WILSON, JOHN A. *The Burden of Egypt.* University of Chicago Press, Chicago. 1951.

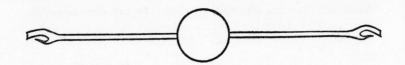

INDEX

226

With this book, Robert Silverberg continues his explorations into ancient worlds. Using evidence discovered by archaeologists, Silverberg skillfully reconstructs the lands of the past, and then guides his readers through them. His books—such as the prize-winning *Lost Cities and Vanished Civilizations* and *Empires in the Dust*—have taken readers to Thebes, Carthage, Pompeii, Troy, Babylon, Machu Picchu and Knossos. His *Sunken History: The Story of Underwater Archaeology* was a Literary Guild Selection, The Young Adults' Division.

A born and bred New Yorker and a veteran writer, Silverberg lives in New York City. He and his wife, an electronics engineer, share the premises with three cats and, at last count, thirteen goldfish.

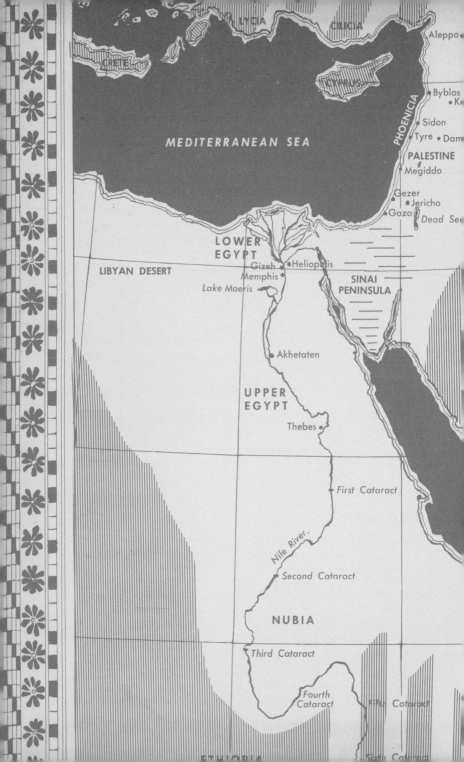